The Railways of
DEVON

The Railways of
DEVON

Martin Smith

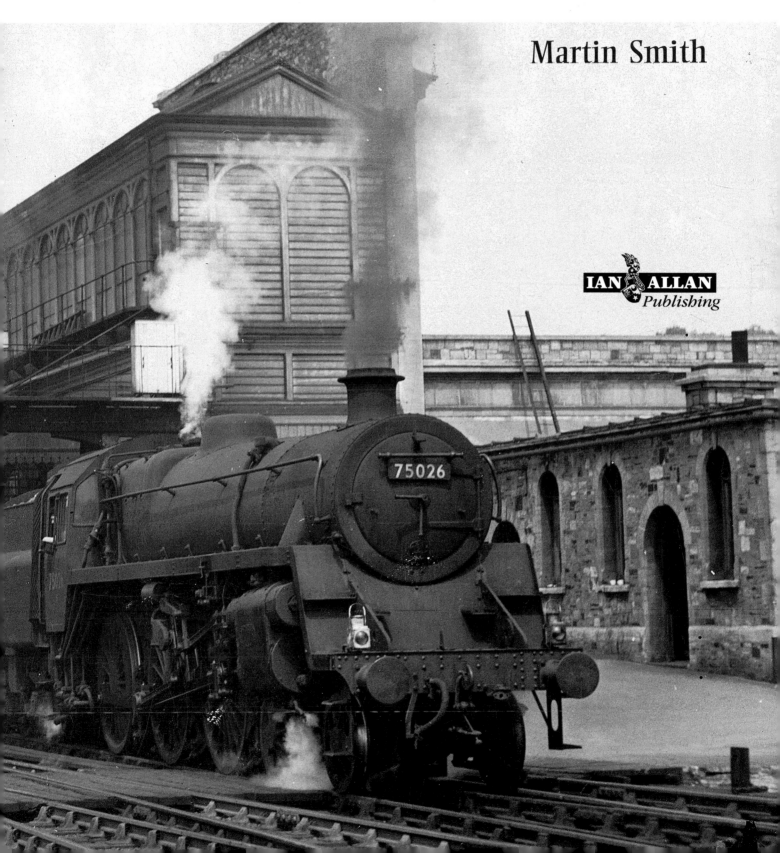

IAN ALLAN
Publishing

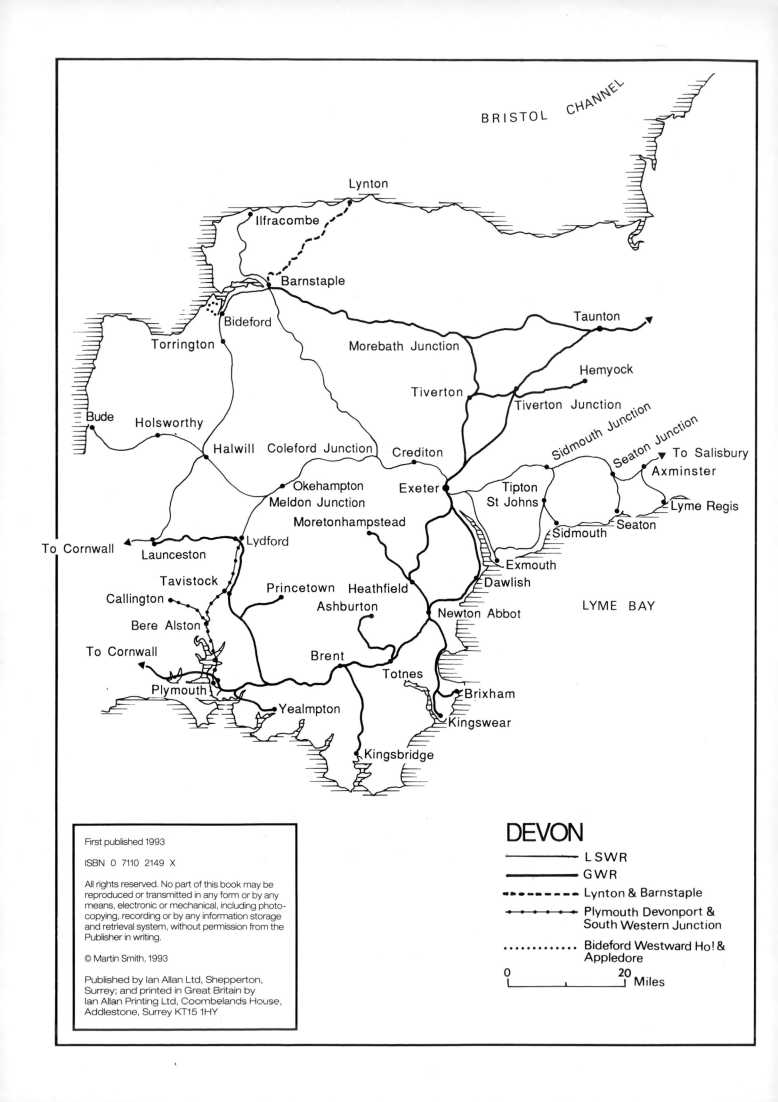

BRISTOL CHANNEL

Lynton

Ilfracombe

Barnstaple

Bideford

Torrington

Taunton

Morebath Junction

Hemyock

Tiverton

Tiverton Junction

Bude

Holsworthy

Halwill   Coleford Junction

Crediton

Sidmouth Junction

Seaton Junction

To Salisbury

Axminster

Okehampton
Meldon Junction

Exeter

Tipton
St Johns

Lyme Regis

Moretonhampstead

Seaton

Sidmouth

To Cornwall

Launceston

Lydford

Exmouth

Tavistock

Princetown   Heathfield

Dawlish

Callington

Ashburton

Newton Abbot

LYME BAY

Bere Alston

To Cornwall

Brent

Plymouth

Totnes

Yealmpton

Brixham

Kingswear

Kingsbridge

DEVON

——————— LSWR

——————— GWR

– – – – – – Lynton & Barnstaple

•–•–•–•–• Plymouth Devonport &
South Western Junction

·············· Bideford Westward Ho! &
Appledore

0   20
|___|___|___| Miles

First published 1993

ISBN 0 7110 2149 X

Published by Ian Allan Ltd, Shepperton,
Surrey; and printed in Great Britain by
Ian Allan Printing Ltd, Coombelands House,
Addlestone, Surrey KT15 1HY

Contents

Acknowledgements

The biggest thank you is due to my wife, Micky, whose patience and assistance belie her total disinterest in railway history. She informs me that, after checking countless pages of my typescript, she has christened the gargantuan spider in our garden shed 'Isambard'. Methinks that is not out of affection.

Sincere thanks are also due to following members of the 'practical help' department: Helen Brent (Morwellham Quay), H. D. Bromidge (Lynton & Barnstaple Railway Association), Paul Burkhalter, Richard Casserley, Mr J. Cogar (Paignton & Dartmouth Railway), M. G. East (Escombe Lambert, Cattewater), Bryan Gibson (Plymouth Railway Circle), Brian Grigg-Trevarthen (ECC), Chris Grove (Bere Ferrers), Roger Hateley (Industrial Railway Society), Sharon Hooton (Regional Railways), D. K. Jones, Colin Judge (Oakwood Press), Chris Leigh, Frank Lismore, Mr D. A. Pearce (Blue Circle Industries), George Reeve, Eric Sawford, P. W. B. Semmens, Alan Smith (Plym Valley Railway), Mr J. Smith (Lens of Sutton), Graham Stacey (LCGB/RAS), Mr D. Steggles (Railway Studies Library, Newton Abbot), F. J. Tapp (Heathfield Terminal), Peter Waller, Bill Wright (South Devon Railway) and the staff of the West Country Studies Library at Exeter, Frome Library (Somerset) and the Public Record Office at Kew.

Martin Smith
Coleford, Somerset.
January 1993

Bibliography

Several excellent reference works have been consulted during the preparation of this book, and they include:

History of the Great Western Railway; E. T. MacDermot, C. R. Clinker, O. S. Nock; Ian Allan.

History of the Southern Railway; C. F. Dendy Marshall, R.W. Kidner; Ian Allan

Locomotives of the Great Western Railway; Railway Correspondence and Travel Society.

Industrial Locomotives of South Western England; ed R. K. Hateley; Industrial Railway Society.

Clinker's Register; C. R. Clinker; Avon Anglia.

L&SWR Engine Sheds; C. Hawkins & G. Reeve; Irwell Press.

Among the other publications which have been perused are:

An Historical Survey of Great Western Engine Sheds; E. Lyons, E. Mountford; OPC.

LSWR Locomotives; M. Bradley; Wild Swan.

LSWR Locomotives; H. C. Casserley; Ian Allan.

Exeter Canal and Quays; J. Hall, J. Yeates; Exeter Canal & Quay Trust.

Bideford, Westward Ho! & Appledore Railway; D. Stuckey; West Country Handbooks.

Railways of the Western Region; G. Body; PSL.

The Barnstaple & Ilfracombe Railway; C. Maggs; Oakwood Press.

The Railways of Bristol and Somerset; M. Smith; Ian Allan.

Great Western Express Passenger Locomotives; M. Smith; Argus Books.

The LSWR in the Twentieth Century; J. N. Faulkner & R. A. Williams; David & Charles.

British Locomotive Catalogue; B. & D. Baxter; Moorland Publishing.

The Golden Age of the Great Western Railway; Tim Bryan; PSL.

Docks and Harbours of Britain; Capt A. G. Course; Ian Allan.

Lines to Torrington; J. Nicholas; OPC.

The Lynton & Barnstaple Railway; L. T. Catchpole; Oakwood Press.

Private and Untimetabled Railway Stations; G. Croughton, R. W. Kidner, A. Young; Oakwood Press.

The British Steam Railway Locomotive; E. L. Ahrons; Locomotives Publishing Co.

Locomotive and Train Working in the Nineteenth Century; E. L. Ahrons; Heffer.

Much information has also been gleaned from a variety of yellowing periodicals, and these include:

Railway Observer, Railways, Railway Magazine, Railway World, Trains Illustrated, Bradshaw's and assorted public and working timetables.

1. The Main Lines

On Wednesday 1 May 1844, the first main line passenger train entered Devon. The company which took full credit for the construction and, ultimately, the opening of the line on which it travelled was the Bristol & Exeter Railway, but the locomotive in charge of proceedings on opening day was the Great Western Railway's 'Firefly' class 2-2-2 *Actaeon*.

It may seem odd that such an auspicious occasion as the inaugural service on a newly-opened railway was entrusted to the locomotive of another company but, in those pioneering days, working or leasing agreements between different railway companies were far from unusual. The B&E, in common with countless other Victorian railways, had been promoted with great optimism, but when construction work had started to make alarming inroads into the company's bank balance, it had soon been realised that the initial aspirations had been a trifle ambitious. Consequently, economies had been needed. One of the areas which the B&E subsequently earmarked as a possibility for reducing capital outlay was the provision of locomotives and rolling stock, and this is where the GWR entered the picture.

The B&E leased its still-uncompleted line to the GWR on 14 August 1840, a little over four years after the former had been formally incorporated, and the latter undertook to provide the locomotives and rolling stock. The agreement had not come as the world's greatest shock as, by 1840, three of the B&E's directors also sat on the board of the GWR and, more significantly, the engineer who had been contracted to mastermind the construction of the B&E was one Isambard Kingdom Brunel. As the history books show, Brunel was not exactly an unfamiliar name to the GWR's hierarchy, and when he was appointed by the B&E there was little likelihood that the company's tracks would be built to anything other than the broad gauge. Brunel was, of course, the champion of the broad gauge and, despite vociferous opposition from railway engineers elsewhere in Britain who built to a gauge of 4ft 8½in, Brunel stuck firmly to his belief that the 7ft 0¼in gauge was far superior. Besides, the construction of the B&E to the same gauge as the GWR was necessary if the leasing agreement were to become operational.

The B&E had opened its first stretch of line between Bristol and Bridgwater on 1 June 1841, but the only trains to operate on that day had been directors' specials; it had been 15 June before the serious business

Above:

The original Bristol & Exeter Railway broad gauge 4-2-4Ts were built in 1853/54 and had 9ft diameter driving wheels; four were later renewed, this time with 8ft 10in drivers. One of the renewals was No 40, and here it is seen in its mid-1870s condition, prior to rebuilding as a 4-2-2 tender engine. It later became GWR No 2002 and was finally withdrawn in 1890. *Ian Allan Library*

of extracting money from fare-paying passengers had commenced. The line had been extended to Taunton on 1 July 1842 and to Wellington on 1 May 1843 but, south of Wellington, there was the little matter of tunnelling under White Ball Hill. The tunnel took two years to construct. It was 1,092yd long and, at its deepest point, was 199ft 6in below the ground; the trackbed rose on a gradient of 1 in 128 from north to south. The border between Somerset and Devon actually crossed White Ball Hill, and so the B&E's southbound passengers were to be presented with the seemingly magical trick of leaving Somerset in daylight, entering a dark cavern, and then re-emerging into the daylight in a completely different county. Generous to the last, the B&E had no intention of charging extra for that wonderment.

The 22-mile stretch between Wellington and Exeter Terminus had stations at Tiverton Road, Cullompton and Hele; the first of those was renamed Tiverton Junction in 1848 and the last became Hele & Bradninch in 1867. A station was added at Stoke Canon in 1860, only to be resited ¼-mile to the south in 1894, and further stations were opened at Burlescombe and Silverton in 1867. At Exeter, there were separate arrival and departure platforms, but both were on the down side of the line being separated by goods sidings and a wagon turntable. This unorthodox arrangement was not unique on the B&E as a similar layout was used at Taunton. Across the station yard from the down platform was a small engine shed but this was to be

replaced by a three-road timber-built shed in 1851; extensive rebuilding of the station site in 1862-64 included the provision of a larger, more modern shed.

Returning to the opening of the B&E through to Exeter on 1 May 1844, the citizens of that city might have viewed the coming of the railway as one of the more significant events in contemporary local history but, to the GWR, the novelty value of opening yet another line was minimal. Messrs Brunel, Gooch *et al* had already notched up a fistful of opening ceremonies but, nevertheless, the inaugural service to Exeter managed to provide something noteworthy, even for them.

The opening to Exeter meant that the GWR had a main line of almost 194 miles, which was far longer than that of any other railway company in Britain. The first train to Exeter ran through from Paddington and the locomotive was driven by Daniel Gooch himself. The six-coach train left Paddington at 7.30am and arrived in Exeter at 12.30pm;

Above:
GWR 4-2-2 No 2001 started life as Bristol & Exeter Railway 4-2-4T No 42, but was extensively rebuilt in 1877 along with its classmates. Whether in their tank or tender forms, they were the crack express locomotives on the B&E main line. *Ian Allan Library*

after the customary indulgence of spa water and sticky buns, the official entourage left Exeter at 5.20pm and arrived back at Paddington for 10pm. That return trip represented an average speed of nearly 42mph and, considering that the science of locomotive engineering was still in its infancy, it was a truly impressive feat. One of the passengers, Sir Thomas Acland MP, went directly from Paddington to the House of Commons and, at 10.30pm, he proudly announced that he had been in Exeter at 5.20pm that same evening. By contrast, Daniel Gooch recorded in his diary that the lengthy stint on the footplate had given him such a sore back that he was unable to walk properly the following day. Such was the price of success.

When the B&E had been incorporated, the residents of Plymouth had seen no reason why they should be excluded from the wonderful world of railways. Consequently, various plans were proposed for a railway between Plymouth and Exeter but, due to the small matter of an outcrop of granite named Dartmoor, the only feasible routes were around the edges of the moors. One scheme was for a line via Crediton, Okehampton and Tavistock while another suggested a route via Torquay but, although the potential of Torquay as a fashionable seaside resort was not to be ignored, the engineering works which would be required west of Torquay would have been immense. The Torquay route was, in fact, suggested by Brunel, but even he had doubts about the sheer expense of construction, and so he came up with an alternative route through Teignmouth, Newton Abbot and Totnes. This eventually gained

Parliamentary approval for the promoters, the Plymouth, Devonport & Exeter Railway. The PD&ER soon changed its title to the South Devon Railway; the renaming was suggested by the B&E and GWR and, considering that those two companies were offering substantial financial backing to help establish a continuous line from London to the gateway of Cornwall, they were not to be ignored.

Construction of the SDR started in 1844 and, like all obedient GWR-supported railways, it was built to the broad gauge. When the subject of motive power cropped up, the directors gave serious thought to the atmospheric system, which had been pioneered by Messrs Samuda Brothers on the West London Railway in 1840 and subsequently patented. This system was a radical departure from the norm. It involved the laying of a cast-iron pipe between the rails, and the provision of stationary pumping houses at regular intervals along the line to pump air through the pipe. Each 'locomotive' would be fitted with a piston which would be pushed through the pipe by the action of air pressure pushing against the vacuum. The SDR's directors consulted Brunel about the potential of the atmospheric system and, perhaps rather surprisingly, he thought it a sensible idea.

For Brunel, there were two major attractions of the atmospheric system. Firstly, he considered that it would be particularly suitable for the steeply-graded and sharply-curved sections of South Devon and, secondly, that it would result in a saving of £8,000pa in operating costs. Not altogether unpredictably, it was that second point

which proved decisive. Brunel surmised that 15in diameter pipes would suffice on the level sections of the line but, over the hills of South Devon, a diameter of 22½in was preferred.

The construction of the SDR slipped well behind schedule. Although Brunel had cautiously delayed his application of the atmospheric system until he had seen a similar one unveiled on the Croydon Railway, this was not the only reason for the delay. A contributing factor was that two particular landowners seemed to be competing for an award for obstructiveness, and it took considerable cajoling, not to mention expense, to obtain the necessary land. Furthermore, at Cockwood Marsh near Starcross, the original idea of an embankment had to be abandoned due to the softness of the mud and instead, a 600ft-long timber viaduct had to be constructed. Near Dawlish, the railway ran alongside the sea and it was necessary to construct a new sea wall; the cliffs above the line required, in some places, partial removal and, in others, tunnelling. In all, there were six tunnels between Dawlish and Teignmouth and these ranged in length from 50yd to 374yd. The longest, Parson's Rock, was to be lengthened to 513yd in 1920.

Because of the slow progress, it became

apparent that the proposed opening date of 1 June 1846 for the entire line was out of the question. As a sop to the critics, the SDR opened the 15-mile section between Exeter and Teignmouth on 30 May 1846 with conventional steam locomotives hired from the GWR. The two locomotives which officiated on the SDR's opening day were inside-framed 2-2-2s which had been built by the Haigh Foundry in 1838. For SDR duties, their GWR names of *Snake* and *Viper* were changed to *Exe* and *Teign* respectively, and the new names were carried until 1851. At Exeter the SDR used the B&E's station, and the approach to the station from the south was over a low timber bridge over the River Exe and a 62-arch stone-built viaduct at St Thomas. The intermediate stations were at St.Thomas in Exeter, Starcross and Dawlish but additional ones were later opened at Exminster in 1852 and Warren platform in 1905, the latter being renamed Dawlish Warren in 1911.

It was 30 December 1846 before the section between Teignmouth and Newton Abbot was opened to the public and, once again, the unfinished state of the atmospheric system necessitated the hiring of locomotives from the GWR; the inaugural train to Newton Abbot was hauled by Sun class 2-2-2 *Antelope*. Totnes was reached on 20 July 1847 and, on 5 May 1848, the line was finally opened through to Plymouth when 2-4-0s *Pisces* and *Cancer* worked double-headed, the former being driven by Daniel Gooch who had, by then, recovered from his bad back. Southwards from Newton Abbot, the line had been difficult to construct. There

were two tunnels, one of 272yd at Dainton summit and the other of 869yd at Marley; the bank at Rattery required a continuous ascent for over 4¼ miles and there were seven viaducts and a skew bridge. The station at Newton Abbot was in the B&E style as it had both platforms on the same side of the line, but it was rebuilt in a less idiosynchratic manner in 1861. The only other stations which were ready when the line opened were those at Totnes and Wrangaton, the latter masquerading under the name of Kings-

Above:
Warren Platform opened as a railmotor halt in 1905, and was later renamed Dawlish Warren. In this 1907 picture, railmotor No 72 is seen disgorging its passengers. *Rail Archive Stephenson*

Below:
These contemporary diagrams explain the principle of the atmospheric system, but it must be emphasised that they do not relate specifically to that of the South Devon Railway.

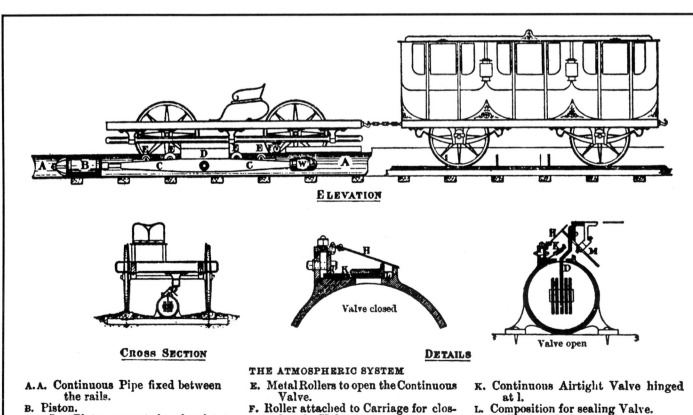

ELEVATION

CROSS SECTION

Valve closed

DETAILS

Valve open

THE ATMOSPHERIC SYSTEM

A.A. Continuous Pipe fixed between the rails.
B. Piston.
C.C. Iron Plates connected to the piston.
D. Plate connecting Apparatus to Carriage.

E. Metal Rollers to open the Continuous Valve.
F. Roller attached to Carriage for closing the Valve.
H. Weather Valve.

K. Continuous Airtight Valve hinged at l.
L. Composition for sealing Valve.
M. Roller attached to Carriage for opening Weather Valve.
W. Counterweight to Piston.

bridge Road between 1849 and 1895. Additional intermediate stations were opened at Brent, Ivybridge and Plympton in 1849, and at Cornwood in 1852.

At Plymouth, the original idea had been for the terminus of the SDR to be at Eldad, but that had been superseded by plans for a terminus at Millbay. When the line opened to Plymouth, it terminated at a temporary station at Laira Green, and it was not until 2 April 1849 that the terminus at Millbay was opened, thereby completing the 52½-mile line from Exeter. Originally, the station at Millbay was equipped with a hydraulic traverser, but even this magnificent piece of machinery was not enough to take the public's attention away from the spartan facilities of the wooden station. It was remarked that, in the case of Millbay station, the GWR seemed intent on trying to raise drabness to an art form. Until it was superseded by North Road station in 1877, Millbay station was called, quite simply, Plymouth. With the advent of North Road, Millbay was no longer in the front of the shop window, and so the GWR managed to stall until 1900 before spending money on the station's reconstruction.

Meanwhile, the equipment for the atmospheric system was being installed slowly but surely. Ten engine houses were constructed between Exeter and Totnes and, during the spring and summer of 1847, experimental trains were run regularly between Exeter and Teignmouth for the purposes of the engineers. None carried fare-paying passengers. It was 13 September before the first revenue-earning atmospheric train worked between Exeter and Teignmouth and, largely due to its smoothness of running and the welcome absence of exhaust smoke, it was very well received. As for performance, the following months saw some impressive running from the atmospheric trains. Speeds of up to 68mph were recorded while, in the muscle stakes, loads of 100 tons were hauled on the level at a constant 35mph. On 10 January 1848, the atmospheric system was extended to Newton Abbot but that was as far as it ever went.

Full credit was due to the SDR's atmospheric superintendent, James Pearson, for getting the trains running, but it was beyond his capabilities to keep them running. It quickly became clear that the atmospheric system did not provide the revolution in railway engineering which had been anticipated. The term 'teething troubles' implies the emergence of a few problems when dealing with something completely new but, in the case of the atmospheric system, the more appropriate term would be 'dental disaster'.

One of the major problems was that leather had been used for the seals in two key components; the first was the valves in the pipes and the second was the 'locomotives'' pistons which were propelled through the pipes. It was soon found that the vacuum created by the pumping of air dried out the natural oil of the leather, thereby making the seals very vulnerable to intruding rain or frost; furthermore, applications of additional grease were found to provide little more than a gastronomic treat for rats. A knock-on effect was that, when the leather started breaking up, more pumping was required to obtain the same vacuum, and the pumping houses were being asked to produce more air than that for which they had been designed. Consequently, the instances of failures in the pumping houses became more and more frequent.

In 1848, it was estimated that the cost of rectifying the problems would be £1,160 per mile, the total for the section to Newton Abbot therefore being around £25,000. Since the atmospheric system had already cost the

SDR in excess of £400,000, the additional expenditure was rejected by the directors. It was decided that, from 10 September 1848, conventional locomotive traction would be adopted, but even apart from the financial implications, this presented major problems. Because of the anticipated extra speed and power of atmospheric workings, the Exeter to Totnes and Rattery to Hemerdon sections had been laid only with single track, while the gradients in South Devon had been engineered more steeply than if a locomotive-operated system had been intended. Today, the 1 in 36 of Dainton Bank is the steepest gradient on any main line in Britain.

Those obliging people at the GWR offered to hire locomotives to the SDR but, mindful of the strenuous work over the South Devon banks, the rate of 1s 4d (6½p) per mile for the Exeter to Newton Abbot section was raised to 1s 9d (8½p) per mile southwards from Newton Abbot. The GWR managed to overlook the fact that it didn't really have any locomotives suitable for work in South Devon but, as the SDR had little option, a working agreement was signed. However, a cheaper alternative materialised in 1851 when Messrs Evans & Geach of Birmingham offered better terms for a ten-year working agreement, and this came into effect on 1 July that year.

The first locomotives supplied by the contractors were 12 4-4-0STs and four 0-6-0STs, both types having inside frames; they followed GWR practice in carrying names instead of numbers. All were designed by Daniel Gooch and the 4-4-0STs, with their 5ft 9in driving wheels and 17in x 24in cylinders, were very similar to his 'Corsair' class for the GWR. The 0-6-0STs were similar to a Gooch design for the Vale of Neath Railway and had 4ft 9in wheels and 17in x 24in cylinders. Further 4-4-0STs and 0-6-0STs were delivered in 1859 and 1865 and, apart from having 1,100 gallon tanks instead of 800 gallon tanks, they were based firmly on the Gooch designs of the original locomotives.

The SDR's locomotive headquarters was at Newton Abbot but, as the widespread use of conventional locomotives had not been anticipated, the premises were not geared up for construction work. The frames of three broad gauge locomotives were actually laid in 1875, but these engines were finished at Swindon Works after the GWR had absorbed the SDR. A proper repair shop was established in 1893, the year after the broad gauge had become extinct, and this was a traverser-equipped building which was modelled on one of the workshops at Swindon. The original SDR engine shed at Newton Abbot was a woefully inadequate twin-road structure, but it was not replaced until 1893, when a standard six-road shed was opened.

At Exeter, a single-road shed sufficed until the extensive rebuilding of the station and yard in 1862-64 while, at Totnes, a twin-road depot was constructed in 1847, mainly to house banking locomotives. It closed in 1904. At Millbay in Plymouth, a twin-road shed was opened in 1849 and, in 1859, a new four-road structure was added, primarily to accommodate the SDR locomotives which worked the newly-opened Cornwall Railway. In January 1901, Millbay's allocation was 74 locomotives but, later that year, the GWR opened a new roundhouse depot at Laira and

this gradually became the main engine shed in the city. Millbay shed was closed in the 1920s but was reopened temporarily between 1925 and 1931. Official records also note the existences of SDR engine sheds at Teignmouth and Laira Green but, in view of their respective closure dates of 1847 and 1849, it is most likely that the 'sheds' were merely sidings with basic servicing facilities, and were of use only when those places were the temporary termini of the still-expanding SDR.

On 18 December 1848, just three months after the SDR had converted to locomotive haulage, the company had opened the five-mile spur from Newton Abbot to a temporary terminus at 'Torquay'. A feature to the north of the terminus was a pumping house for the atmospheric system, but the building had never had its pumping engine installed. The only intermediate station on the new line was at Kingskerswell but it was not opened until 1853. The terminus at 'Torquay' was renamed Torre on 2 August 1859 when a three-mile extension into Torquay itself was opened. Nominally, the extension was owned

by the Dartmouth & Torbay Railway, which had been promoted as a subsidiary of the SDR in case the extensive civil engineering work proved too costly but, despite the need for 20 bridges, one viaduct and a 133yd tunnel (which was opened out in 1910) on the three-mile extension, the bank had not been broken.

The ultimate goal of the Dartmouth & Torbay Railway was Kingswear and, after a series of piecemeal openings, the completed line was eventually unveiled to the travelling public on 16 August 1864. At first, the only intermediate stations between Torquay and Kingswear were at Paignton and Brixham Road (later renamed Churston); Preston platform and Sands halt were added in later years, but the former lasted only until 1914. Between Churston and Kingswear, Britannia halt opened in 1898 to serve the nearby Naval college, but the halt's exclusive use kept it out of the public timetables; its precise closure date is uncertain, but it is known that it masqueraded under the name of Kingswear Crossing after 1917. When the line was opened throughout to Kingswear, temporary locomotive servicing facilities at Torre were closed. A permanent single-road engine shed was subsequently opened at Kingswear and, apart from the replacement of the original 23ft 5in turntable by one of 55ft 8in in 1900, the shed and yard remained little altered until closure in 1924.

Kingswear might have seemed a strange target, particularly in view of the difficulty of engineering the line. Apart from considerable earthworks, there was a 495yd tunnel and a stone viaduct near Greenway, and two timber viaducts, one of 200yd and the other 170yd, on the approach to Kingswear. The reason why the railway company earmarked Kingswear as a target was simply that the fashionable town of Dartmouth was on the opposite bank of the River Dart. Obviously, a railway into Dartmouth itself would have been ideal but, while the Kingswear line had been difficult to construct, the topography on the Dartmouth side of the river would have caused even Brunel to throw up his

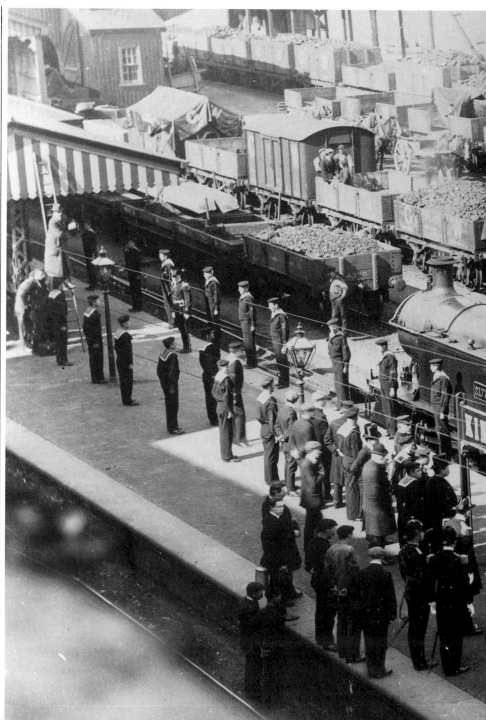

hands in despair. A ferry service provided the connection between Kingswear and Dartmouth and, at Dartmouth, full 'railway station' facilities were maintained for the ferry traffic. All that was missing were the trains. The Dartmouth & Torbay Railway, complete with its ferries, was officially absorbed by the South Devon Railway in 1872.

Even before the railway had arrived at Torbay, the area had become well established as a fashionable resort. However, the availability of a rail connection provided a tremendous boost and, in years to come, Torbay was, arguably, one of the very best examples of how the railways changed the face of the great British holiday. As early as 1874, the SDR had to lay a third track between Newton Abbot and Aller in order to cope with the traffic on the Torbay line.

While the 'atmospheric caper', as it became known locally, was going on in South Devon, changes were afoot on the B&E. Its directors became well aware of the success of the main line to Exeter and, con-

Above:
The 200yd Longwood Viaduct, near Kingswear, photographed in 1921, the year in which it was rendered redundant by a new alignment of the railway. The nearby 170yd Noss Creek Viaduct was similarly affected by the alteration of the route. *LCGB/Ken Nunn Collection*

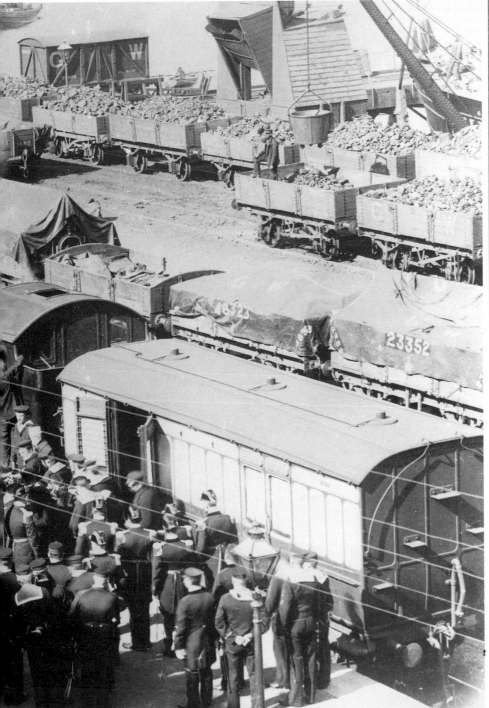

sequently, they became increasingly frustrated at seeing the GWR reap a considerable proportion of the benefits. Eventually, it was considered that the B&E could go it alone and, therefore, the lease with the GWR should not be renewed. It was 1 May 1849 when the B&E formally became a self-sufficient concern and, in preparation for that day, the company had started ordering its own locomotives during the summer of 1847.

The first of the B&E's own locomotives were delivered early in 1849. For passenger duties, the company opted for 4-2-2s which, with their 7ft 6in driving wheels and 16½in x 24in cylinders were, in effect, smaller versions of Gooch's famous 'Iron Duke' class. Twenty were delivered during 1849. Ten were built by Stothert & Slaughter, the Bristol company which was the forerunner of the famous Avonside Engine Co, and the other 10 came from Longridge & Co of Bedlington. For freight work, Stothert & Slaughter supplied eight 0-6-0s with 5ft 0in wheels and 16in x 24in cylinders; these were very similar to locomotives which the company had previously built to a Gooch design for the GWR. The absence of small shunting engines was not unusual as, in common with many railways of the age, shunting tended to be looked after by horses. In contrast to the GWR and SDR, the B&E numbered its locomotives. The 4-2-2s were given Nos 1-20 and the 0-6-0s took Nos 21-28.

The B&E erected temporary locomotive workshops alongside the engine shed at Exeter. The master plan was to establish a permanent workshop in the city at which the company could not only maintain, but also

build, its own locomotives, and this idea was later favoured by James Pearson. Pearson was appointed as the B&E's locomotive superintendent in June 1850 although, at that time, he was still being paid a retainer by the South Devon Railway to supervise the disposal of its atmospheric equipment. Exeter was Pearson's home town and, understandably, he was quite happy to remain there but his directors eventually had other ideas. Being a Bristol-based company, the B&E's hierarchy saw no reason why the provincial outpost of Exeter should have the locomotive works, and so alternative plans were drawn up for a workshop in Bristol. Bristol Works opened in September 1854 and the makeshift facilities at Exeter were retained for routine repairs.

As the 1850s progressed, the business community in Plymouth became increasingly worried by the Cornwall Railway's plans to build a line from Plymouth to Falmouth; it was considered that through rail access to the port of Falmouth would present stiff competition for Plymouth. Nevertheless, the Cornwall Railway's proposals passed the Parliamentary stages and, on 4 May 1859, the company opened its broad gauge line between Plymouth and Truro to the public. From the outset, the Cornwall Railway was worked by the SDR and, considering that the latter had had to rely on the GWR for motive power only a few years earlier, it demonstrated the ambitiousness of the SDR's directors.

On the Devon side of the Tamar, the West Cornwall's only station was at Devonport. On the 3½-mile stretch between Cornwall Junction, on the SDR's line into Plymouth, and the crossing of the Tamar, there was a 125yd tunnel at Devonport, and timber viaducts at Stonehouse Pool (107yd), Keyham (144yd) and Weston Mill (400yd). Structurally, the

viaducts were very sound and none of the three was replaced until the 1900s but, to many first-time railway travellers, they looked somewhat death-defying. The public's impression of the timber viaducts was not exactly boosted when, just two days after the railway opened, a locomotive and its train parted company with the track on Grove Viaduct, just on the Cornish side of the Tamar, and plummeted 30ft into the water.

The best known engineering work on the Cornwall Railway's line from Plymouth was, of course, the Royal Albert Bridge. Where it crosses the Tamar, the river is 1,100ft wide and up to 70ft deep at high water; as if to compound the challenge to Brunel's engineering capabilities, the Admiralty insisted that any bridge across the river should have at least two spans of 200ft each and a mini-

mum headroom of 100ft. Work on the bridge had commenced in 1853 but, after excavations had revealed deep sand and mud, Brunel had abandoned the idea of a timber bridge. Instead, plans were drawn up for combining the arch and suspension methods in a bridge which had two main spans, each 455ft long, 56ft high and weighing 1,060 tons. Due to the immense cost involved, the original plans for a double-track bridge were dropped in favour of single track, and this brought the eventual outlay down from £325,000 to £225,000.

The bridge was formally opened by HRH The Prince Consort on 2 May 1859, two days before the public opening of the Cornwall Railway. The tragedy was that, during the previous year, Brunel's health had deterio-rated. At the ceremonial opening of the bridge, Brunel was working abroad and, when he returned to Britain, his trip across the famous bridge was in an open truck which had been laid on specially because of his very poor health. Isambard Kingdom Brunel died on 15 September 1859 at the age of just 53 and, fittingly, an inscription was ultimately applied at each end of the Royal Albert Bridge. It read, quite simply: I. K. BRUNEL. ENGINEER, 1859.

Back on the B&E's and SDR's main lines through Devon, things ticked over reasonably steadily during the 1850s. Between Paddington and Exeter, Gooch's 'Iron Duke' 4-2-2s were used on the crack expresses and the schedule allowed 4½hr. This was decelerated to 4¾hr in 1852, but the fastest down

Right:
This view of the approach to the LSWR's Queen Street station in Exeter was taken from New North Road circa 1910. The locomotives waiting for up expresses are (left) Drummond 'T9' class 4-4-0 No 727 and (right) Adams 'T3' class 4-4-0 No 576. The locomotive on their right appears to be a 'Jubilee' class 0-4-2. *Bucknall Collection/Ian Allan Library*

train became known as the 'Flying Dutchman' after the racehorse which won both the Derby and the St Leger in 1849. However, during the 1840s and 1850s, the GWR and its associated companies had found their beloved broad gauge under constant threat and, in the south of England, one of the prime antagonists was the London & South Western Railway.

As early as 1848, the standard gauge LSWR had received assent to extend westwards from Salisbury but, as this had been little more than a measure to block possible GWR expansion, it had come as little surprise that the LSWR had showed no enthusiasm for constructing its authorised line. It took a Board of Trade directive in 1855 to coax the LSWR to extract its corporate digit but, even then, progress was not exactly swift. The LSWR eventually reached Yeovil in 1860 and, on 19 July that year, the extension to Exeter was finally opened for business. The obligatory directors' special had run the previous

day and three locomotives had been required to haul the 20-coach train. The newest was Joseph Beattie's 6ft 6in 2-2-2 of 1857, No 151 *Montrose*, and the others were John Gooch's 7ft 2-2-2s of 1852/53, No 115 *Vulcan* and No 122 *Britannia*. The journey had taken seven hours, and the day had been marked by a total eclipse of the sun. The GWR had refrained from suggesting that those two points might not have been coincidental.

On the Devon section of the LSWR's main line, there were stations at Axminster, Colyton, Honiton, Feniton and Whimple. Colyton was renamed Colyton Junction in 1868 and Seaton Junction the following year; Feniton became Ottery Road in 1861 only to be rechristened Sidmouth Junction in 1874. Additional stations were later opened at Broad Clyst and Pinhoe, and an unadvertised stopping place, Roundball halt, was established in 1909 between Honiton and Sidmouth Junction to serve the local rifle ranges; it vanished in the 1920s. The inaugural LSWR passenger train to Exeter left Waterloo at 9am and arrived in Exeter at 2.10pm. The timing of 5hr 10min wasn't bad but, nevertheless, it was 40min slower than the schedule which the GWR had established in 1845. This was despite the LSWR's route of 171½ miles being 22½ miles shorter than the GWR's. The LSWR had its terminus at Queen Street in Exeter which was, at first, isolated from the GWR. However, a connection between the two unneighbourly neighbours seemed essential, particularly in view of the LSWR's interests in the branch line to Crediton which used the B&E's station at St Davids. The problem was that any physical link between Queen Street and St Davids had to negotiate the 150ft drop from the LSWR's hilltop site.

Nevertheless, a connecting line was opened in 1862 and, even by present day standards, it was a daunting one; the line left Queen Street and dropped on a gradient of 1 in 37, part of which passed through the curved St Davids tunnel while another part ran on a sharply-curved embankment. This apparent afterthought did little to improve the LSWR's image in Exeter, as local folk had

Left:
Millbay station in Plymouth is shown in this 25in Ordnance Survey map. Unfortunately, the quality of the map leaves a little to be desired but, as the original dates from 1868, excuses are considered unnecessary. *Crown Copyright*

previously become used to a smart broad-gauge station and, by contrast, Queen Street was stark and poorly-equipped, even by the standards of the day. During the late 19th century, Queen Street came in for constant criticism but there was to be no significant improvement in its facilities until the late 1920s, when the Southern Railway reluctantly footed the bill. Queen Street was not given its more familiar title of Exeter Central until 1933.

While the LSWR's link to the B&E's station at St Davids was under construction, the B&E realised that improvements at its own station would be beneficial. The original layout of both platforms on the same side of the line might have been adequate in the 1840s, but it was a positive hindrance to operations in the 1860s. The rebuilding of St Davids started in 1862 and the outcome was a completely new station, which was unveiled in July 1864. It had three platforms, one of 510ft, a second of 640ft and a third of 750ft, and these served four platform roads; the station was protected by an overall roof which was 363ft long and had a 132ft span. During the rebuilding, the whole station yard was also relaid, and this necessitated the removal of the original engine shed and the construction of a new four-road shed on an adjacent site. Further improvements were carried out at Exeter in 1903, when a new goods depot was opened at Alphington Road, and the station and shed at St Davids were both extended again in 1912-14. This last bout of rebuilding included the replacement of the station's overall roof by a series of awnings, and a new two-storey frontage.

The LSWR's locomotives in Exeter were given bed and breakfast in a three-road engine shed which had been constructed just beyond the east end of Queen Street station but, by the 1870s, the expansion of the company's network into other parts of Devon meant that the shed had been outgrown. An alternative site was sought for a larger shed, and suitable land was found just over a mile to the east of Queen Street where the branch to Exmouth diverged. The new 11-road shed at Exmouth Junction was opened in 1887, but the old facilities at Queen Street were retained for stabling. A useful legacy of Queen Street shed was the turntable, which obviated the need for light running to Exmouth Junction for turning. However, the original 42ft turntable at Queen Street was well past its sell-by date, and so a new 50ft model was installed.

Coleford Junction was three miles west of Crediton on the route of the North Devon Railway, the 'missing link' between Exeter and Crediton belonging to the logically-named Exeter & Crediton Railway, a B&E-worked broad gauge line which had opened in May 1851. The LSWR had originally set its sights on working the E&CR as a standard gauge line and, predictably, that had resulted

in much squabbling with the B&E. The friction between the LSWR and the B&E had not been helped when, in July 1854, the North Devon Railway had commenced operating from Crediton to Barnstaple on its broad gauge line. A fuller account of the in-fighting between the rival factions is related in chapter 3, but suffice to say that the LSWR later secured the lease of the E&CR and converted it for mixed gauge operation, thereby permitting standard gauge working from Exeter to Coleford Junction and, ultimately, Okehampton and beyond.

Beyond Okehampton the LSWR was authorised in February 1863 to make a connection with the Launceston & South Devon Railway near Lidford (later spelt Lydford). Two years later, the extension of the main line to Launceston, complete with a branch to Bude was authorised. Construction of the new line was not easy as the northern edge of Dartmoor presented stiff challenges for engineers and labourers alike. There was the little matter of the 950ft summit south of Meldon Junction, and also the valley of the West

Above:
The line between Okehampton and Lydford was opened on 12 October 1874, and its best-known feature was the Bouch-style Meldon Viaduct. This picture of the precarious-looking but, nevertheless, long-lived structure was taken in 1906. *Rail Archive Stephenson*

Okement River, which necessitated the building of a 150ft high viaduct.

Partly as a result of the obstacles, the new LSWR lines tended to open in a piecemeal fashion. The line to Lydford was opened throughout on 12 October 1874 and Launceston was reached on 21 July 1886, but it was 1899 before the main line to Padstow was completed. Between Coleford Junction and Lydford, there were intermediate stations at Bow, North Tawton, Okehampton Road, Okehampton and Bridestowe. By October 1871, the line had reached only as far as the station at Okehampton Road but, when the next section was opened, complete with the 'new'

Right:
Adams '460' class 4-4-0 No 526 was photographed near Okehampton on 14 July 1924, still wearing old LSWR livery. *Bucknall Collection/Ian Allan Library*

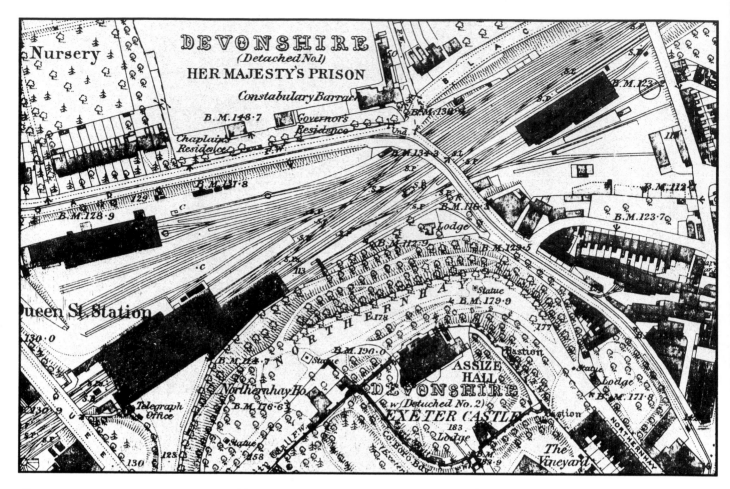

This 25in Ordnance Survey map of 1890 shows Queen Street (later Central) station in Exeter almost in the same condition as when it opened. The structure near the turntable in the upper part of the map is the old engine shed. *Crown Copyright*

Okehampton station, Okehampton Road was renamed Belstone Corner; it was rechristened Sampford Courtenay in 1872. The Launceston line had intermediate stations at Ashbury, Halwill & Beaworthy, Ashwater and Tower Hill. Halwill & Beaworthy was renamed Halwill Junction in 1887 in recognition of the branch to Bude, but although the word 'Junction' was officially dropped from the station's title in 1923, the general public continued to refer to it as Halwill Junction.

The main engineering contractor on the construction of the LSWR's main lines west of Exeter was Robert Relf. He had his own standard gauge locomotives for use on his contracts, and four of these were eventually purchased by the LSWR. Two were Manning Wardle 'E' class 0-4-0STs of 1876, which were named *Pioneer* and *Jessie;* the LSWR bought them both in 1881 and gave them Nos 407/08. The LSWR used them for shunting duties on the Sutton Harbour and Cattewater branches in Plymouth, where they worked until 1891. In that year, No 408 was withdrawn, but No 407 was transferred to Guildford for shed pilot duties and was not scrapped until 1921. The other two contractor's locomotives which passed to the LSWR

were also Manning Wardle machines, one being an 'E' class 0-4-0ST of 1872 and the other an 'I' class 0-6-0ST of 1862. The 0-4-0ST was originally named *Lydford,* but the LSWR renamed it *St Michael* and gave it No 457; the 0-6-0ST, which was named *Lady Portsmouth,* became LSWR No 392. Of those two, No 457 worked alongside No 407 *Pioneer* at Plymouth, and was repurchased by Robert Relf in 1893 for the engineering work on the GWR's main line between Brent and Kingsbridge; the other locomotive, No 392 *Lady Portsmouth,* was used by the LSWR mainly in the London and Bournemouth areas.

The LSWR repeatedly drew up grandiose plans to reach West Cornwall but, as things turned out, it had to be content with Wadebridge and Padstow on the north coast. Plymouth, however, was a different matter. The Okehampton Railway, which had nominally constructed the LSWR-worked line through mid-Devon, had changed its name in 1865 to the Devon & Cornwall Railway. When the D&CR unveiled its plans to reach Plymouth, the GWR was not taken in as it knew, quite correctly, that the D&CR was little more than an LSWR subsidiary.

The development of a standard gauge route between Okehampton and Plymouth was marked by a series of agreements in the 1860s. The first, in 1862, between the LSWR and the GWR/SDR confirmed that the LSWR was not to have any interest west of Okehampton. In return, the LSWR gained the Andover-Redbridge line. However, in the same year proposals for a standard gauge line to Lydford were made. The sections in the

hill allowing for operation by the LSWR were
withdrawn when it became clear that these
ran counter to the agreement. In 1865 the
D&CR plans, in conjunction with those of
the Cornwall Central, caused the issue to be
raised again. This time an agreement was
reached between the LSWR and the
GWR/SDR/B&E, which permitted standard
gauge access to Plymouth, but on
unfavourable terms. This agreement was
scheduled to be guaranteed through a parliamentary bill, but a dispute arose between the
LSWR and B&E which led to the repudiation
of both the 1865 and 1862 agreements. The
scene was set for unrestricted competition
on the traffic to Plymouth.

The suggestion of a competing route to
Plymouth set the alarm bells ringing in the
GWR camp, and strongly-worded letters
bounced back and forth between the GWR
and LSWR directors, the latter being unable
to admit their interest in the D&CR but,
somewhat suspiciously, fighting its case all
the same. Things came out into the open in
1872 when the LSWR absorbed the D&CR.
The LSWR reached Lydford in October 1874,
and built a junction which provided a link
with the South Devon Railway's Launceston
branch. In theory this junction was of little
use, as the SDR line from Lydford into Plymouth was broad gauge while the LSWR's
line was standard gauge. But the LSWR had
an ace up its corporate sleeve. It called on
powers which had been granted in 1866 to
compel the SDR to convert the line into Plymouth to mixed gauge.

The SDR had little option but to comply
with the LSWR's demand and, as if to add
insult to injury, the SDR was compelled to
build a new mixed gauge station at North
Road in Plymouth for joint use by the LSWR.
On 17 May 1876, LSWR trains started working into Plymouth, but North Road station
was not ready for opening until 28 March the
following year. This was no real disappointment to the LSWR as its long-awaited arrival

Table 1.1: Locomotives built for the South Devon Railway

Type	Built	Total	Wheels	Cylinders	GWR Nos	Wdn	Notes
4-4-0ST	1851-53	12	5ft 9in	17in x 24in	2096-2105	1873-84	Two withdrawn in pre-GWR days.
0-6-0ST	1854/55	4	4ft 9in	17in x 24in	2139-42	1877-85	
4-4-0ST	1859-65	16	5ft 6in	16½in x 24in	2106-21	1876-92	
0-6-0ST	1860-64	8	4ft 6in	16½in x 24in	2143/44/48-53	1877-92	
4-4-0ST	1866	6	5ft 8in	17in x 24in	2122-27	1885-92	
0-6-0ST	1866	2	4ft 9in	16½in x 24in	2154/55	1886/92	
0-4-0WT	1868	1	3ft 0in	9in x 12in	2180	1883	
0-6-0ST	1869	1	3ft 0in	12½in x 16in	2170	1905	Converted to SG in 1892*
2-4-0T	1871	1	3ft 0in	9in x 16in	2171	1907	Converted to SG in 1878*
2-4-0ST	1871	1	4ft 0in	12in x 17in	2137	1899	Converted to SG in 1892*
0-6-0ST	1872-74	10	4ft 9in	17in x 24in	2160-69	1889-1905	Built as convertibles*
4-4-0ST	1872/75	4	5ft 9in	17in x 24in	2128-31	1892	
0-4-0WT	1873	3	3ft 0in	10in x 16in	2172-74	1882-1913	Two converted to SG in 1893 *
0-4-0ST	1874/75	5	3ft 0in	14in x 18in	2175-79	1906-10	Converted to SG in 1892/93*
2-4-0ST	1878	3	4ft 0in	11½in x 17in	1298-1300	1926-36	Completed by GWR as SG locos

Notes

*The GWR renumbered the locomotives which were converted to the standard gauge. BG No 2170 became SG No 1326.
BG No 2171 became SG No 2.
BG No 2137 became SG No 1316.

BG Nos 2160-62/64-69 became SG Nos 1317-25 (BG No 2163 withdrawn 1889). BG Nos 2172/74 became SG Nos 1327/28.
BG Nos 2175-79 became SG Nos 1329-33.
NB: SG Nos 1298-1300 never ran as BG locomotives and, therefore, did not carry BG numbers.

Table 1.2: Secondhand locomotives purchased by the South Devon Railway

Type	Built	Total	Wheels	Cylinders	GWR Nos	Wdn	Notes
4-4-0ST	1864	2	5ft 3in	16½in x 24in	2132/33	1892	Ex-Carmarthen & Cardigan Ry 1868/72
4-4-0ST	1872	2	5ft 2in	17in x 24in	2134/35	1889/92	Ex-Carmarthen & Cardigan Ry 1872
2-4-0ST	1853	1	5ft 0in	15in x 22in	2136	1888	Ex-West Cornwall Ry 1866
0-6-0ST	1852	1	5ft 0in	17in x 24in	2138	1889	Ex-GWR 1872
4-4-0ST	1863	1	5ft 6in	16½in x 24in	2145	1885	Ex-Llynvi & Ogmore Ry 1868
0-6-0T	1862	2	4ft 6in	16½in x 24in	2146/47	1884/86	Ex-Llynvi & Ogmore Ry 1868
0-6-0ST	1865	1	4ft 9in	17¼in x 24in	2156	1889	Ex-West Cornwall Ry 1866
0-6-0T	1865/66	3	4ft 6in	17in x 24in	2157-59	1887-92	Ex-GWR 1872

in Plymouth was adequate to keep the directors smiling and, furthermore, the LSWR had completed its own smart and spacious terminus at Devonport in time for opening day. These days, a main line station in Devonport might seem like a poor substitute for one in central Plymouth but, in the mid-19th century, Devonport was the larger and more prosperous community.

The original intention had been to provide a sturdy stone-built station at North Road, but in order to hasten completion the station was constructed in wood. North Road was not significantly improved until 1908, and it was the 1920s before it really claimed the status of Plymouth's premier station. About ½-mile to the east of North Road, a station had opened at Mutley in 1871 and this was to become jointly used. Mutley later became known as 'the gentry's station' and, for many years, the LSWR had its own staff there to look after the well-heeled clientele. For the motive power between Exeter and Plymouth, William Beattie had designed a class of six 4-4-0Ts, Nos 318-323, but they proved to be exceptionally rough riders and were soon replaced by older Beattie locomotives.

Even after some 18 years, the SDR had not fully recovered from the financial disaster of the atmospheric system and, having become totally browned off with the LSWR intrusion, the SDR sold out to the GWR. At the time of the absorption on 1 February 1876, the SDR's portfolio showed 123½ miles of track and 85 broad gauge locomotives. The majority of the locomotives were either 4-4-0STs or 0-6-0STs, but the remainder provided a motley collection. There were second-hand acquisitions from the Llynvi & Ogmore and the Carmarthen & Cardigan Railways, plus two engines which had been acquired from the West Cornwall Railway and had subsequently been converted from narrow gauge tender locomotives to broad gauge tanks. The older of the WCR duo was *Penwith* which dated to 1853, but the other, *Redruth*, claimed the distinction of having been built at the WCR's workshops at Carn Brea.

Ten of the SDR's small tank locomotives were later converted to the standard gauge and, furthermore, 10 0-6-0STs and four 4-4-0STs had been originally built with a view to eventual conversion. The SDR's broad gauge locomotives became GWR

Nos 2096-2179, and most of those later converted to standard gauge eventually took numbers in the '13xx' series. At the time of the absorption, three small broad gauge 2-4-0STs were actually under construction at Newton Abbot Works, although most of the parts had been supplied by the Ince Forge Co. The building work was finished off at Swindon, but the trio emerged from the works in 1878 as standard gauge 2-4-0 side tanks; they became GWR Nos 1298/99/1330. No 1299 was fitted with a crane in 1881 for duties as the Swindon Works shunter and the locomotive was not retired until 1936.

On 1 January 1876, exactly one month before the SDR had amalgamated with the GWR, the B&E had done exactly the same thing, although the B&E/GWR merger did not officially come into effect until 1 August. Despite the steady inroads into the broad gauge system, the B&E had, at the time of absorption, 125½ miles of broad gauge track, 69½ miles of mixed gauge but just 18½ miles of standard gauge; there was also a 3ft gauge siding at Westleigh Quarries, near Burlescombe. None of the standard gauge track was in Devon.

The B&E passed 125 locomotives to the

Right:
GWR 2-4-0 Crane Tank No 1299 had been intended to start life as a broad gauge 2-4-0ST on the South Devon Railway. Here, it is seen near the end of its long life at Swindon in April 1932. *Rail Archive Stephenson*

Below:
This photograph of a full-house at Plymouth Friary was taken from Tothill Road bridge in the early 1920s. The locomotives cannot be positively identified, but the one at the near end of the middle road seems to be a 'O2' class 0-4-4T. The building on the left of the picture is the goods shed. *Lens of Sutton*

GWR and these comprised 95 broad gauge, 28 standard gauge and a pair of 3ft gauge shunters for work at Westleigh Quarries. The broad gauge contingent became GWR Nos 2001-95, and among them were four 4-2-4Ts which had been rebuilt from older Pearson 4-2-4Ts; the originals, which had driving wheels of 9ft diameter, were known to have notched up speeds in excess of 80mph. The B&E's broad gauge locomotives were never converted to the standard gauge, and so they became extinct in 1892. The standard gauge locomotives became GWR Nos 1353-82 and, although none had been built before 1867, only 12 were to remain in service after 1890. The long-service awards went to a pair of Bristol-built 0-6-0Ts of 1874/75 which became GWR Nos 1376/77. No 1377 survived until 1927, by which time it had spent 46 years at Weymouth hauling

boat trains through the streets; its classmate also worked at Weymouth but was transferred to the Tanat Valley line in North Wales in 1927, and was withdrawn from Oswestry shed in 1934.

The arrival of the LSWR in Plymouth in 1876 prompted improvements in the services of the GWR. The LSWR's route from Waterloo to Plymouth was 19 miles longer than the GWR line from Paddington but, west of Exeter, neither company's line was suitable for fast running. In 1877, the fastest GWR train from Paddington to Plymouth took 6hr 15min, while the crack LSWR service took 6hrs 55min. The GWR introduced a new service in 1879 which reduced the time to Plymouth to 5hr 55min, and this was nicknamed the 'Zulu' after the South African wars which were, at that time, hogging the headlines. The LSWR replied in 1882 with a

6hr 8min express to Plymouth which, as far as Exeter, was actually 15min faster than the GWR's 'Zulu'. However, the great advantage of the LSWR's service was that it took third-class passengers while the GWR, not the least class-conscious of railway companies, stuck to first and second-class only.

In 1890, the GWR introduced a new fast train which left Paddington at 10.15am and took 4hr 5min to Exeter and 5hr 35min to Plymouth; because of its continuation to Penzance, it became known, albeit unofficially at first, as the 'Cornishman'. The main reason behind the inauguration of the new service was that, on 2 June that year, the LSWR had acquired an alternative route between Lydford and Plymouth. That route belonged to the independent Plymouth, Devonport & South Western Junction Railway which, in later years, was to upgrade a

tramway to Callington for use as a conventional standard gauge branch. The new 22½-mile main line between Lydford and Plymouth was double throughout and ran to Devonport station at Plymouth, thereby turning Devonport from a terminus into a through station. When the line opened, the LSWR trains made a stop at Devonport but terminated at North Road. However, the LSWR set to work on converting the 13-year old goods station at Friary into a passenger terminus and it opened in its new guise on 1 July 1891. The new Friary station had two platforms, each of which had bays; a run-round track was provided between the two main platform roads.

When the LSWR had first arrived in Plymouth, there had been a small engine shed at Devonport but, with the shift of emphasis to Friary, a new twin-road engine shed was constructed in the yard of Friary station. Nevertheless, Devonport shed was retained until 1919 as an out-station for locomotives engaged on the LSWR's dock branches. With the LSWR's constantly increasing activities in Plymouth, the original shed at Friary was outgrown very quickly, and so a new three-road shed was opened in 1908. The main line locomotives which were housed at Friary after the opening of the LSWR's own route into Plymouth were, on the whole, Adams 4-4-0s of the '380' and '460' classes. For local services, the customary 0-4-4Ts gradually took over and went on to form a sizeable proportion of Friary's stud; for dock shunting, a

Above:
Bere Alston station was photographed circa 1910 and an unidentified LSWR locomotive, possibly a 'T1' class 0-4-4T, approaches the down platform with a short freight train. The open trucks in the siding beyond the up platform were, almost certainly, for mineral traffic originating on the PD&SWJR's Callington branch. *Lens of Sutton*

Below:
GWR 'Bulldog' class 4-4-0 No 3340 *Marazion* is seen at Brent on a Newton Abbot to Plymouth working on 23 July 1910. The locomotive was later renumbered 3328, but lost its nameplates in 1931. *LCGB/Ken Nunn Collection*

number of the small, but deceptively powerful, 'B4' 0-4-0Ts were drafted in over the years.

At Okehampton, mid-way between Exeter and Plymouth, an engine shed was built in 1895, primarily to house the locomotives engaged on local duties on the Exeter-Plymouth route and branch work to Holsworthy (and later to Bude). In 1897, a major quarry was started at nearby Meldon, and the task of transporting the stone was, logically, given to Okehampton locomotives. The original shed was a wooden, single-road structure, but it was destroyed by fire in 1920, and its replacement was built from concrete blocks. The 50ft turntable, which was installed in 1895, was not replaced until the 1940s.

The PD&SWJR line into Plymouth, which included gradients of up to 1 in 75, had been an expensive one to build. It had numerous bridges and also three tunnels, two of which were under the community of Devonport itself but, despite the line's strategic importance to the LSWR, that company had contributed only a very small proportion to the PD&SWJR's corporate piggy bank. Between Lydford and Devonport, there were intermediate stations at Brentor, Tavistock, Bere Alston, Bere Ferrers, Tamerton Foliot, St Budeaux and Ford. At first, St Budeaux station was suffixed 'for Saltash' but, later, the suffix was changed to 'Victoria Rd.' and, until 1898, the stations at Bere Alston and Bere Ferrers were named Beer Alston and Beer Ferris respectively; until 1906, Tamerton Foliot was spelt 'Tamerton Foliott'.

And so, by 1891, the main line map of Devon was more or less complete, but this did not mean the end of major changes for the foreseeable future. The GWR's beloved broad gauge had been under fire ever since the 1840s and, gradually, much of the network had been converted to either mixed or standard gauge; indeed, by 1876, all but one mile of the main line between Taunton and Exeter had become mixed gauge. West of Exeter, however, there was a greater degree of isolation and, consequently, there had been less urgency about conversion. Further provision of standard gauge rails could, quite easily, have resulted in the LSWR gaining running powers. In Plymouth, the LSWR intrusion had necessitated the laying of mixed gauge rails in the late 1870s for access to North Road station and on to Friary, but there was no way that the GWR was going to make things easy elsewhere for its arch-rival.

By the beginning of 1892, over 100 of the

GWR's 171 miles of exclusively broad gauge track were in Devon. This was changed irreversibly in May that year. At dawn on Saturday 21 May 1892, work commenced on the conversion of the GWR's remaining broad gauge lines and, by Monday 23rd, the broad gauge was extinct. The last broad gauge locomotive to leave Plymouth was 'Standard Goods' 0-6-0 *Europa* which started its journey to the scrap sidings at Swindon at 4am on Saturday 21 May.

The removal of broad gauge rails meant that the GWR found it less difficult to double the remaining sections of the old SDR main line between Exeter and Plymouth. In 1884, the stretch between Parsons Rock Tunnel and Teignmouth had been doubled, and this

had involved the opening up of East Cliff Tunnel and the rebuilding of Teignmouth station. After the gauge conversion, the GWR got to work on doubling the troublesome Rattery to Hemerdon section and building a new viaduct at Ivybridge, but it was 1902 before work was started on doubling the Dawlish-Parsons Rock section. Eventually, on 1 October 1905, the GWR could boast a continuous double line from Paddington to Plymouth. In that same year, doubling was completed on the Kingswear line as far as Paignton.

The year before the gauge conversion, the South West had been hit by severe blizzards. The worst had been on Monday 9 March and, quite innocently, the 3pm Plymouth express

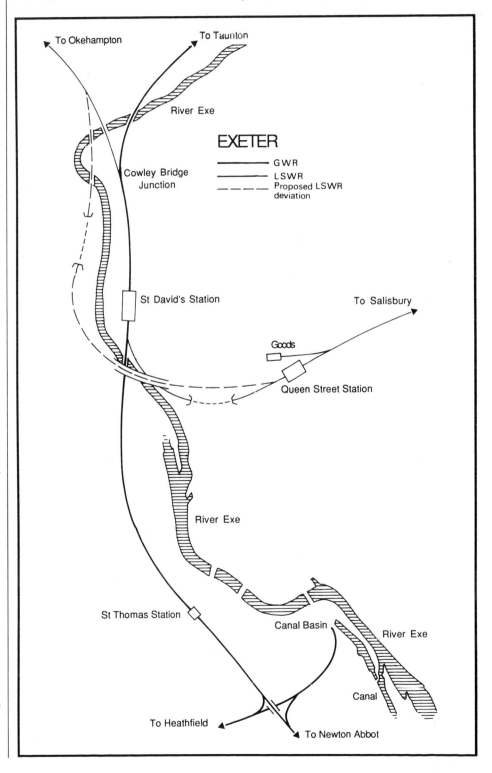

Right:

In 1905, the LSWR proposed a new line at Exeter to circumvent the GWR's station at St Davids completely; the LSWR's enthusiasm for the new line stemmed from the anticipated demand for the fastest possible services from the Ocean Terminal at Plymouth to Waterloo. The GWR opposed the LSWR scheme by stating that the proposal was in breach of an Act of 1884 and the scheme was, therefore, defeated. As things turned out, the LSWR's flirtation with ocean liner traffic was not to be long lived anyway.

had left Paddington on time that day but had got only as far as Brent before encountering impassable snowdrifts. The train had been scheduled to arrive in Plymouth at 8.55pm that evening but had eventually made it at 11.55pm on Friday 13th. However, things were not always that desperate.

Although the GWR's first timetabled non-stop run between Paddington and Plymouth was made in 1 July 1904, the company had worked a non-stop train on the route on 10 March 1902, and this had been made possible by the provision of water troughs near Taunton. The journey of 1902 had not been an ordinary one, however, as the train had carried HM King Edward VII and Queen Alexandra. The locomotive in charge had been 'Atbara' class 4-4-0 No 3374 *Baden Powell* which had been renamed *Britannia* for the special duty. The double-framed 4-4-0s had been developed by the GWR principally for fast mixed traffic duties in Devon and Cornwall, and the first to appear had been the 'Duke' class of 1895. The 'Atbara' and 'Flower' classes had been express passenger versions of the original design, and the ultimate development was the 'City' class, introduced in 1902. However, it was usually

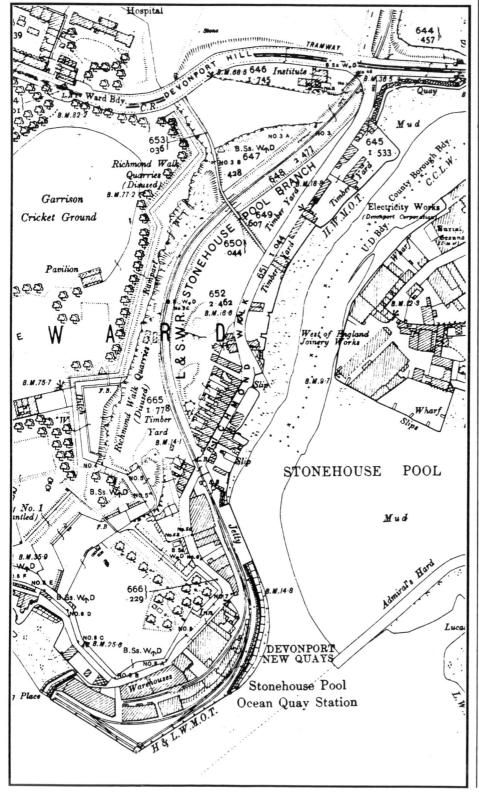

THE GREAT WESTERN COMPANY GIVE THE FOLLOWING NOTICE OF SPEED RESTRICTIONS ON PORTIONS OF THAT COMPANY'S LINE OVER WHICH THIS COMPANY'S TRAINS RUN.

EXETER DIVISION.

Name of Place.	Direction of Train.		Miles per hour.	Affecting London & South Western Trains.
	From	To		
Exeter Station, West End, over Curve West of St. David's Platforms.	St. David's Station...	Queen Street Station (S. W. R.).	15	Up Trains.
	Queen Street Station (S. W. R.).	St. David's Station...	10	Down Trains.
Cowley Bridge Jct.	Main Line (G. W. R.)	Branch (S.W. Line to Plymouth and North Devon).	25	Down Trains.
Cowley Bridge Jct.	Branch (S.W. Line from Plymouth and North Devon).	Main Line (G. W. R.)	25	Up Trains.

PLYMOUTH DIVISION.

Name of Place.	From	To	Miles per hour.	Affecting London & South Western Trains.
Devonport Jct. ...	Down Main (G. W. R.)	Devonport (L. & S.W.)	20	Up Trains.
Devonport Jct. ...	Devonport (L. & S.W.)	Up Main Line (G.W.R.)	20	Down Trains.
North Road (West)	North Road ...	Devonport Junction	25	Up Trains.
North Road (West)	Devonport Junction	North Road ...	25	Down Trains.
North Road (Down Platform Line).	Through Down Trains	... ...	20	Up Trains.
North Road (Up Platform Line).	Through Up Trains ...	... ...	20	Down Trains.
Lipson Junction...	Main Line	No. 1 Curve	15	Down Trains.
Lipson Junction...	No. 1 Curve	Main Line	15	Up Trains.

No. 1 CURVE.

Name of Place.	From	To	Miles per hour.	Affecting London & South Western Trains.
Mount Gould Jct.	Lipson Junction ...	Friary or Cattewater Junctions.	20	Down Trains.
Mount Gould Jct.	Friary or Cattewater Junctions.	Lipson Junction ...	20	Up Trains.
Friary Junction ...	Mount Gould Junction	Friary	20	Down Trains.
Friary Junction ...	Friary	Mount Gould Junction	20	Up Trains.

the 'Duke' and their direct descendants, the 'Bulldogs', which predominated west of Exeter as the larger driving wheels of the 'Atbaras', 'Flowers' and 'Cities' were less suited to the sharp gradients.

The GWR usually allocated its newest and most powerful locomotives to the Paddington-Plymouth run, not only because of the nature of the line westwards from Exeter, but also because the ocean liner traffic at Plymouth generated considerable prestige. Until 1904, the GWR had the boat traffic virtually to itself, passengers from transatlantic liners being transferred by tender to the GWR's Ocean Terminal near Millbay. As early as 1863, the Duke of Connaught Hotel had been opened near the quay, primarily to serve the boat passengers. However, the American Line decided that, from 1904, its ships should call at Plymouth *en route* to Southampton, and this presented the LSWR with a golden opportunity. The LSWR already provided a service for the American Line at Southampton, and the terms of the contract were extended to the proposed arrivals at Plymouth.

In anticipation of its new traffic, the LSWR built its own passenger terminal at Stonehouse Pool in Devonport and, considering the speed with which the building was constructed, the premises were very well equipped. The rail connection to the new terminal was provided by the steeply-graded, 1¼-mile line to Stonehouse Pool, which had been in operation as a freight branch since 1886; it left the LSWR line on the east side of Devonport station, and almost immediately entered a tunnel which passed underneath the goods shed. On 9 April 1904, the arrival of the American Line ship SS *St Louis* in Plymouth Sound marked the commencement of business.

For the services, the LSWR introduced sets of 'Ocean Special' coaches which were some six inches wider than ordinary carriages and considerably more luxurious. Each set had sleeping cars which were the only such carriages ever to be used by the LSWR. Unfortunately, a bad accident at Salisbury on 1 July 1906, in which 24 passengers and four railway staff were killed, was largely blamed on the excessive speed of an 'Ocean Special' train, and so the edict was issued for the 'Ocean Specials' to be timed as for other

expresses. This was a severe, if self-inflicted, blow to the LSWR, as the GWR opened its fast avoiding line through southern Somerset the very same day, thereby reducing the distance between Paddington and Plymouth by 20 miles.

The White Star Line announced its intention to start calling at Plymouth as from May 1907, but the LSWR's dreams of future dominance of the ocean liner trade at the port soon faded. The writing on the wall was seen even before the White Star Line's first arrival as, in February 1907, only eleven passengers disembarked from the American Line ship, the SS *New York*, at Plymouth. Just three of those took the LSWR boat train to Waterloo. Matters had not been helped earlier when the LSWR's application to carry the mails from the American Line and White Star Line's ships had been rejected. The Post Office had been quite happy with the excellent service provided by the GWR, and had seen no reason to change. Admittedly, the GWR had been flavour of the month with the Post Office due, in part, to the events of 9 May 1904. On that date, the GWR had transported five vans of mail from the German Lloyd ship, SS *Kronprinz Wilhelm*, over the 246¾ miles from Plymouth to Paddington in 3hr 37min. That trip had included a descent from White Ball summit into southern Somerset at an alleged speed of 102.3mph. The locomotive on that famous run was, of course, 'City' class 4-4-0 No 3440 *City of Truro*. The LSWR admitted defeat in 1910 and conceded the ocean liner traffic at Plymouth to the GWR; the roof of the LSWR Ocean Terminal was removed two years later.

Elsewhere on the main lines, it was 1905 when the LSWR introduced its first 4-6-0s and, although they did good work on the fastest Waterloo-Exeter expresses, it was generally considered that the 4-4-0s, particularly the 'Greyhounds', were just as good. During World War 1, the 4-6-0s were seconded for hauling the heaviest military trains, usually to Southampton, and were replaced on the Exeter expresses by 4-4-0s, but even allowing for the deceleration of schedules, the 4-4-0s proved the equal of the 4-6-0s. It was not until the introduction of Urie's 'King Arthurs' in 1918 that the face of motive power on the LSWR's Exeter expresses was really revolutionised.

World War 1 made surprisingly little difference to railway activities in Devon. The Admiralty's base at Devonport obviously generated additional traffic but, apart from that, the troop trains to and from Plymouth Docks provided the only regular evidence of the hostilities. During the war, the Government assumed control of all of Britain's railways, but when peace was restored, it was clearly impossible to implement a 'return to normal' policy overnight. It took five years to reorganise the national railway network, and this was done in the form of the Grouping.

2. The GWR Branches

Isambard Brunel rated crows very highly. When engineering his broad gauge railways, he agreed that the shortest distance between two points was a straight line. Consequently, Brunel was reluctant to divert the course of the main lines to serve medium-size or smaller towns and, instead, he often preferred to construct branch lines to the towns in question. The first passenger-carrying branch line in Devon was the one to Tiverton, and it provided a good illustration of Brunel's policy.

When the Bristol & Exeter Railway's main line was in the planning stage, the important wool town of Tiverton was less than five miles away from the line, but a relatively minor deviation into the town itself was considered out of the question due to the nature of the topography which would have made the route much longer. Instead, a station named Tiverton Road was opened on the main line, and this had to suffice until a branch could be constructed into the town. The main line through Tiverton Road opened on 1 May 1844 but it was 12 June 1848 before the 4¾-mile branch was opened. Today, a journey of under five miles to a

main line station might sound like a doddle for seasoned commuters but, in the 1840s, that sort of journey meant spending around one hour travelling over bumpy tracks in a horse-drawn coach. Those days were long before the advent of Quells.

The opening of the broad gauge branch to Tiverton resulted in the main line station at Tiverton Road being renamed Tiverton Junction. In engineering terms, the branch had not been difficult to construct but the Grand Western Canal Co had proved awkward when it had come to the railway passing under the canal at Halberton. At the time the branch opened, the B&E was being worked by the GWR and so it fell to the latter to provide the motive power. The B&E took over the responsibility for working its own lines on 1 May 1849 and, for the Tiverton branch, the company acquired a steam railmotor which had been designed and built by William Bridges Adams at the Fairfield Works in Bow; it was only the second such machine to have been constructed in Britain. The railmotor had a vertical tubular boiler and two 8in x 12in cylinders which powered a pair of 4ft 6in driving wheels. The carriage section,

which was mounted on two axles, accommodated 16 first and 32 second class passengers, while all luggage was carried on the roof. The B&E gave the railmotor No 29 and retained the builder's name of *Fairfield*, but the contraption was not altogether satisfactory. It was passed on to the Clevedon and, later, the Weston branches but was sold in 1855 and the power unit was converted to an 0-4-0T for an industrial user in Bridgwater. The railmotor's replacement on the Tiverton branch was a small B&E 2-2-2T. It is believed that the B&E opened a single-road engine shed at Tiverton Junction in 1848 for the branch line locomotive but the B&E's records do not confirm the date.

The Tiverton branch had an uneventful existence until June 1884 but, in that year, it was converted to the standard gauge in readiness for the completion of a branch to Morebath Junction, on the GWR's Taunton-Barn-

Below:
In this 1890 25in Ordnance Survey map of Tiverton, the site of the original terminus station can be seen. *Crown Copyright*

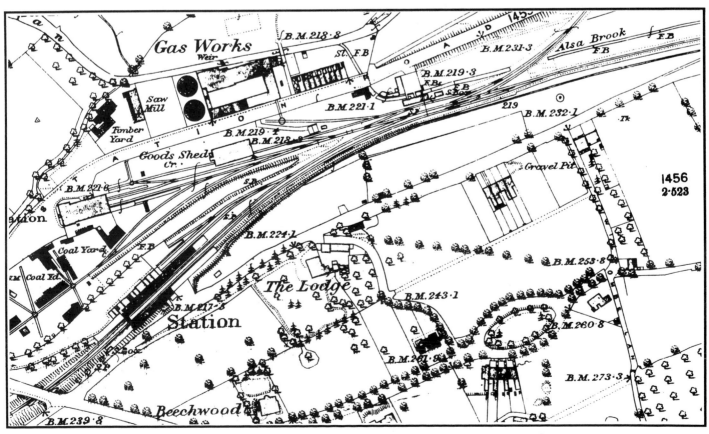

staple line. On 1 May 1885, a new station was opened at Tiverton and the original one was relegated to the status of a goods depot. Due to the lightweight nature of the branch, the choice of standard gauge locomotives was restricted and, inevitably, the '517' class 0-4-2Ts eventually monopolised the passenger duties with 0-6-0STs being used on the daily freight service. In the 1880s, there were usually ten trains each way on weekdays with a journey time of 10min; 40 years later, little had changed.

When it came to branch lines, the South Devon Railway was not to be left out, but when it opened its branch to Sutton Harbour in Plymouth in May 1853, the occasion was a low-key affair. The lack of pomp and ceremony at the opening of the 1¾-mile branch was not just because of its freight-only status, but also because it was worked by horses. Clearly, a horse and train of wagons were considered less of a public attraction than a locomotive-hauled train of local dignitaries. Even in its non-mechanical state, the Sutton Harbour branch had an erratic early existence. It was closed from May 1856 to October 1857 largely to permit further upgrading, as the route and some of the track had been inherited from an old 4ft 6in gauge tramway company. A ¼-mile spur from the Sutton Harbour branch to North Quay was opened on 6 November 1879, but the LSWR had just beaten the SDR to it; on 22 October, the LSWR had opened a short extension from Friary goods depot to the same quay.

Locomotive traction did not appear on the SDR's Sutton Harbour branch until 19 April 1869 and, in view of the lightweight nature of the line, a small 0-4-0WT was built specially. The locomotive had a vertical boiler, 3ft diameter wheels and cylinders of 9in x 12in; named *Tiny*, it was withdrawn in 1883, by which time it was wearing GWR

No 2180. After its retirement from active duties, it was used as a stationary boiler at Newton Abbot but, in 1927, was overhauled and installed as a static exhibit on the down platform of the station. *Tiny* is now part of the National Collection and currently resides at the preserved station at Buckfastleigh. That locomotive's usual replacements on Sutton Harbour duties were SDR 0-6-0ST *Taurus* and 2-4-0T *Prince;* they eventually became GWR Nos 2171/37 respectively and both were converted to the standard gauge in 1892.

The second SDR branch to open during the 1850s was the one to Tavistock. Nominally, the branch belonged to the South Devon & Tavistock Railway, but it was worked by the SDR from the outset and formally absorbed soon after. The 15¾-mile broad gauge branch was opened to passengers on 22 June 1859 and for goods the following February. It had been a tricky line to engineer and, apart from extensive earthworks, it had required three tunnels, the longest of 641yd at Yelverton, and six timber viaducts on stone piers, that at Walkham taking first prize with its 364yd length and 132ft height. The intermediate stations were at Bickleigh and Horrabridge, additional ones at Marsh Mills and Yelverton being opened in 1861 and 1885 respectively.

Another nominally independent company, the Launceston & South Devon Railway, constructed the 15-mile extension from Tavi-

stock to Launceston which opened for passenger traffic on 1 July 1865. The SDR worked this section simply as a continuation of the Tavistock branch. With the opening of the Launceston extension, the single-road engine shed at Tavistock was rendered redundant and subsequently closed. Demolition ensued in 1900 but, perversely, a new 45ft 3in diameter turntable was installed in the yard that same year. At Launceston, a single-road stone-built shed was opened with the extension and, apart from being lengthened from 80ft to 100ft in 1899, was to remain virtually unaltered until its closure in 1962.

On the Launceston extension, the intermediate stations were Mary Tavy, Lydford, Coryton and Lifton; Mary Tavy was renamed Mary Tavy & Blackdown in 1907. Traffic figures were steady but, considering the prominence of Tavistock and Launceston, hardly spectacular. By 1922, Tavistock was served by 11 trains in each direction on weekdays, but only four of those worked to, or originated from, Launceston. Motive power was, by then, usually the '45xx' class 2-6-2Ts. The first '45xxs' to have been used on the Launceston branch had appeared during 1912, when Nos 2161/65/71/79 had made regular forays on to the line; under the GWR renumbering scheme of December 1912, those four had become Nos 4500/04/10/18 respectively.

On 4 July 1866, a broad-gauge branch line opened from Newton Abbot to Moretonhampstead. It was 12½ miles long and was worked by the SDR; at first, the only intermediate stations were at Bovey and Lustleigh, but Teigngrace was added in 1867. In 1874, a further station was opened at Chudleigh Road only to be renamed Heathfield in 1882. The stone-built single-road engine shed at Moretonhampstead opened with the line in 1866 and was to

remain virtually unchanged until its closure in 1947.

Initially, the SDR displayed little interest in the Moretonhampstead branch and the services were infrequent. However, the boom in tourism in the late 19th century had a knock-on effect and the branch's fortunes improved. In 1905, the GWR attempted to introduce a motor bus service between Moretonhampstead and the pretty village of Chagford, but the county council refused to foot the bill for road improvements. Undeterred, the GWR did further battle with the authorities, and the improvements were made in time for the bus service to be launched in the summer of 1906. The LSWR hadn't been as fussy about giving its customers a smooth ride as, in 1904, it had inaugurated its own motor-bus service between Exeter and Chagford, with or without unmade roads. The LSWR bus service is noteworthy as, between 1905 and 1908, the two vehicles used on the route were Clarkson's steam buses. Private bus operators eventually muscled in on the route, but the LSWR's own buses flew the flag until 1924. By the summer of 1922, the rail service on the Moretonhampstead branch had stabilised at eight trains each way on weekdays, with an additional one running each way between Newton Abbot and Bovey only. The average journey times for the entire trip were around 45min and services were, most usually, in the capable hands of '45xx' class 2-6-2Ts.

In Exeter, the SDR had chosen to ignore the fact that, since 1846, it had passed within ½-mile of the docks. Exeter had been a port since Roman times and the Ship Canal had, since its opening in 1566, been used in preference to the tidal River Exe for access to the centre of the city. During the late 16th century, the Ship Canal had helped to promote Exeter to the status of the fourth busiest port in Britain, with the produce of the local wool trade providing the port's mainstay. The canal had been lengthened in 1724 and widened in 1827 but, although the usefulness of rail-linked quays had been appreciated throughout the country since the tramway era, the South Devon Railway had been slow to appreciate Exeter's maritime importance. Remarkably, it was 17 June 1867 before the SDR got round to opening a branch to the City Basin in Exeter. The branch was only ¼-mile long and it left the Teignmouth line to the south of St Thomas station. Standard gauge rails were added in 1871 and, at the same time, the down line between St Davids and the branch junction was converted to mixed gauge. One of the few mixed gauge trains to run used to operate over this line.

South of Exeter, the SDR's secondary main line to Kingswear had opened in 1864 and had passed through Brixham Road station. The abandonment of the small fishing port of Brixham two miles from the railway might have seemed like a legacy from the Brunel era, but the local topography ruled out the possibility of a main line into the town and out the other side. Nevertheless, Brixham was to have its own railway and the local superhero who provided it was one R. W. Wolston. Wolston had extensive business interests in Brixham, and he promoted the broad gauge Torbay & Brixham Railway to link the port to the station at Brixham Road. Wolston purchased most of the shares in his own company and, when the contractor who had been engaged to construct the line defaulted, Wolston completed the line with his own workforce. After all that, he purchased a secondhand 0-4-0WT named *Queen* to work the line.

The Torbay & Brixham Railway opened on 28 February 1868 and joined the SDR line at Brixham Road, that station subsequently being renamed Churston. The enterprising Mr.Wolston was realistic enough to accept that his solitary locomotive would not be adequate to cope with all eventualities, and so he entered into a working agreement with the SDR. Whether by oversight or intention, the SDR failed to credit Wolston with the amounts due and, despite owning a busy little line, Wolston started to receive regular letters from his bank manager. The SDR's 'omission' was eventually rectified but, smarting at having been found out, the SDR spitefully introduced excessive charges for the T&BR's use of Churston station. Once again, matters went to litigation and Wolston was awarded £2,000 compensation. With renewed confidence, the T&BR opted for full independence and purchased an additional

Right:
The Torbay & Brixham Railway's 0-4-0WT *Queen* had been built in 1852 for the contractor engaged on construction of the Portland breakwater in Dorset. It was purchased for the T&BR in 1868 and was absorbed, first into South Devon Railway stock and, later, into GWR stock. It was withdrawn in 1883. *Ian Allan Library*

Above:
Messrs Avonside of Bristol built broad gauge 0-4-0ST *Raven* for the South Devon Railway in 1874. It became GWR No 2175 and was subsequently sold to the Torbay & Brixham Railway. However, the T&BR was absorbed by the GWR in 1883, and *Raven* returned to GWR stock; it was converted to the standard gauge in 1892 and was given No 1329. The locomotive was sold to the Wantage Tramway in 1910 but was eventually considered rather heavy for the line, and was sold for scrap 10 years later. *Ian Allan Library*

locomotive; this was 0-4-0T *Raven* which the GWR had previously acquired on its absorption of the SDR. Eventually, in 1883, Wolston sold the T&BR to the GWR for £12,000. The Brixham branch had no intermediate stations. Its engine shed, a single-road structure at Brixham, was replaced in 1897 and lasted until 1929; the shed allocation list for 31 December 1920 show that the sole resident at Brixham was '517' class 0-4-2T No 571.

During the 1860s, the Devon & Somerset Railway set its sights on linking Taunton, in Somerset, to Barnstaple and readily entered into a working agreement with the B&E. This inevitably meant that the line was to be built to the broad gauge and, naturally, the LSWR was not amused by the prospective challenge to its hard-won domination of North Devon. For a while, however, the LSWR thought that its fears of a nasty broad gauge tentacle into North Devon could have been unfounded as the Devon & Somerset lurched from one financial crisis to another. Nevertheless, the line opened as far as Wiveliscombe on 8 June 1871; it took until

1 November 1873 to cross the border into Devon and arrive at Barnstaple.

The 44¾-mile branch to Barnstaple had been a pig to construct and promised no easier a time for the operators. Heavy gradients abounded and 1 in 60 was encountered with disturbing frequency; there were two substantial wrought-iron viaducts, one of 162yd and the other 232yd long, and three tunnels, the longest being the 440yd bore at Bathealton. On the Devon side of the border, there were intermediate stations at Venn Cross, Morebath, East Anstey, Molland, South Molton, Castle Hill and Swimbridge; Molland was retitled Bishop's Nympton & Molland in 1876 and Castle Hill was renamed Filleigh in 1881. At Barnstaple, the B&E had its own terminus at Victoria Road which had a medium-size goods yard and a twin-road engine shed. The timber-built shed was to survive more or less in its original form for nearly 80 years.

Economics had dictated the construction of the Taunton-Barnstaple branch as a single track line and, in order to conserve financial resources to the utmost degree, only three crossing loops were provided. Although the line was worked by the financially-sound B&E, the services for the first few years were abysmal, and the local traders demonstrated their feelings by boycotting the railway and reverting to road transport for the collection and delivery of their goods.

The turning point in the branch's fortunes came in two stages, both after the B&E had been absorbed by the GWR. Firstly, there was the line's conversion to the standard gauge in 1881 and then, in 1887, the opening of a 1¼-mile connecting spur between the GWR and the LSWR stations in Barnstaple. The connecting loop was laid because the GWR had, at last, become aware of the poten-

Below:
'517' class 0-4-2T No 1466 spent much of its life in Devon, and here it is seen at Buckfastleigh station in the early 1900s. *Lens of Sutton*

For a terminus at the end of a short rural branch, Brixham station was comparatively expansive. This early 1900s picture is undoubtedly posed, and it shows what seems to be a '850' class 0-6-0ST. *Lens of Sutton*

tial of North Devon, this awakening being largely due to the LSWR's success in the area. In 1874, the LSWR had reached Ilfracombe and the arrival of the railway had turned the town into a popular holiday resort. The GWR stood no chance of finding its own route to Ilfracombe and so, in 1886, it inaugurated a horse-drawn coach service to the town from Victoria Road station in Barnstaple. Predictably, the LSWR was not overwhelmed, but the road service got some of the inter-company hostilities out of the way so that the GWR could then peacefully persuade the LSWR to haul GWR carriages through to Ilfracombe. The opening of the connecting loop between the GWR and LSWR in Barnstaple in 1887 was intended specifically for those through carriages.

A further improvement of the GWR layout at Barnstaple was unveiled in 1905 when a short spur was opened at the GWR's end of the connecting loop. This enabled through running from Taunton to Ilfracombe without a reversing manoeuvre at Victoria Road station and, as the years progressed, the public came to prefer the shorter GWR route from London to Ilfracombe via Taunton to the cir-

cuitous LSWR route via Exeter. After the GWR had opened its eyes to the usefulness of the Barnstaple branch in the 1880s, the line had become better-managed but, even so, the route rarely found itself at the top of the list when money was made available for major improvements. The limited potential for vast profits from the line was underlined when the Devon & Somerset Railway, which had built the line, was officially absorbed by the GWR in 1901. The D&SR's arrears of interest to shareholders amounted to over £500,000.

In the 1880s, usual weekday services between Taunton and Barnstaple comprised five passenger trains each way, with average

journey times of a little under two hours. By the summer of 1922, the timetables showed little improvement apart from the addition of two trains each way which stopped only at Wiveliscombe, Dulverton and South Molton. These were no faster than the regular 'all stations' services. Remarkably, other limited-stop services which operated only on Fridays were actually slower than the normal trains. Towards the end of the 19th century, passenger services on the line were usually worked by 'Metro' class 2-4-0Ts while 'Dean Goods' 0-6-0s were the normal workhorses for freight duties. 4-4-0s started to be used in the early 1900s and the December 1920 allocation lists show that '3521' class 4-4-0 No 3547 was resident at Barnstaple shed. That locomotive was one of a class which had started life as 0-4-2Ts in 1887, had been converted to 0-4-4Ts in the early 1890s and then rebuilt as 4-4-0s in 1899-1902.

Back in South Devon, the last passenger branch to be opened by the South Devon Railway before the end of its independent existence was the 9½-mile line from Totnes to Ashburton. An earlier scheme had proposed a branch from Newton Abbot to Ashburton and, arguably, that had made more commercial sense, but the route to Totnes had the great advantage of being able to follow the less-tortuous gradients of the Dart Valley. The Totnes-Ashburton branch opened to passengers on 1 May 1872 and had intermediate stations at Staverton and Buckfastleigh. The Dart Valley had had, at one time, a thriving wool industry but although much of the trade had gone by the 1870s, the area retained about half of Devon's remaining wool trade. In the line's early years, more traffic was generated at Buckfastleigh than at Newton Abbot.

One of the locomotives to be used regularly during the early years of the Ashburton branch was the SDR's 0-6-0ST *Taurus* which, in its later life, was transferred to the Sutton Harbour branch in Plymouth. Eventually, the delightful little 0-4-2Ts took over most passenger duties on the branch and '517' class No 845 was shown on the 1920 allocation list of the single-road shed at Ashburton. By 1922, the passenger service on the branch comprised six trains each way on weekdays with an average journey time of 25min.

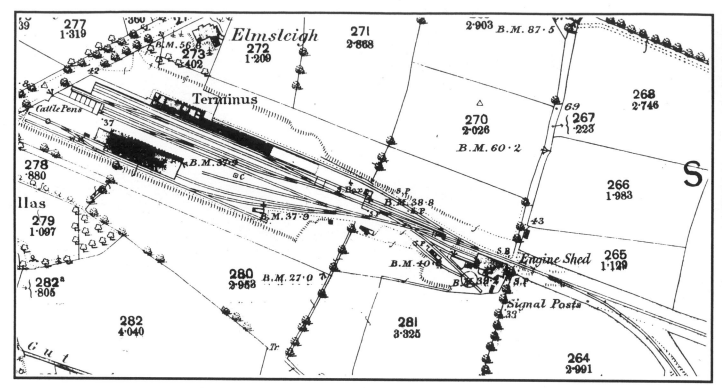

There was, at that time, no Sunday service. At Totnes, a ¾-mile goods spur was opened from the main line to a quay on the River Dart on 10 November 1873, but this was worked exclusively by horses until August 1874. When the Totnes quay line had been authorised, its Act had prohibited the use of 'locomotives, stationary engines, ropes or "atmospheric agency"'. Although the SDR was, in the light of past events, hardly likely to use atmospheric traction on the quay line, the authorities were taking no chances whatsoever of a re-enactment of the earlier fiasco.

Moving across to northeast Devon, the B&E had, during its final years of independence, undertaken to work the Culm Valley Light Railway but, at the time the B&E was absorbed by the GWR, the CVLR was not quite ready for opening. The B&E's working agreement was inherited by the GWR and so, when the CVLR opened its 7¼-mile branch from Tiverton Junction to Hemyock on 29 May 1876, it fell to the GWR to provide the motive power. The Hemyock branch had been authorised as a light railway and, therefore, had been built on a comparatively ban-

CULM VALLEY BRANCH.

Narrow Gauge.

Single Line worked by Train Staff. The Train Staff Stations are Tiverton Junction and Hemyock.

Section.	*Form of Staff and Ticket.*	*Colour of Ticket.*
Tiverton Junction and Hemyock.	Square.	Green.

TIVERTON JUNCTION TO HEMYOCK.

Down Trains.

Miles.	STATIONS.		Week Days only. 1	2	3	4	5	6	7	8	9
			Pass.	Pass.	Pass.	Pass.					
			A.M.	P.M.	P.M.	P.M.					
	Tiverton Junction	dep.	9 25	12 30	4 25	7 35	....	....	....	....	....
2	Cold Harbour Siding	,,	C R	—	—	—	..	..	..	..	..
2¾	Uffculme	,,	9 49	12 50	4 44	7 54	....	....	....	....	....
5	Culmstock	,,	10 4	1 0	4 59	8 9	..	..	..	..	..
6¼	Whitehall Siding	,,	C R	—	—	—	....	....	....	....	....
7¼	**Hemyock**	arr.	10 20	1 15	5 10	8 20	....	....	....	....	....

HEMYOCK TO TIVERTON JUNCTION.

Up Trains.

Miles.	STATIONS.		Week Days only. 1	2	3	4	5	6	7	8	9
			Pass.	Pass.	Pass.	Pass.					
			A.M.	A.M.	P.M.	P.M.					
	Hemyock	dep.	8 30	10 30	2 35	5 20	....	....	....	....	....
1	Whitehall Siding	,,	—	—	—	—	....	....	....	....	....
2¼	Culmstock	,,	8 46	10 46	2 51	5 36	..	..	..	..	..
4½	Uffculme	,,	9 1	11 1	3 6	5 51	....	....	....	....	....
5¼	Cold Harbour Siding	,,	—	CR	—	—	..	..	..	..	..
7¼	**Tiverton Junction**	arr.	9 15	11 15	3 20	6 5	....	....	....	....	....

Extract from the Regulations made by the Board of Trade for the working of the Culm Valley Light Railway.

"That the said Railway shall be worked between Tiverton Junction and Hemyock Station by one Engine in steam combined with the absolute Block Telegraph system; that the rate of speed of the Trains shall not exceed fifteen miles an hour on any part of the said Railway; and that the Locomotive Engines, Carriages and Vehicles used on the Railway shall not have a greater weight than eight tons upon the rails on any one pair of wheels."

Left:
The GWR working timetable for autumn 1886 devoted a whole page to the hectic activity on the Hemyock branch. The reference to 'narrow gauge' emphasises that the broad gauge was still in existence elsewhere at the time.
Author's collection

tamweight scale. In order to take advantage of the light railway specifications, the branch workings were to be restricted to a maximum axle weight of 8 tons and a top speed of 25mph. Furthermore, the line had had to be constructed to the standard gauge, but the potential problem of interchange traffic at Tiverton Junction had been circumvented in March 1876 when the GWR had finished laying mixed gauge rails between Taunton and Exeter.

For working the Hemyock branch, the B&E had built a pair of small 0-6-0Ts which had 3ft 6in diameter wheels and 12in x 18in cylinders; they had been built at Bristol Works and had become GWR Nos 1376/77 after the absorption. In its first full year of operation, the branch carried 46,000 passengers, 9,000 tons of freight and 3,700 parcels, but these figures were not to last. In the best tradition of small Victorian railway companies, the CVLR soon became familiar with the word 'overdraft' but, to be honest, the GWR had hardly helped matters. It leaked out that potential freight traffic from the branch's catchment area was, with the GWR's knowledge, being taken by road to Honiton for transport by the LSWR. Despite the GWR's attitude to the CVLR, it became inevitable that the former would take over the latter lock, stock and barrel; this it did in 1880.

The CVLR's branch to Hemyock had, at first, intermediate stations at Uffculme and Culmstock, but two halts were added after the Grouping. In the 1870s, there were five trains each way on weekdays with an average journey time of 45min for the 7¼ miles. By 1922, the weekday service had been reduced to four trains each way, but the journey times varied between 33min and 1hr 5min. The original 0-6-0Ts were replaced in 1878 by a pair of 2-4-0Ts, GWR Nos 1298/1300, and these were the regular branch locomotives until the 1920s. A timber-built single-road engine shed was erected at Hemyock and lasted until 1929, but the parent shed for the branch line locomotives was always the one at Exeter. Despite the general unprofitability of the branch and the leisurely nature of the services, the line performed a useful function for the local community. Encouraged by the railway, a milk factory opened at Hemyock and, in later years, a textile mill was established between Tiverton Junction and Uffculme.

By the 1880s, the growth of Britain's railway network was slowing down because most of the areas which had warranted a railway had, by then, already got one. Consequently, most new lines of the period were built by major companies or nominal subsidiaries and, even then, only after much deliberation. One of the independent concerns which had not read the instruction book was the Teign Valley Railway, which had battled through nine Acts of Parliament to obtain authorisation for a branch line of just 7¾ miles. When the legal battles were over, the company celebrated by going into receivership.

The Teign Valley's dream had been for a line from Heathfield (formerly Chudleigh Road), on the GWR's Moretonhampstead branch, to the village of Ashton, but somebody had not done his (or her) homework. The proposals had received assent, but authorisation had been for a standard gauge line in one of the last bastions of broad gauge exclusivity. At the time of the little company's demise, no construction work had been undertaken, let alone the opening of the line, and so it might have seemed somewhat philanthropic of the GWR to announce that it would itself build the line. However, the GWR's reason for taking on board a branch of the wrong gauge which ran, in effect, to nowhere of use, was that the LSWR was waiting in the wings to take over the corpse of the Teign Valley company. To the accountants of the GWR, a relatively minor

Above:
Although this picture was taken on 22 July 1939, the casual way of life at Heathfield station, the junction for the Teign Valley branch, was little different from that of the previous fifty-odd years. 'Metro' 2-4-0T No 3590 is seen at the head of a three-coach train. *Lens of Sutton*

expense was permissible if the LSWR were to be kept out.

The GWR opened the 6¾-mile branch from Heathfield to Ashton on 9 October 1882 and, the following year, it was extended for one mile to a goods depot at Teign House. The freight extension was intended to serve local quarries and also a number of mines, where a large-scale extraction of tin and copper had been planned, but the industrialisation of the area hardly got off the ground. The branch remained as the only exclusively standard gauge GWR-operated line in the immediate area until the mass gauge conversion of 1892. There were intermediate stations at Chudleigh and Trusham, and the branch locomotive was housed at a small engine shed at Ashton.

In 1883, the Exeter Railway was incorporated to extend the Heathfield branch from Teign House to Exeter, but this stretch did not open until 1 July 1903; it had intermediate stations at Christow, Longdown and Ide. The GWR worked the original section and the extension as one complete branch of 17½ miles and the usual motive power for passenger trains was '517' class 0-4-2Ts. The working of the entire branch as one unit rendered the engine shed at Ashton superfluous and it was closed in 1908. In 1904, a ¼-mile freight spur was laid at the northern end of the branch, where it joined the main Dawlish line, to connect with the existing goods branch to the City Basin at Exeter.

The Heathfield-Exeter branch did little more than break even but, despite its single-track status, the GWR viewed it as useful insurance; if ever the main line via Dawlish were to be closed, the Heathfield branch would be available as an alternative route. The matter of gradients as steep as 1 in 56 seemed unimportant. By 1922, the summer service on the branch comprised four trains each way on weekdays and five on Saturdays with an average journey time of just under one hour. An additional daily train made one trip from Heathfield to Christow and back. The impecunious Teign Valley Railway, which had promoted the original section, and the Exeter Railway both retained nominal independence until 1923. An additional station on the branch, Alphington Halt, was opened on 2 April 1928 and served a fast-growing village.

The year after the first section of the Heathfield branch had been unveiled, the GWR opened another standard gauge branch in Devon. On 11 August 1883, services commenced on the branch from Yelverton, on the Tavistock and Launceston line, to Princetown. Much of the Princetown branch was built on the route of the old Plymouth & Dartmoor Tramway, which the GWR had purchased for £22,000, and the nature of the local landscape had necessitated a rather circuitous route. As the crow flies, the distance between Yelverton and Princetown is under six miles but the railway's route covered 10½

miles. Princetown stands 1,373ft above sea level and, consequently, all but one mile of the branch rose on a gradient which, at its sharpest, was 1 in 40. Apart from the severe gradients, there was an abundance of tight curves and the GWR must have been grateful that the broad gauge had not been required.

For its traffic, the branch depended largely on Britain's criminal population. Princetown was the location of Dartmoor Prison and, as long as the judiciary kept dispatching miscreants to the gaol, the railway offered the only sensible means of transportation for men and provisions. However, the branch had an additional source of regular traffic at King Tor Quarry where granite was still extracted. At first, the Princetown branch trains ran to Horrabridge, as the station at Yelverton was not opened until 1 May 1885; the only intermediate station on the branch itself until the 1920s was at Dousland. Branch locomotives were housed at the single-road engine shed at Princetown which opened with the line and remained almost unchanged throughout its 73-year life. By the early 1920s, services on the Princetown branch usually comprised six trains each way on weekdays with an average journey time of 30-35min. The regular locomotives were, by then, the Churchward '44xx' class 2-6-2Ts which had been introduced in 1904 as the first of the GWR's standard lightweight Prairie Tanks.

The mid-1880s saw a flurry of activity around Tiverton. On 1 August 1884, a standard gauge branch was opened between Morebath Junction, on the Taunton-Barnstaple line, and a point just over two miles

Below:
The track layout at Princetown station can be clearly seen in this 1905 Ordnance Survey map. The scale of the original was 25in to the mile. *Crown Copyright*

north of Tiverton. The reason for not extending into Tiverton itself was that a branch from Exeter to the Tiverton area was nearing completion and the objective was to link the two new branches as one unit. This came about on 1 May 1885 when the branch from Exeter was opened and, to round things off neatly, a new station was built at Tiverton to serve the branch to Tiverton Junction as well.

The new branch between Tiverton and Morebath Junction was built and owned by the Tiverton & North Devon Railway which had been in existence since the early 1870s, but the Tiverton-Exeter branch was exclusively GWR property. That latter section joined the main line just to the south of Stoke Canon, a little over three miles north of Exeter St Davids station, but a new junction station was built at Stoke Canon in 1894. On the section between Exeter and Tiverton, the intermediate stations were at Brampford Speke, Thorverton and Cadeleigh & Bickleigh while, on the section north of Tiverton, the only intermediate station was at Bampton. Cadeleigh & Bickleigh was abbreviated to Cadeleigh in 1906 while Brampford Speke closed in 1917, only to reopen two years later. Although Morebath Junction was the physical extent of the two branches, there was no station at that point for many years and so the branch trains through the Exe Valley terminated at Dulverton. The branch was single-track throughout but the stations at Thorverton, Tiverton and Bampton all had crossing loops.

Until after the Grouping, services between Exeter and Dulverton were sparse. In 1886, six passenger trains were scheduled each way on weekdays with journey times of around 65-70min for the 24¾ miles; by 1922, the weekday service was five trains in each direction. Locomotives were supplied by Exeter shed but, although official records show an engine shed at Stoke Canon, this had been opened by the B&E in 1862 and had closed in 1879, well before the branch was built. Pas-

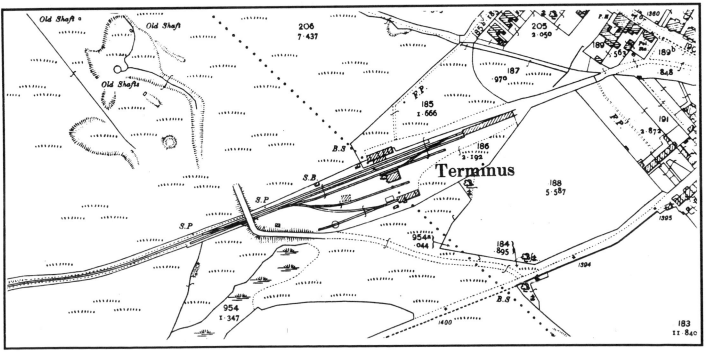

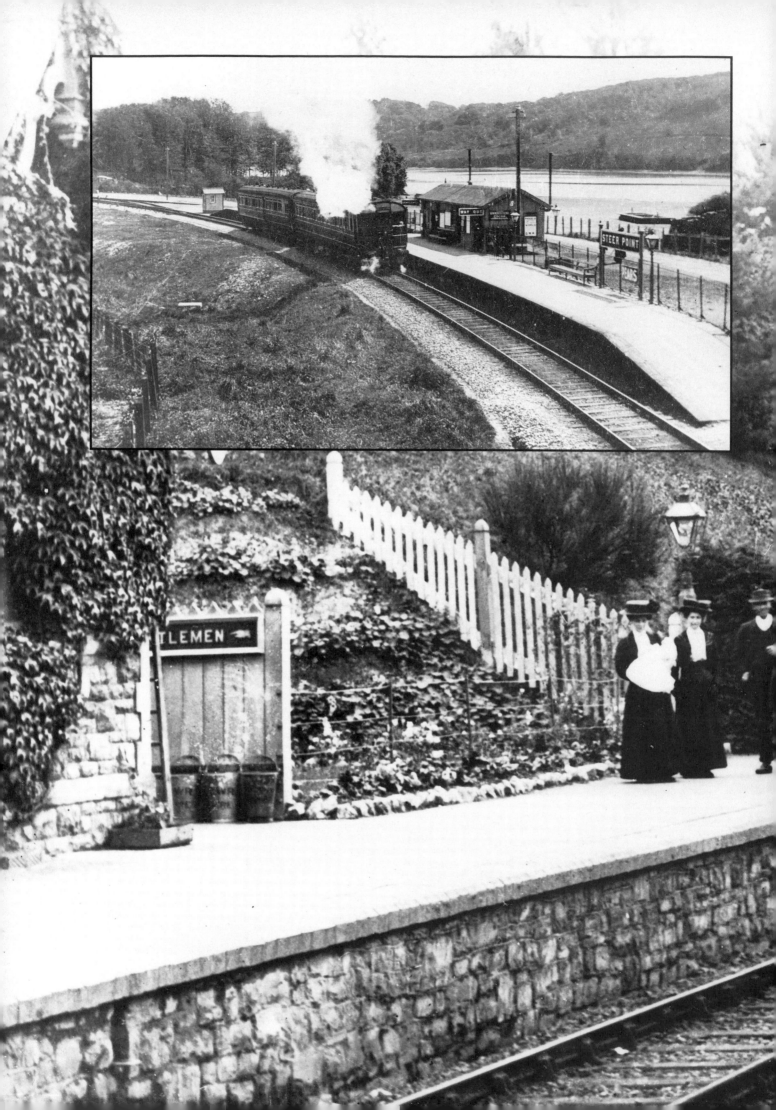

Inset:
Steer Point station on the Yealmpton branch was alongside the Yealm Estuary and well-removed from any centre of population. In this early 1920s picture, an unidentified steam railmotor departs for Plymouth. *Lens of Sutton*

Below:
Bampton station was on the delightful Exe Valley line, and it remained largely unaltered throughout its life. This early 1920s photograph shows part of the goods yard at the southern end of the station. *Lens of Sutton*

senger trains were normally worked by '517' class 0-4-2Ts while the daily freight tended to be handled by the ubiquitous 0-6-0STs.

In South Devon, plans for a branch to Kingsbridge had been around since the 1860s but the locals had been unenthusiastic. They had considered that their coach services had been adequate to take them to the great beyond whereas a railway could have brought the great beyond to them. In the close-knit communities of the Kingsbridge district, comparative isolation provided the luxuries of peace and quiet. Nevertheless, the GWR insisted on constructing a 12½-mile branch from Brent to Kingsbridge, and the line opened on 19 December 1893.

The Kingsbridge branch had intermediate stations at Avonwick, Gara Bridge and Loddiswell and, after its opening, the main line station at Kingsbridge Road, to the west of Brent, reverted to its original name of Wrangaton. The branch locomotive lived at Kingsbridge and, from the early 1900s, '44xx' and '45xx' class 2-6-2Ts tended to be the usual steeds for passenger duties. Passenger services eventually stabilised at six trains each way on summer weekdays but, perhaps sur-

prisingly, a fair amount of freight traffic was generated by the harbour at Kingsbridge.

In Plymouth, the LSWR opened its short branch to Plymstock in 1892 and this was extended to Turnchapel in 1897. Plymstock became a junction station on 17 January 1898 when a GWR branch opened eastwards from there to Yealmpton. It had intermediate stations at Billacombe, Elburton Cross, Brixton Road and Steer Point; Mount Gould & Tothill halt, on the west side of the River Plym, was added in 1905 but it closed in 1918. The GWR's services to Yealmpton started at Millbay and used the loop between Lipson Junction and Mount Gould Junction which had been laid in 1891; the journey from Millbay to Yealmpton was 10¼ miles.

The Yealmpton branch had originally been part of an LSWR scheme for a line to the small resort of Modbury, and the GWR had feared that the LSWR might eventually extend from Modbury to Torbay. Rather than become involved with the wasteful blocking measure of counter-proposals, both companies had reached an untypically amicable agreement. The terms had been that the GWR should construct the branch between

Plymstock and Yealmpton while the LSWR should be responsible for the extension to Modbury; each company was to have running powers over the tracks of the other. As things turned out, the LSWR abandoned the Modbury scheme and, furthermore, the company seemed disinterested in exercising its legal running powers over the GWR's branch to Yealmpton.

The opening of the Yealmpton branch in 1898 virtually completed the GWR's portion of the branch line map of Devon. However, there was a significant boom in the suburban services around Plymouth in the early 1900s. In 1903, the GWR tried out its first steam railmotors on the Stroud Valley branch in Gloucestershire and, within a few years, the railmotors were in use throughout much of the GWR's network. Plymouth saw its first railmotors in 1904 and halts were opened at Laira, Wingfield Villas, Dockyard and St Budeaux specifically for the new services. A new station had opened at Keyham in 1900 and this came into its own with the introduction of the suburban railmotor services across the River Tamar to Saltash.

Eventually, the main GWR railmotor working in the Plymouth area was operated as a shuttle service between Plympton and Defiance platform, ¾ mile beyond Saltash, although not all of the advertised workings ran the whole length of the route. By the early 1920s, around 25 local workings were scheduled for either all or part of the route on weekdays, and they warranted over three-quarters of a page in Bradshaw's. Another guide as to the impact of the railmotors in Plymouth was that, in 1903, North Road station had accommodated about 100 trains each weekday but, by 1907, the number had risen to over 250. Furthermore, railmotor platforms were opened at Plym Bridge, Shaugh Bridge and Whitchurch Down on the Launceston branch, and at Mount Gould & Tothill on the Yealmpton branch.

But it was not just railway operations which changed after the appearance of the railmotors in Plymouth. A consequence of the vast improvement in local communications was that the residential suburbs grew rapidly and St Budeaux, in particular, became the Devon equivalent of the Metropolitan Railway's 'Metroland', albeit without railway-company property development. If anything, the Plymouth railmotors became victims of their own success. Such was the residential and commercial growth in and around Plymouth that the 'Three Towns' – ie Plymouth, Devonport and Stonehouse – became united in 1914 and the new local council started to integrate the three, previously unconnected, tramway systems. The case of road transport seeing off rail services may have become more familiar in the 1950s, but Plymouth saw its effects by the early 1920s.

The GWR's Devon-based railmotors were not confined to Plymouth. A number were allocated to Exeter, from where they worked the Heathfield and Dulverton branches, and also on the main line to Dawlish. The heyday of the railmotors might have been shortlived but, in its other spheres of branch and suburban activity in Devon, the GWR's success story echoed that of the main lines. By the early 1900s, the tourist trade was booming and, outside of urban areas such as Plymouth and Exeter, the railways were the only sensible means of transportation for those who didn't wish to spend almost all of their annual break in transit. But it was not only the coastal resorts which attracted the holidaymakers. Walking holidays became very popular, and places such as Moretonhampstead, Ashburton and the Exe Valley attracted many of the visitors who fancied setting off on foot to explore the less-publicised attractions of Devon. The GWR's country branches were, of course, ready and waiting to provide the necessary transportation.

SPECIAL RAIL MOTOR CAR ARRANGEMENTS.

Thursday, March 28th.

PLYMOUTH SUBURBAN SERVICE.

The usual Wednesday and Saturday Relief Cars will run on this day as under :

1- 0 p.m.—LAIRA JUNC. to PLYMOUTH (coupled to ordinary Car and Trailer).	6-27 p.m.—PLYMOUTH to SALTASH.
	7- 0 p.m.—SALTASH to PLYMOUTH.
	8-35 p.m.—PLYMOUTH to SALTASH.
1-45 p.m.—PLYMOUTH to SALTASH.	9- 0 p.m.—SALTASH to PLYMOUTH.
2-10 p.m.—SALTASH to PLYMOUTH.	11- 5 p.m.—PLYMOUTH to ROYAL ALBERT BRIDGE.
2-30 p.m.—PLYMOUTH to KEYHAM.	
2-45 p.m.—KEYHAM to PLYMOUTH.	11-23 p.m.—ROYAL ALBERT BRIDGE to PLYMOUTH.
4-40 p.m.—PLYMOUTH to SALTASH.	
5-30 p.m.—SALTASH to PLYMOUTH.	11†50 p.m.—PLYMOUTH to LAIRA JUNC.

Good-Friday, March 29th.

PLYMOUTH SUBURBAN SERVICE.

An extra Car and Trailer to leave Laira for Millbay at 12-15 p.m., and stand at Plymouth (Millbay) and work as required by Mr. HUNT.

The Station Masters, Plympton to Defiance inclusive, must keep themselves closely in touch with Mr. HUNT, and advise him if the traffic is becoming heavy, and Mr. HUNT will arrange to relieve the Suburban Traffic, where necessary, with the spare Car and Trailer. If the traffic promises to be light the extra accommodation must be dispensed with. Mr. HUNT to arrange.

The 11-0 a.m. Plymouth to Tavistock and 11-55 a.m. Tavistock to Plymouth will be worked by Engine and Coaches on this day.

Mr. HUNT to arrange for the front Vehicle to be reserved for those passengers using Lipson Vale and Laira Halts.

Easter-Monday, April 1st.

PLYMOUTH SUBURBAN SERVICE.

The usual Wednesday and Saturday Relief Cars will run on this day as under :

1- 0 p.m.—LAIRA JUNC. to PLYMOUTH (coupled to ordinary Car and Trailer).	6-27 p.m.—PLYMOUTH to SALTASH.
	7- 0 p.m.—SALTASH to PLYMOUTH.
	8-35 p.m.—PLYMOUTH to SALTASH.
1-45 p.m.—PLYMOUTH to SALTASH.	9- 0 p.m.—SALTASH to PLYMOUTH.
2-10 p.m.—SALTASH to PLYMOUTH.	11- 5 p.m.—PLYMOUTH to ROYAL ALBERT BRIDGE.
2-30 p.m.—PLYMOUTH to KEYHAM.	
2-45 p.m.—KEYHAM to PLYMOUTH.	11-23 p.m.—ROYAL ALBERT BRIDGE to PLYMOUTH.
4-40 p.m.—PLYMOUTH to SALTASH.	
5-30 p.m.—SALTASH to PLYMOUTH.	11†50 p.m.—PLYMOUTH to LAIRA JUNC.

YEALMPTON BRANCH SERVICE.

An extra Car and Trailer to work attached to all trips from 9-17 a.m. ex Plymouth, up to and including 9-3 p.m. ex Yealmpton.

Empty Car and Trailer to leave Laira for Millbay at 8-50 a.m. punctually.

A man will be stationed at Lipson Vale and Dockyard Halts, commencing duty at 12-0 noon, to book passengers and collect tickets.

Chief Inspector SCANTLEBURY to provide men.

The Junior Conductor of each Car will alight at Laira Halt on the Up journey, after 12-0 noon, and book passengers for the Return trip, and rejoin his Car on its return from Plympton.

Left:
The arrangements for the GWR's railmotor operations in the Plymouth area for Easter 1907 were explained in this official staff notice. *Author's collection*

3. The London & South Western Branches

In Southwest England, the London & South Western Railway had an odd attitude to branch lines. Whereas other railway companies tended to complete a main line and then build branches which were connected to it, the LSWR thought nothing of having branch lines which were completely isolated from any of its main lines. The prime example of this was in Cornwall, where the LSWR took over the Bodmin & Wadebridge Railway in 1846. It was 1895 before the LSWR main line arrived at Wadebridge to provide a connection between the branch and the outside world. Had the LSWR had its own way in Devon, a similar situation would have occurred, albeit for a less outlandish period.

As early as 1847, the Exeter & Crediton Railway had virtually completed its 5¾-mile double-track branch between the communities of its title and, furthermore, the stations at Crediton and St Cyres (renamed Newton St Cyres in 1913) were ready and waiting. All that remained to be done was the laying of the short stretch of track at the junction with the B&E at Cowley Bridge, 1¼ miles north of St Davids station in Exeter. From the moment the E&CR had been incorporated, the LSWR had wanted to work the line, clearly with a view to an eventual takeover, but one trifling fact which the LSWR had seemed to have overlooked was that, at the time, its nearest main line had been in Hampshire.

As things turned out, the LSWR's eccentric aspirations had become hypothetical as the E&CR had elected to built to the broad gauge so that the Bristol & Exeter Railway could work the line. This had been strongly opposed by the LSWR but construction work had, nevertheless, been put in hand. In a fit of pique, the LSWR had sought the necessary legal loopholes and had obtained an injunction to prevent the E&CR from completing and opening the line but, by then, only the junction at Cowley Bridge was missing. The absurd situation of an almost-finished railway, complete with fully-equipped stations, doing absolutely nothing continued throughout 1847 but, at the end of the year, the LSWR enforced its legal rights by tearing up the broad gauge tracks and replacing them with those of the standard gauge.

To the people of Crediton, the petulant LSWR was hardly the flavour of the month when it put the brakes on the opening of the railway. The licensee of the Ship Hotel, in particular, was not amused as he had arranged for horse-drawn coaches to bring the crowds from the station to his hostelry

where, most thoughtfully, he had ordered large quantities of 'refreshments' for the anticipated throng. In truth, however, it was not the town of Crediton which had attracted the interest of the railway company in the first place. Other schemes were afoot for railways extending from Crediton to North Devon and the LSWR was determined to secure access to that part of the county. The E&CR's line was an integral part of the LSWR's master plan to strike out for territory which was, theoretically, the domain of the broad gauge companies. When the residents of North Devon realised that the arrival of their railway was being constantly hampered by the LSWR there was uproar, and the LSWR eventually waved the white flag. Consequently, the B&E reaffirmed its interest in the line by reinstating the broad gauge rails between Exeter and Crediton. On 12 May 1851, the line opened for business with the B&E providing the motive power.

Had the LSWR secured the contract to work the E&CR in 1847, it would have resulted in the ludicrous situation of a completely isolated branch line, as the LSWR main line from Waterloo did not reach Exeter until July 1860. However, when that main line arrived, the LSWR considered that it was time to renew the battle plans for the conquest of North Devon. After much wran-

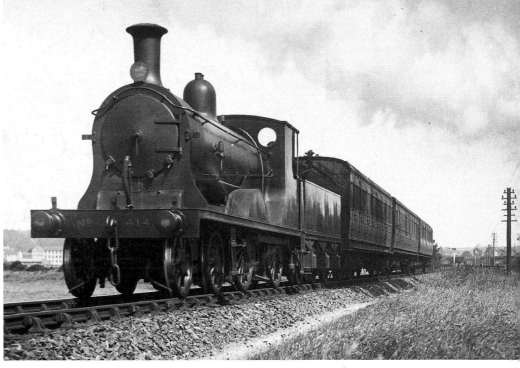

Above:
Although the inclusion of the LSWR's North Devon route in a chapter about branch lines is open to debate, no excuses are offered for printing this superb picture of Drummond 'L11' class 4-4-0 No 414 at the head of a Bideford train near Barnstaple. Although this photograph was taken in June 1925, the locomotive still sports its LSWR livery. *M. W. Earley*

gling, the LSWR secured the lease of the Crediton branch, with effect from 1 February 1862, and a third rail was laid for mixed gauge operation. Furthermore, the B&E was compelled to convert the section between St Davids station in Exeter and Cowley Bridge Junction to mixed gauge in order to provide the LSWR with access to the Crediton branch. The LSWR's decision not to remove the broad gauge rails from the Crediton branch was not an act of neighbourliness, as the terms of its hard-won lease of the line stipulated that the B&E should be permitted to operate goods trains to Crediton. It was a small price to pay, and the B&E's freight trains were grudgingly accommodated until 1903.

Throughout the 1850s, work progressed

EXETER TO CREDITON.

Mixed Gauge.   **Double Line.**

EXETER TO CREDITON. Down Trains.				Week ~~D~~ays.			
		B.G. 1			B.G. 2		
Miles from Exeter.	STATIONS.	G.W. Goods.			G.W. Goods.		
		arr.	dep.		arr.	dep.	
		A.M.	A.M.		P.M.	P.M.	
	Exeter	....	6 25		....	5 0	
4	St. Cyres ..	6 35	6 45		5 10	5 15	
7	Crediton	6 53	....		5 23	....	

CREDITON TO EXETER. Up Trains.				Week Days.			
		B.G. 1			B.G. 2		
Miles from Crediton.	STATIONS.	G.W. Goods.			G.W. Goods.		
		arr.	dep.		arr.	dep.	
		A.M.	A.M.		P.M.	P.M.	
	Crediton	....	7 15		....	6 10	
3	St. Cyres ..	—	7 20		—	6 18	
7	Exeter	7 30	....		6 27	....	

Above:
The GWR's right of access to Crediton by means of the broad gauge rails is confirmed by this extract from the company's working timetable for autumn 1886. *Author's collection*

on the branch between Crediton and Barnstaple and, once again, the LSWR and the B&E found themselves with horns firmly locked. Northwards from Crediton, the line was promoted by the Taw Vale Railway, which later changed its name to the North Devon Railway, and was being constructed by one of the prominent civil engineers of the period, Thomas Brassey. The LSWR contributed, quite illegally, to the cost of the branch's construction, but the company became familiar with the term 'own goal' when the authorities insisted that the line should be built to the broad gauge. This was, of course, of no use whatsoever to the LSWR. At first, the B&E was quite smug at the LSWR's come-uppance but the B&E itself was not to profit from the affair. The contract to work the branch was awarded not to the B&E but to Thomas Brassey.

On 1 August 1854, the North Devon Railway opened its 35½-mile branch throughout from Crediton to Fremington, just beyond Barnstaple. Today, the choice of Fremington as a railway terminus might sound strange but, in the mid-19th century, the village had a quay which provided a very useful alternative to that at Barnstaple, where the navigation of the Taw Estuary proved troublesome; at its peak, Fremington Quay handled some 50,000 tons of coal annually. The emphasis on freight at Fremington was confirmed by

the fact that the community was not served by passenger trains until 2 November 1855, when the six-mile extension to Bideford opened. The extension was worked by Thomas Brassey simply as a continuation of the existing branch from Crediton, but the usurped LSWR did not let its case rest and, by 1863, the latter had obtained the leases on the lines through to Bideford. Standard gauge trains started working into Bideford on 1 March 1863 but, as if to echo the Crediton story, a third rail was retained until 1876 to give a daily B&E goods train access to Bideford. Between Crediton and Barnstaple, there were intermediate stations at Yeoford, Copplestone, Morchard Road, Lapford, Eggesford, South Molton Road, Portsmouth Arms, Umberleigh and Chapeltown. The last-named of those was closed as early as August 1860, but reopened in June 1875 under the amended name of Chapelton. On the Bideford extension, the intermediate stations were at Fremington and Instow.

On 18 July 1872, the 5½-mile extension southwards from Bideford to Torrington opened and, by this time, the LSWR had for-

Below:
Fremington station was not officially opened until 1855, although the railway had arrived to serve the adjacent quays the previous year. As can be seen from this 25in Ordnance Survey map of 1886, Fremington Quay was well equipped with siding accommodation.
Crown Copyright

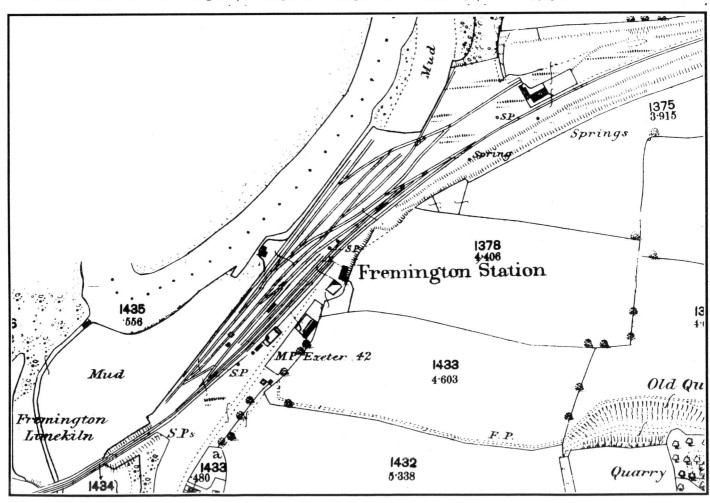

verted to the standard gauge. Those locomotives had all been built by the Bristol firm of Stothert & Slaughter and, as far as it is possible to tell from existing records, were all used on Brassey's North Devon contract along with three Birkenhead-built engines.

Brassey had three engine sheds, one at Crediton, one at Bideford and the other at Barnstaple. Crediton shed passed to the LSWR and survived until the 1870s, and Bideford shed, despite being retained by the LSWR, became redundant with the opening of the Torrington extension in 1872, and was eventually sold for private use. At Barnstaple, the LSWR considered Brassey's shed to be of no practical use and, therefore, the company built its own. The Brassey shed in Barnstaple was, it seems, left to decay and appears to have been condemned in 1878.

At the start of the LSWR's working agreement for the North Devon line in 1863, most of the duties were performed by Joseph Beattie's 2-4-0WTs and, despite their small stature, they seem to have been regarded as very capable engines. For the Torrington extension, the LSWR drafted in Beattie 2-4-0s Nos 61 *Snake* and No 89 *Saturn*, along with veteran 2-2-2 No 30 *Vulture*, which had been built by John Viret Gooch in 1844. From the 1880s, however, Adams's 4-4-2 Radial Tanks and '380' class 4-4-0s started to be used regularly on the North Devon line. During the early 1900s, a number of the displaced 'Jubilee' class 0-4-2s were dispatched to North Devon for mixed

mally taken over the North Devon Railway. The opening of the extension required the construction of a new through station at Bideford; this was situated a little under ½-mile to the south of the original terminus at Cross Parks, which subsequently became the town's goods depot. When each section of the line between Crediton and Torrington had been opened, it had consisted of only a single track but the stretch between Crediton and Coleford Junction (west of Yeoford) was doubled in the 1870s when the LSWR extended towards Plymouth. Further doubling was started in 1906, but although many earthworks and bridges were widened in preparation, only the Coleford Junction-Copplestone and Umberleigh-Barnstaple sections were actually laid with double tracks.

During the mid-19th century, the railways provided a significant boost to holiday resorts all over Britain and, in Devon, the prime area around Torbay had fallen to the broad gauge companies. The LSWR was never likely to reap the same rewards from North Devon but, nevertheless, the Barnstaple area provided a steady mixture of local and holiday traffic. One drawback of the Barnstaple line was that, when compared to the broad-gauge lines in South Devon, it was slow. In the early 1900s, it still took over two hours to cover the 54 miles between Exeter and Torrington and, even during the peak summer months, there were usually only eight trains each way. By 1922, the year before the Grouping, the services were neither faster nor more frequent. It may seem debatable to classify the LSWR's route to North Devon as a branch line but, during the 1860s, the company clearly regarded Ply-

mouth as its most important target in the county. Consequently, the services on the other LSWR routes in Devon tended to take a back seat.

On the North Devon line, the broad gauge locomotives used by Thomas Brassey until the expiry of his contract in 1863 are, these days, poorly documented. Brassey certainly built his own locomotives at Birkenhead but, if the records are correct, the ones used in North Devon were mainly second-hand acquisitions. It is known that Brassey purchased five 2-2-2s, one 2-4-0 and a pair of 0-6-0s from the Bristol & Gloucester Railway in 1855-57 after that company had been bought by the Midland Railway and con-

traffic duties and these were later augmented by Drummond 'L11' and 'K10' class 4-4-0s.

The hub of the LSWR's locomotive operations in North Devon was Barnstaple shed. Constructed in 1862/63 to replace the dilapidated Brassey shed, it was a twin-road timber-built structure at the east end of the station. Apart from the provision of a larger turntable in the 1890s, the shed was to be little altered throughout its long life. When the Torrington extension was opened in 1872, a single-road shed and 42ft turntable were provided on the west side of that station; a larger 50ft turntable was installed in 1898, but was taken out in 1925 when the line was extended beyond Torrington to Halwill Junction.

Even with the Torrington extension of 1872, the LSWR was far from finished in North Devon and, on 20 July 1874, the company opened the 15-mile extension from Barnstaple to Ilfracombe. Ilfracombe had been the target of several previous schemes but, by the time the LSWR had extracted its corporate digit, the area had fallen into economic decline; although, paradoxically, the LSWR had severe problems in rounding up enough labourers to construct the line. Largely due to the labour shortages, it had taken four years to complete the Ilfracombe extension, but the nature of the route itself had not exactly helped matters. There was a three-mile climb at 1 in 40 on the approach to Mortehoe from the south and then a two-mile descent of 1 in 36 towards Ilfracombe; in Barnstaple, the River Taw had to be crossed by a 'quarter circle'-shaped bridge which was linked to the junction by an 'S'-shaped trackbed.

The intermediate stations on the Ilfracombe extension were at Wrafton, Braunton and Mortehoe, the last-named originally being spelt 'Morthoe' and suffixed 'for Lee and Woolacombe'. The original LSWR station in Barnstaple, which had opened in 1854 to serve the line from Crediton, was on the west side of the River Taw; it was equipped with a 400ft-long island platform in preparation for the opening of the Ilfracombe extension and was subsequently renamed Barnstaple Junction. At the end of the bridge, on the east bank of the Taw, Quay station was opened as a more central location for traffic on the Ilfracombe line, and was renamed Barnstaple Town in 1886. However, the station was cramped and so a new station was built on an adjacent site, albeit only slightly less constricted than its predecessor; the 'new' Barnstaple Town station was opened on 16 May 1898 and also accommodated the narrow gauge Lynton & Barnstaple Railway.

At Ilfracombe, a single-road engine shed was built at the east side of the station and was equipped with a standard turntable; a larger 60ft turntable was installed in 1895. There was a definite need for a turntable at Ilfracombe as the difficult nature of the line from Barnstaple meant that lightweight tank engines would be of little use. William Beattie ordered five Beyer Peacock 0-6-0s specially for freight duties on the line, and three similar locomotives were built by the LSWR itself in 1875/80. These smart-looking 0-6-0s had 4ft 6in diameter wheels and inside cylinders of 16in x 20in. They became known as the 'Ilfracombe Goods' and were officially limited to loads of no more than fourteen axles on the gradients around Mortehoe; two of the class, LSWR Nos 282/83, were given the honour of hauling the first train on opening day. When superseded by newer 0-6-0s and mixed traffic 4-4-0s, six of the 'Ilfracombe Goods' were sold to light railways in the Colonel Stephens empire. The last of the 'Ilfracombe Goods' to survive was LSWR No 324 which had been built in 1875; after its withdrawal by the LSWR in 1910, it was sold to the Shropshire & Montgomeryshire Railway where it was rechristened No 3 *Hesperus*. It was not scrapped until 1941.

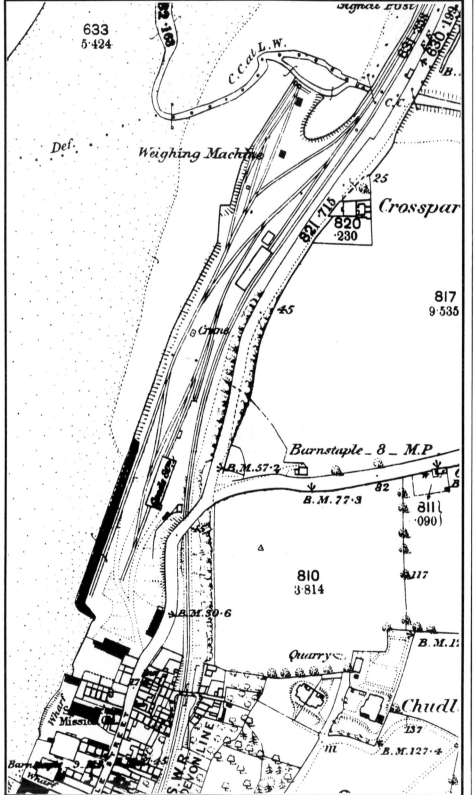

Left:
The goods depot, which can be seen to the west of the running line in this 1889 25in Ordnance Survey map of Bideford, was the town's passenger terminus until the line was extended to Torrington in 1872. *Crown Copyright*

Table 3.1: Locomotives used by Thomas Brassey on the North Devon Railway

Due to the sparseness of official records, it cannot be guaranteed that this list is definitive. However, cross-referencing of several respected sources has enabled the compilation of a list which is, in the opinion of this writer at least, as accurate as possible.

Brassey's locomotives were, by necessity, broad gauge; they were taken into LSWR stock in 1863. Some had been obtained secondhand by Brassey and, in the following list, the abbreviations 'B&G', 'MR' and 'S&S' denote Bristol & Gloucester Railway, Midland Railway and Stothert & Slaughter respectively.

Name	Built	Builder	Type	Wheels	Cylinders	Weight	LSWR No	Origins
Creedy	1854	Brassey	2-4-0	5ft 6in	17x24 (o)	?	176	
Yeo	1854	Brassey	2-2-2	6ft 0in	15x24 (o)	?	177	
Dart	1854	Brassey	2-2-2	6ft 0in	15x24 (o)	?	178	
Venus	1844	S&S	2-4-0	5ft 0in	15x18(i)	17½t	179	Originally B&G No 2, latterly MR No 469
Star	1844	S&S	2-2-2	6ft 6in	15x21(i)	18t	180	Originally B&G No 4, latterly MR No 460
Barum	1844	S&S	2-2-2	6ft 6in	15x21(i)	18t	181	Originally B&G No 5, latterly MR No 461
Exe	1844	S&S	2-2-2	6ft 6in	15x21(i)	18t	182	Originally B&G No 6, latterly MR No 462
Tite	1844	S&S	2-2-2	6ft 6in	15x21(i)	18t	183	Originally B&G No 8, latterly MR No 464
Mole	1844	S&S	2-2-2	6ft 6in	15x21(i)	18t	184	Originally B&G No 9, latterly MR No 465
Dreadnought	1844	S&S	0-6-0	4ft 6in	16x21(i)	26t	185	Originally B&G No 10, latterly MR No 466
Defiance	1844	S&S	0-6-0	4ft 6in	16x21(i)	26t	186	Originally B&G No 11, latterly MR No 467

Above:
William Adams's handsome 'Jubilee' class 0-4-2s were not ideally suited to hilly West Country lines because of their four-coupled wheel arrangement. Nevertheless, this did not prevent some members of the class from having spells in Devon, and even the steeply-graded Ilfracombe line received their attentions for a while. In 1928, the locomotive in the picture, No 535, became one of the first of the class to be withdrawn. *Ian Allan Library*

For passenger duties on the Ilfracombe extension, the original intention had been to use purpose-built outside-cylindered 0-6-0s, and Joseph Beattie had prepared the design for these well in advance of the opening of the line. However, the drawings were shelved when William Beattie took over the locomotive superintendent's job from his father and, consequently, many of the passenger turns to Ilfracombe in the late 19th century were handled by the 'Ilfracombe Goods' 0-6-0s. Adams's 'T1' class 0-4-4Ts and 'Jubilee' class 0-4-2s started to appear on the line in the late 1890s along with Drummond's 'M7' 0-4-4Ts.

On the Ilfracombe line, doubling work was undertaken in 1889-91 but the bridge over the River Taw at Barnstaple remained single track. Almost from the outset, the branch had brought about a reversal in Ilfracombe's fortunes. Before the railway had arrived, things had looked pretty grim for the isolated community but the railway had brought the tourists. The regeneration of Ilfracombe was sustained, and this is illustrated by the timetables for the summer of 1909 which advertised 17 trains each way on weekdays and three on Sundays; the average journey times to and from Barnstaple were around 40min. By the summer of 1922, Sunday services to Ilfracombe had been discontinued and weekday passenger services had dropped to 14 trains each way. However, this was still a healthy number and, interestingly, the 1922 timetables advertised a through carriage between Brighton and Ilfracombe on one train each day. No comment is offered here about the respective merits of

Left:
The curving bridge across the River Taw led to Barnstaple Town station, which can just be seen in the distance in this 1912 photograph. The locomotive appears to be an 'M7' class 0-4-4T. *Rail Archive Stephenson*

Below:
Beattie's 'Ilfracombe Goods' 0-6-0 No 282 was given No 0282 in the duplicate list in 1899, and was renumbered 349 later that year. Thus, the photograph can be dated but, alas, the location cannot be confirmed. *Bucknall Collection/Ian Allan Library*

Brighton and Ilfracombe, but it has been suggested that Ilfracombe hoteliers were a little less wise to a plethora of 'Mr & Mrs Smiths'.

After having had its corporate ears well and truly boxed by the broad gauge lobby in the 1850s, the LSWR sheepishly accepted that the least traumatic method of constructing a branch line was to undertake the task itself or, failing that, to guide the hand of a compliant subsidiary. When a branch to Exmouth was considered, the LSWR found that a potential subsidiary was, most conveniently, already in existence. The obliging subsidiary-in-waiting was the Exeter & Exmouth Railway, which had originally been promoted as a broad gauge concern with a connection to the South Devon Railway at Exminster, from where the proposed line would cross the River Exe by means of a bridge. Those plans had lain dormant for some time and so, when the LSWR courted

the Exeter & Exmouth with promises of grandeur and wealth, the latter happily sided with the former. In truth, the LSWR did not have to work very hard on the courtship. In the 1840s, Exmouth had been a modestly prosperous town with a population of around 5,000, but the SDR's arrival on the opposite bank of the Exe had passed the initiative to Dawlish and Teignmouth. The lack of a railway at Exmouth had resulted in a gradual decline in the town's fortunes which, the LSWR pointed out to its subsidiary, was ripe for reversal.

Exmouth got its railway on 1 May 1861. The 10½-mile branch between Exeter and Exmouth ran for its entire length on the east side of the Exe estuary, and had intermediate stations at Topsham, Woodbury Road and Lympstone. At Exmouth, the station had one platform and a small goods yard while, opposite the platform, was a single-road engine shed and a 42ft turntable. At first, the usual

motive power on the branch took the form of Beattie 2-2-2WTs, and it was one of these, No 36 *Comet*, which had hauled the 11-coach train on opening day. The ubiquitous Beattie 2-4-0WTs started to appear in the mid-1870s, and were superseded by Adams's 4-4-2 Radial Tanks in the early 1890s. The coming of the railway to Exmouth did, indeed, provide the boost the town needed. Not only did Exmouth benefit from the tourist trade but, just three years after the railway had arrived, a new dock was opened in the town to act as a direct, and more accessible, alternative to the Canal Basin in Exeter. During the 1890s and early 1900s, Adams's 'B4' class 0-4-0Ts were the usual dock shunters at Exmouth, the parent shed at Exmouth Junction normally having an allocation of three members of the class.

Flushed with success after the opening of the Exmouth branch in 1861, the LSWR looked longingly at the independent Seaton

Above:

Drummond 'M7' class 0-4-4T No 22 is seen leaving Ilfracombe c1912/13. The original engine shed, which survived until the late 1920s, can be seen in the distance behind the locomotive. *Lens of Sutton*

Left:

Ilfracombe was promoted as a 'genteel' resort, and suitably-worded advertisements were included in official railway publications. This example of over-sell featured in the LSWR guide for 1912. *Author's collection*

349.—SEATON AND BEER.

Incorporated by 26 and 27 Vic., cap. 118 (13th July, 1863), to construct a line from the Colyton station of the South Western to Seaton. Length, 4¼ miles. Capital, 36,000*l.* in 10*l.* ordinary shares, 12,000*l.* on loan. Opened 16th March, 1868. Arrangements with South Western, which works the line at 45 per cent.

CAPITAL.—Additional capital to that authorised by parliament has been raised under certificate from Board of Trade, to the extent of 12,000*l.* in 5 per cent. preference, and 4,000*l.* on loan.

No. of Directors—5; minimum, 3; quorum, 3. *Qualification,* 200*l.*

DIRECTORS:

Sir WALTER CALVERLEY TREVELYAN, Bart., Nettlecomb, Somerset, and Wallington, Northumberland.

Deputy-Chairman—GEORGE EVANS, Esq., Seaton, Axminster.

William Dommett, Esq., Chard.
John Babbage, Esq., Nettlecomb, Taunton.

John Latoysonere Scarbrough, Esq., Coly House, Colyton, Devon.

OFFICERS.—Sec., C. E. Rowcliffe, Stogumber, Taunton; Eng., W. R. Galbraith, Victoria Street, Westminster, S.W.; Solicitors, Radcliffe and Davies, 20, Craven Street, Strand, W.C.

Left:

Although it was worked by the LSWR, the Seaton & Beer Railway was an independent concern. These corporate details appeared in Bradshaw's Manual for 1869.

& Beer Railway which had been incorporated in 1863 to construct a branch from the main LSWR line at Colyton to the coastal town of Seaton. The LSWR's offer of a working agreement was accepted by the smaller company and the line was opened on 16 March 1868. Seaton later became a moderately prosperous seaside resort, largely thanks to the railway, but at the time the railway was opened, there was a degree of philanthropy in the air. During the mid-1850s, the harbour at Axmouth, on the opposite bank of the River Axe to Seaton, was in decline and so the railway had to depend on the future of Seaton as a tourist spot or, alternatively, keep its fingers crossed for the success of a proposed expansion of the harbour at nearby Beer. The plans for Beer harbour came to nothing and even the existing fishing trade dwindled, but the sedate appeal of Seaton saved the day for the railway. To tidy things up neatly, the LSWR officially absorbed the Seaton & Beer Railway in 1885.

The 4½-mile long Seaton branch was single track and had intermediate stations at Colyton and Colyford. The junction station on the main line had originally been called Colyton but this was changed to Seaton Junction with the opening of the branch. At Seaton, there was a single-platform station which had a small goods yard; a timber-built single-road engine shed opened with the line but was replaced when the entire station site was modernised in 1937. The first regular locomotives on the Seaton line were Beattie 2-2-2WTs, and it is known that No 12 *Jupiter* and No 33 *Phoenix* worked on the branch very early on. These were replaced by 'O2' and 'T1' 0-4-4Ts in the 1890s, and like the locomotives on the Exmouth line, were serviced at the parent shed in Exeter. The timetables for the summer of 1909 show nine passenger services each way on weekdays with one goods and two mixed trains. There was provision in the working timetable for an additional 'as required' early morning goods service. By 1922, a similar number of services were offered and the journey time remained at around 15min.

Eight miles along the coast from Seaton was Sidmouth, where a railway had been partially completed as early as 1836. That line had been conceived in connection with a plan for a new harbour but both the harbour scheme and the unfinished railway had passed into oblivion. A revived scheme of 1862 had fared little better. The LSWR took stock of the situation at Sidmouth and knew a good thing when it saw one; the prospect of a part-finished trackbed into a seaside resort seemed too good to ignore. The fly in the ointment was that the residents of Sidmouth didn't really want a railway.

Sidmouth was a genteel seaside town which took pride in the 'selectivity' of its residents and visitors. The thought of the town being invaded by nasty, grubby away-day excursionists presented all sorts of horrors for the refined locals but, eventually, a compromise was reached. The railway was permitted into Sidmouth, but the station had to be sited almost one mile from the sea front. The astute residents of Sidmouth reckoned that this would give them access to the great beyond as, of course, many of them had their own transport to take them to the station while, conversely, day trippers would find the walk to the sea too daunting and, consequently, would inflict themselves on other resorts. That was precisely how things turned out after the railway opened on 6 July 1874 and, remarkably, the situation changed little throughout the line's 93-year life. All that was missing was an 'inspection' of visitors.

The 8¼-mile Sidmouth branch left the LSWR's main line at Feniton which, pre-

Sidmouth station was almost one mile from the sea front, and so the abundance of cabs seen in this late-Victorian photograph was not a case of over-supply. *Lens of Sutton*

The Railway Station, Sidmouth.

Above:
This early 1900s picture seems to show a lengthy train arriving at Ottery St Mary but, judging from the rigid stances of the assembled throng, a posed shot with a static 0-4-4T and train is a strong possibility. *Lens of Sutton*

dictably, was renamed Sidmouth Junction. The line followed the Otter Valley for much of its route but the approach to Sidmouth included gradients which peaked at 1 in 45; there were intermediate stations at Ottery St Mary and Tipton, the latter being retitled Tipton St John in 1881. At Sidmouth, there was a single-road engine shed which had, on its approach road, a turntable. The turntable proved to be an extravagance as, although the original intention had been to use one of the 'Ilfracombe Goods' 0-6-0s on the branch, it seems that the line was worked by tank engines from the outset; it was the Beattie 2-4-0WTs which dominated in the early years, with 0-4-4Ts muscling in during the 1890s. Nevertheless, the little-used turntable remained *in situ* until the closure of the shed in 1933. During the early 1900s, there were usually 10 or 12 passenger services and one goods train each way on weekdays, the average journey time being 25min.

In West Devon, the LSWR spent much of the 1870s working on its main line towards Plymouth. That line had been considered the most vital of several LSWR-backed schemes which had been promoted around the same time and, therefore, most other plans had been treated with little urgency. However, on 20 January 1879 the LSWR eventually arrived at Holsworthy. The ultimate target of that line was Bude, just over the border in Cornwall, but it was to be 1898 before the residents of Bude saw their first train.

Although Holsworthy was the point at which the LSWR's horse-drawn coaches started their journey to the seaside town of Bude, Holsworthy itself was, by the 1870s, a market town in decline. The LSWR's prime objective in the area was, in fact, neither Holsworthy nor even Bude but, instead, a main line extension to Launceston and, from there, a link with the isolated Bodmin & Wadebridge Railway in North Cornwall. The construction of the branch to Holsworthy and Bude was, to an extent, a case of killing two birds with one stone. The Launceston extension left the main Plymouth line at Meldon Junction, 2¾ miles west of Okehampton; 10 miles beyond Meldon was Halwill where, in 1886, the line to Launceston and, later, beyond would continue. By the end of 1879, however, work on the Launceston line had not progressed beyond Halwill, and so the contemporary LSWR map of West Devon showed only a branch line from Meldon Junction, through Halwill, and on to Holsworthy.

Until the opening of the Launceston extension, the proposed junction station at Halwill was named Halwill & Beaworthy. Between there and Holsworthy, the only intermediate station was at Dunsland Cross. For motive power on the Holsworthy branch, three brand new '46' class 4-4-0Ts were dispatched to Okehampton and these were representatives of William Adams's maiden design for the LSWR. In later years, the '46s' were rebuilt as 4-4-2Ts and, unwittingly, became the predecessors of the famous Radial Tanks. The Okehampton trio of '46s', LSWR Nos 123/24/30, were themselves replaced by new Radial Tanks in 1883, but 'O2' class 0-4-4Ts were eventually used for most of the passenger duties. A single-road engine shed was installed at Holsworthy but it became redundant when the branch was extended to Bude.

The opening of the extension across the Cornish border into Bude on 10 August 1898 completed the 18½-mile branch from Halwill Junction. The new line had necessitated the resiting of Holsworthy station, and between there and Bude, the only intermediate station was Whitstone & Bridgerule. Outside of Holsworthy, there was a viaduct of nine 50ft arches which was by far the largest concrete structure of its day. The station at Bude was some distance from the town centre, but this was a deliberate sop to the residents of nearby Stratton who felt somewhat miffed at not having their own station. From the station at Bude, a freight branch diverged to the town's canal basin, where consignments of sand were brought from the beach by means of a horse-operated tramway. There was a single-road engine shed and a 50ft turntable in the station yard at Bude, these being unveiled in time for the opening of the line.

At first, most of the passenger services on the Bude branch were handled by tank engines, particularly the Adams 4-4-2Ts and 'O2' class 0-4-4Ts, with ageing Beattie 0-6-0s taking care of the freight turns. In the early 1900s, Drummond's 'M7' 0-4-4Ts became the standard LSWR branch engines and these gradually took over many of the Bude workings but, by the Grouping, 4-4-0s had started to be used for mixed traffic duties. An average of ten passenger trains ran each way on the Bude branch on summer weekdays during the 1905-10 period, with journey times of around 35min for the run from Halwill Junction. At that time, there was one passenger and one freight train each way on Sundays. By the summer of 1922, six passenger trains operated on the Bude branch each way on weekdays but there was no Sunday service. Of the weekday trains, four in each direction had through carriages to or from Waterloo.

The Bude branch generated an adequate flow of passenger traffic but it was never one of the world's greatest money-spinners. This was, arguably, because it had arrived comparatively late in the day and, by the time it had finally materialised, the GWR's publicity machine had performed a very effective job on the rival attractions of South Devon and the Cornish Riviera. Those through carriages to Bude which were advertised in the 1922 timetable took, at best, 5hr 40min to get from Waterloo while, in the same amount of time, the GWR could convey passengers from Paddington right through to Truro in the heart of Cornwall.

After the LSWR acquired its own main line route into Plymouth in 1890, the company looked at the potential of local services in the city. On 5 September 1892, the LSWR opened its branch between Friary and Plymstock, on the east bank of the River Plym, and an extension which curved westwards to Turnchapel was opened on 1 January 1897. The complete branch was only 2½-miles long but it had an intermediate station on the extension at Oreston; at Turnchapel, the branch continued for ¼-mile beyond the station to a wharf but this section was for goods trains only.

After having watched the GWR introduce railmotor services at Plymouth in 1904, the LSWR did precisely the same the following year, albeit on a much smaller scale. During the summer of 1905, one of the two railmotors which Drummond had built for the Basingstoke & Alton Light Railway was transferred to Friary shed for duties on the Turnchapel branch. Further railmotors were constructed at the end of 1905 and two of these were allocated to Friary in 1906 for local services. Latching on to the GWR's example, the LSWR opened railmotor halts at Albert Road, Camel's Head and Weston Mill on the main line and at Lucas Terrace on the Turnchapel branch from Friary.

Within a few years, the local service between Friary station and St Budeaux (LSWR) comprised over 15 trains each way on weekdays while, on the Turnchapel branch, around 20 daily passenger services plied in each direction. At Plymstock station on the Turnchapel branch, the LSWR also had to accommodate the GWR branch trains to Yealmpton. By 1922, the LSWR weekday service of 22 trains each way on the Turnchapel branch and the GWR's seven trains each way on the Yealmpton branch meant that 58 passenger trains stopped at Plymstock every day. On top of that, some 10 or 12 freight trains passed through but, remarkably, the atmosphere at Plymstock was, more often than not, one of rare cordiality. By then, however, the LSWR's railmotors had all been withdrawn and local services tended to be handled by 0-4-4Ts.

During their comparatively brief lives, the LSWR railmotors also appeared at Exeter. Two new railmotors were dispatched to Exeter in 1906 for services between Queen Street and Topsham, on the Exmouth Branch. Halts were constructed at Lion's

Holt (renamed St James Park in 1946), Mount Pleasant Road, Polsloe Bridge and Clyst St Mary & Digby and, in anticipation of increasing the machines' sphere of activity, Whipton Bridge halt was opened on the main line. Both of the Exeter-based railmotors were transferred to the London area, the first in 1912 and the other in 1915.

The last passenger branch to open in Devon before the end of the century was the line between Tipton St Johns, on the Sidmouth branch, and Budleigh Salterton. Promoted and constructed by the independent Budleigh Salterton Railway, it opened on 15 May 1897 and was worked by the LSWR; the inevitable absorption followed in 1912. Despite the inclusion of the name 'Budleigh Salterton' in the independent company's title, the station in that town spent the first eleven months of its working life with the official title of Salterton. The only intermediate stations on the branch were at Newton Poppleford and East Budleigh. The LSWR

Above:
Until the opening of the extension to Bude in 1898, Holsworthy was a terminus. This picture, which was taken in 1895, gives a rare glimpse of Holsworthy's wooden engine shed; it can be seen just to the left of the carriages. *Lens of Sutton*

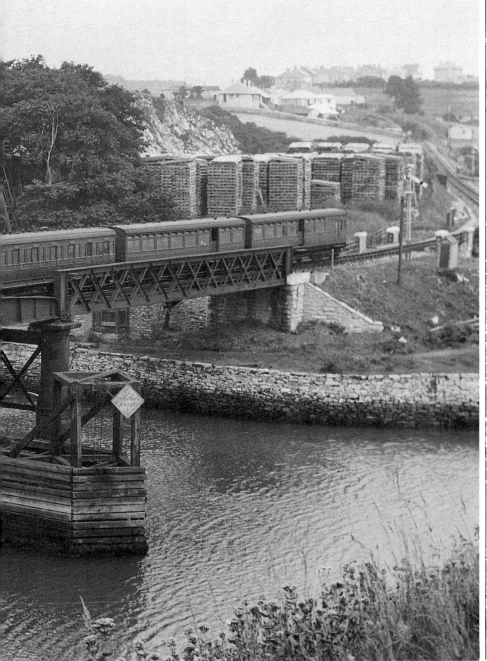

Left:
'O2' class 0-4-4T No 218 was photographed arriving at Turnchapel on 8 July 1924, but it was still wearing its pre-Grouping livery. The locomotive ended its days in 1966 as No W33 *Bembridge* on the Isle of Wight. *H. C. Casserley*

itself undertook the construction of an extension from Budleigh Salterton to Exmouth which opened on 1 June 1903 to complete the 11¼-mile run from Tipton St John; the new section had an intermediate station at Littleham. The extension to Exmouth necessitated the reconstruction of Budleigh Salterton station, and the small engine shed which had been provided in 1897 became superfluous.

The LSWR was quick to make full use of the new route into Exmouth and, particularly during the peak holiday season, a number of through trains from Waterloo to Exmouth were routed via Budleigh Salterton, thereby avoiding Exeter completely. Later, a circular Exeter-Sidmouth Junction-Budleigh Salterton-Exmouth-Exeter service was introduced. Throughout most of the line's LSWR and, indeed, Southern Railway days, the usual motive power on passenger workings took the form of 'O2' and 'M7' 0-4-4Ts which were supplied by Exmouth shed; freight duties on the Budleigh Salterton, Sidmouth and Exmouth branches tended to be performed by 'G6' 0-6-0Ts until the 1930s. For many years, the summer passenger services between Tipton St Johns and Exmouth comprised 10 or 12 trains each way on weekdays and the usual journey time was around 30min.

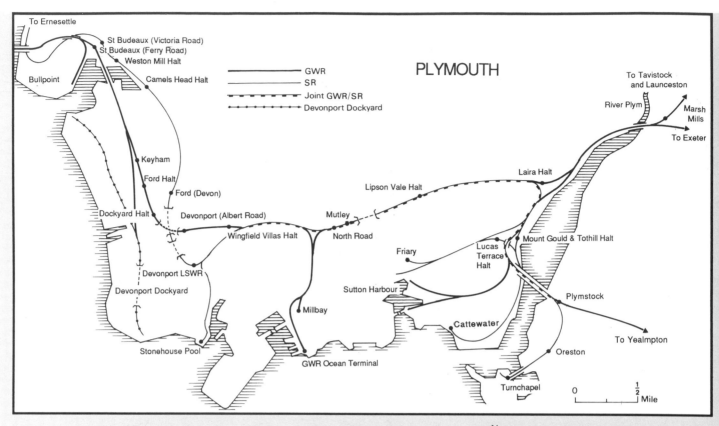

PLYMOUTH

To Ernesettle
St Budeaux (Victoria Road)
St Budeaux (Ferry Road)
Weston Mill Halt
Bullpoint
Camels Head Halt

GWR
SR
Joint GWR/SR
Devonport Dockyard

To Tavistock
and Launceston
River Plym
Marsh Mills
To Exeter

Keyham
Ford Halt
Ford (Devon)
Dockyard Halt
Devonport (Albert Road)
Mutley
Lipson Vale Halt
Laira Halt

Wingfield Villas Halt
North Road
Mount Gould & Tothill Halt
Devonport LSWR
Friary
Lucas Terrace Halt
Devonport Dockyard
Sutton Harbour
Plymstock
Millbay
Cattewater
Stonehouse Pool
Oreston
To Yealmpton
GWR Ocean Terminal
Turnchapel

0   ½   Mile

Above:
Railways of Plymouth.

Right:
LSWR railmotor No 5 was built in 1905, and was one of an order for nine identical vehicles. Some of the nine worked on the Friary and Turnchapel branches in the Plymouth area, while similar machines were later used in the Exeter area. *Ian Allan Library*

Welcome to the sunny South West. This early 1900s picture shows that it can rain even in Lyme Regis. *Lens of Sutton*

Just across the East Devon border, in the westernmost corner of Dorset, lies the well-known beauty spot of Lyme Regis. As early as 1845, the first of several schemes had been promoted to build a railway to Lyme Regis but the nearest any of them had come to fruition was when the Lyme Regis Railway had cut its first sod in 1874. It seems that the cost of the ceremonial spade had been the last straw for the impecunious little company as, before the real construction work had got underway, the company had passed into receivership. In the late 1890s, other schemes had been proposed for a railway to Lyme Regis and these had been better-financed, but the great argument had been whether a branch should join the main line at Chard Road in Somerset or Axminster in Devon. The latter won the day.

The 6¾-mile single-track branch between Axminster and Lyme Regis opened on 24 August 1903 and, although built by an independent local company, it was worked by the LSWR. The branch abounded in tight curves and sharp gradients but, even so, it stood no hope of reaching the centre of Lyme Regis. The terminus was perched 250ft up on a hill just beyond the town but, nevertheless, the branch generated considerable tourist traffic and, within a few years, over 60,000 passengers were using the line annually. On the minus side, the availability of a rail connection at Lyme Regis meant that the town's ancient harbour, the Cobb, lost virtually all of its little trade it had left.

At Axminster, the branch services used a bay platform on the up side and, after leaving the station, the branch crossed over the main line by means of a flyover. The small engine shed at Axminster, which had been built in the 1860s to house the locomotives which assisted on Honiton bank, was demolished to make way for the necessary embankment. There was a freight connection to the branch on the down side of Axminster station but this was little used and was taken out in 1915. The only intermediate station on the branch was at Combpyne which had a crossing loop until 1930, and the single-platform terminus at Lyme Regis had a small goods yard and a timber-built engine shed. The shed was destroyed by a fire in 1913 and was replaced by one of asbestos which cost the princely sum of £400. The LSWR knew all about fire-proofing, if not asbestosis.

From the outset, the nature of the Lyme Regis branch placed severe limitations on the type of locomotives which could be used. At first, two LBSCR 'Terrier' 0-6-0Ts, No 646 *Newington* and No 668 *Clapham*, were purchased specifically for the line but they proved unsuccessful. After the LSWR had taken over complete ownership of the line in 1907, the tracks were relaid and, consequently, 'O2' 0-4-4Ts were tried but, even with half-loads of coal and water, the axle weights of the 'O2s' were rather too close to the limits for comfort. In 1913, the LSWR's new locomotive superintendent, Robert Urie, decided to modify two of the Adams '415' class 4-4-2Ts, better known as the Radial Tanks, for trials on the branch and this involved increasing the play on their bogies and restricting the water capacities of each to 800 gallons. It worked.

The two Radial Tanks which were modified were on the LSWR's duplicate list and carried Nos 0125/0419; classmate No 521 was similarly treated in 1914. Apart from trials of two other locomotives in 1928-30, the Radial Tanks went on to handle all workings on the Lyme Regis branch until the 1950s, and No 0125 was to remain in action on the line until 1961. In the early years of the branch, most trains were mixed; the summer timetable for 1909 listed eight passenger or mixed services each way on weekdays and this increased to nine by the summer of 1922. The journey time of 20min for the 6¾ miles hardly changed from the day the line opened to the time it closed in 1965.

The GWR and its predecessors might have had the high-profile branch lines of South Devon but the LSWR didn't do so badly elsewhere in the county. The LSWR and, later, the Southern maintained a monopoly of East Devon where the coastal resorts were somewhat less brash, and the branch lines which served them retained an air of subtle efficiency. From the railway enthusiast's point of view, the Lyme Regis branch was, arguably, one of the most charismatic little lines anywhere in southern England and, although Lyme Regis itself was just over the border in Dorset, all but the last half-mile or so of the branch was firmly ensconced in Devon.

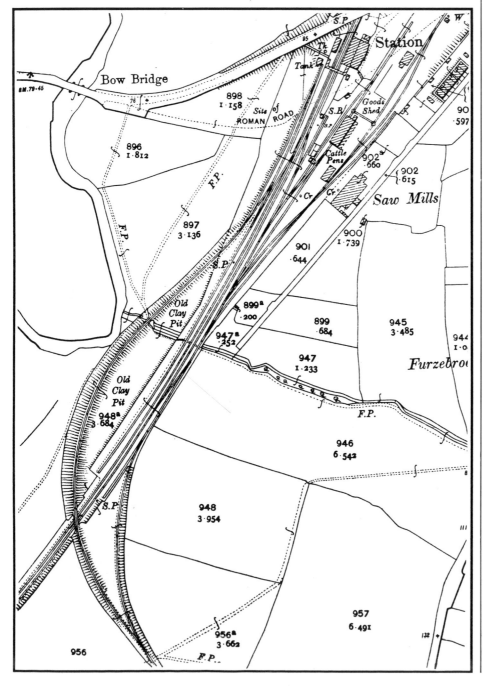

Left:
This reduction from the 25in Ordnance Survey map of 1905 shows Axminster station, complete with the short-lived loop between the down side and the Lyme Regis branch. The tank, which is marked at the rear of the up platform, provided the water for the Lyme Regis branch engines. *Crown Copyright*

4. The Independents

In Devon, as elsewhere in Britain, there were numerous instances of independent railway companies which, from the outset, relied on other companies to provide the locomotives, rolling stock and, usually, the staff as well. For example, the Seaton & Beer Railway was totally dependent on the LSWR for its motive power and rolling stock, but retained a nominally independent existence until 1885, despite never having worked any of its own services. Another example is provided by the Teign Valley Railway, which was virtually bankrupt even before its line was completed. The GWR stepped in to assist with the final stages of construction and, predictably, worked every single service from the moment the line opened.

The instances of small independent railway companies which owned their own locomotives and rolling stock, and operated their own services, are as rare in Devon as elsewhere. The Bristol & Exeter and the South Devon Railways were very large concerns but, nevertheless, they gave up their respective struggles for independence as early as 1876 and sold out to the GWR. If such prominent companies as the B&E and SDR couldn't survive alone, the future for small, localised independents must have looked pretty grim. However, there were three locomotive-operating independents in Devon which defied the trends, and each had a very different story.

The Plymouth, Devonport & South Western Junction Railway

If the precise definition of an 'independent railway company' isn't contentious enough, then the inclusion of the Plymouth, Devonport & South Western Junction Railway in a book about Devon might, despite the company's title, be considered grounds for a good argument. The original section of the PD&SWJR was the main line between Lydford and Plymouth, which was worked by the LSWR from the outset and was, indisputably, in Devon. However, the PD&SWJR's branch line was between Bere Alston and Callington and, for most of its length, was most definitely over the border in Cornwall. Furthermore, the old narrow gauge tramway which was inherited by the PD&SWJR and subsequently converted into the standard-gauge Callington branch, didn't actually reach Devon. Nevertheless, there is little doubt that the company's close connection with the Devon side of the Tamar more than justifies its inclusion in this book.

When the LSWR started operating into Plymouth in 1876, it had to exercise running powers over the GWR line between Lydford and Plymouth, which had to be converted for mixed gauge operation. It did not come as the world's greatest surprise when the GWR gave priority to its own trains over the jointly-used section, and since the stretch of line in question was only single track, the LSWR services were frequently subjected to delays. Among the business community of Plymouth, this prompted a bout of 'things must be done'.

The first scheme to provide the LSWR with its own route between Lydford and Plymouth was proposed in 1882, and involved the laying of an LSWR track alongside the GWR one but, although this proposal received Parliamentary assent, it was not acted upon. In 1883, an alternative scheme was put forward, whereby the LSWR would have a completely separate route into Plymouth from that of the GWR. The new route from Lydford passed through Tavistock, Bere Alston, St Budeaux and Devonport on its way to a central station at Plymouth. The com-

Below:
The PD&SWJR's Callington branch was a charismatic little line. One of its most-celebrated features was the wagon lift on Calstock Viaduct but, by the time this photograph was taken on 14 June 1926, the lift was seldom used. The locomotive at the head of the mixed train on the viaduct is ex-LSWR 'O2' class 0-4-4T No 223. *H. C. Casserley*

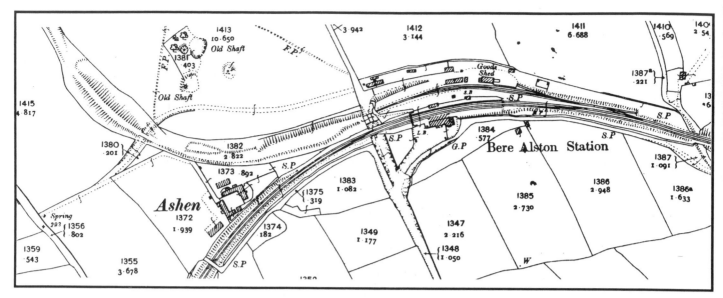

Above:
This Ordnance Survey map of Bere Alston station was published in 1906, and the work to prepare the way for the PD&SWJR's Callington branch is evident. *Crown Copyright*

pany which promoted this new line was the Plymouth, Devonport & South Western Junction Railway.

To outsiders, the PD&SWJR appeared to be little more than a subsidiary of the LSWR, but it had been conceived in Plymouth, and not Waterloo, and had been financed almost exclusively by Devon money. Construction work commenced on 2 April 1887, and the line proved to be a difficult and expensive one to build. The idea of a new station in Plymouth was shelved in order to reduce costs, but even so, there were enough engineering features on the 22¼-mile double-track line to keep the contractors busy. In all, there were three tunnels and over 50 bridges, including an eight-arch viaduct over the River Tavy and a smaller viaduct near Tamerton Foliot. The line opened on 2 June 1890, but was leased to, and worked by, the LSWR.

However, the PD&SWJR wanted a little more out of life than to act simply as a route

for the LSWR, and so it cast its corporate eyes across the River Tamar. Just over the border in eastern Cornwall, the area around Kit Hill and Callington had a number of mines where copper, tin and arsenic were extracted. The mining industry in that area had grown during the 1850s and 1860s, and so a tramway had been built to link the mining area with a wharf on the River Tamar. It was a descendant of this tramway which eventually passed to the PD&SWJR.

The original tramway had been promoted by the Tamar, Kit Hill & Callington Railway Co, although the company's title had been changed, first to the Callington & Calstock Railway, and later to the East Cornwall Mineral Railway. In was the ECMR which had the distinction of opening the 7¾-mile 3ft 6in gauge line throughout on 7 May 1872, although some isolated sections had been operational before that date. The tramway started at Kelly Bray, some 1¼ miles north of Callington, and finished at a quay on the Tamar at Calstock, whence barges could transport the minerals to Plymouth for transfer to larger vessels. On leaving Kelly Bray, the tramway passed Redmoor and Holmbush mines, then Monks Corner and Kit Hill mines, and near Gunnislake there

were the workings at Drakewalls and Clitters United.

At Calstock, the quay was some 350ft below the level of the tramway, and so the wagons had to descend an incline of 1 in 6 which was worked on the counterbalance principle, but with the assistance of a stationary engine. The maximum loading on the incline was two full wagons or three empties. At the lower end of the incline, a ½-mile long horse-operated spur provided the connection to the quay. The section between the top of the incline and Kelly Bray was locomotive-operated, and two new 0-4-0STs had been purchased from Neilson & Co of Glasgow in 1871 in readiness for the completion of the tramway. The locomotives carried Works Nos 1660/61, and had outside cylinders of 10½in x 18in and wheels of 3ft 1in diameter; the machines weighed in at 13 tons apiece. The legal speed limit on the tramway was 16mph, but in view of the locomotives' design, there was little real likelihood of their drivers receiving any penalty points.

In 1876, the ECMR received assent to construct a spur to a quay at Morwellham, just to the north of Calstock, and also an extension to the GWR at Tavistock. More significantly, a further ingredient of the same Act was for conversion to the standard gauge. The problem of how the company was going to finance the new work became hypothetical when, in the late 1870s, the mining industry went into a rapid nosedive. After protracted negotiations with sundry semi-autonomous railway companies, the ECMR formally sold out to the PD&SWJR on 4 January 1894. For a price of £21,500 in cash plus £48,250 in shares, the PD&SWJR had emphasised its independence by securing a line which it could operate itself.

Left:
East Cornwall Mineral Railway 3ft 6in gauge 0-4-0ST No 2 was rebuilt as a standard gauge 0-4-2ST in 1907/08, by which time it had become part of PD&SWJR stock; it was sold in 1912. This picture is believed to have been taken at Callington. *Ian Allan Library*

Despite the continuing decline of the mining industry in East Cornwall, the PD&SWJR continued to work the tramway, but looked towards revitalising the old plans for conversion to a standard gauge passenger-carrying railway, complete with a connection to the Lydford-Plymouth line. Assent for the upgrading was gained in 1900, the nominal subsidiary of Bere Alston & Calstock Light Railway being created for the purpose, and the scheme soon came under the scrutiny of the GWR. During the early 1900s, the GWR evolved an inexpensive way of testing the water for possible branch lines, and this was to establish a motor bus service on a likely route in order to assess its potential. The GWR looked at the possibility of a branch of its own between Saltash and Callington, and introduced a bus service between those communities on 1 June 1904. The buses were poorly patronised and, therefore, not only was the service discontinued, but it put the dampers on the idea of a branch railway.

Undeterred by the GWR's findings, the PD&SWJR pressed on with its conversion of the tramway, and the new railway opened in all its glory on 2 March 1908. It had not been a case of merely laying new rails on the trackbed of the old tramway. Southwards from Gunnislake, a new route had had to be engineered to take the line over the Tamar to Bere Alston, and this section had necessitated the construction of a viaduct with 12 spans, each of 60ft width. On the Cornish side of Calstock viaduct, there was a remarkable wagon lift which could raise or lower a 20-ton truck to Calstock quay, 112ft below the rail level of the viaduct. Despite the

diminishing need for the wagon lift over the years, it remained *in situ* until 1934, when it was sold and dismantled. When the wagon lift opened, the incline at Calstock quay fell into disuse, and the stationary engine was eventually sold in 1913.

The transformation of the freight-only tramway into a standard gauge passenger-carrying railway was interrupted only for two days; the work was supervised by one Holman Frederick (later Lieutenant-Colonel) Stephens, who was best known for his management of numerous light railways throughout much of southern Britain. Stephens's administrative expertise proved invaluable, as the daily transportation of some 200 tons of minerals was, it was decreed, to be subject to minimal interruption.

The new Callington branch left the main line at Bere Alston, where branch trains used the rear of the up platform. On the branch itself, there were intermediate stations at Calstock, Gunnislake, Chilsworthy, Latchley and Luckett; in March 1910, Seven Stones halt was opened between Latchley and Luckett to serve the workers at the nearby Phoenix Mines, and also for excursion traffic to the Phoenix Pleasure Ground, but the halt closed in September 1917. At Calstock station there were three sidings, while Gunnislake had an island platform and the only crossing loop on the branch. The branch terminus at Callington had a single platform, a modest goods yard and a twin-road engine shed. Throughout the branch, there were ferocious gradients, peaking at 1 in 33 on the approach to Callington. The topography of the route is well illustrated by the six-mile stretch between Calstock and Luckett, which rises 562ft.

Some of the branch's stations were to have identity crises. In ECMR days, the 'stations' at Gunnislake, Latchley, Luckett and Callington had been merely freight transfer points, and had been named Drakewalls

Depot, Cox's Park Depot, Monks Corner Depot and Kelly Bray respectively. It took the PD&SWJR until 1909 to revamp and rename all five although, for a short period in 1908/09, Luckett and Callington stations had masqueraded under the respective names of Stoke Climsland and Callington Road. The latter name was more appropriate as the station was situated at a considerable distance from the settlement it purported to serve. But whether it was Callington Road, Callington for Stoke Climsland (1909-1949), or just plain Callington, the locals still referred to it as Kelly Bray. Even Bere Alston station had not been immune, as until 1898 it had been named BEER Alston.

The reopening of the branch as a standard gauge railway in 1908 necessitated a review of the motive power situation. The two Neilson 0-4-0STs of 1871, which had carried ECMR Nos 1 and 2, were still active and No 2 was rebuilt as a standard gauge 0-4-2ST. It seems that the parts were supplied by R. W. Hawthorn & Co, but it remains unconfirmed whether the work was carried out by Hawthorns or at Callington. The rebuilt locomotive was used mainly as the station pilot at Callington, but it is known to have made the occasional forays on to the branch with passenger trains. In July 1912, it was sold for £250 to the Hundred of Manhood & Selsey Tramway in Sussex, which happened to be part of the 'Colonel Stephens' empire. It became that company's No 3 and was christened *Hesperus*, a name which cropped up on most of the Colonel's railways at some time or other due to his enthusiasm for classical mythology. The locomotive was finally retired in 1927. The fate of the other 0-4-0ST, No 1, is a bit of a mystery. Some reports suggest that it was rebuilt as a standard gauge 0-4-2ST, others say not. Its demise in 1909 is, however, confirmed, though there are conflicting reports as to whether it was cut up at Callington or by a South Wales scrap merchant.

Below:
This picture of Gunnislake station was taken shortly after the Grouping, as 0-6-2T No 757 *Earl of Mount Edgcumbe* appears to have acquired its curious mix of post-1923 lettering. *Lens of Sutton*

Out of necessity, the PD&SWJR lashed out on three brand new locomotives for its standard gauge operations, and all were supplied by Hawthorn Leslie in 1907. The first was a 0-6-0T, which became No 3 and was named *A. S. Harris*. It was intended for freight duties and had outside cylinders of 14in x 22in, 3ft 10in wheels and weighed in at 35¼ tons. The other two were 0-6-2Ts with 16in x 24in outside cylinders and 4ft driving wheels; they weighed 49t 19c apiece and were regarded as the passenger locomotives. The 0-6-2Ts became Nos 4 and 5, and were named *Earl of Mount Edgcumbe* and *Lord St Levan* respectively. All three locomotive names were inspired, if not insisted upon, by the company's directors. The company's locomotive headquarters were at Callington, where the superintendent was one H. E. Kemp, but the PD&SWJR's close connection to the LSWR meant that Callington was regarded, in effect, as a sub-shed of Plymouth Friary.

The original coaching stock for the branch comprised eight carriages which had been purchased from the North London Railway, and these were replaced in 1921 by second-hand acquisitions from the LSWR. Freight wagons were supplied largely by the mining companies. It is unrecorded whether the PD&SWJR applied its own livery to the coaches, but the locomotives were treated, at first, to a smart dark blue plumage with gleaming brass domes. In 1914, the 0-6-0T was repainted in GWR green while, in 1915/16, the 0-6-2Ts were given LSWR green liveries.

In view of the gradients on the Callington branch, the PD&SWJR locomotives were subjected to strict loading limits. These were not the same for all three, however, as the two types of locomotives had different capabilities; in the tractive effort stakes, 0-6-0T No 3 was rated at 13,345lb and the 0-6-2Ts at 18,495lb. On passenger duties, No 3 was limited to three bogie coaches, whereas Nos 4 and 5 were allowed up to six, provided that the rails were dry. Freight loading limits varied according to gradients of each section of line. For example, on the steepest sections, the 0-6-0T was permitted 10 wagons and the 0-6-2Ts were allowed 14, while on the easier parts, the two types were permitted 18 and 30 wagons respectively.

After the PD&SWJR's regeneration of the Callington branch, traffic figures were fairly healthy despite the ever-diminishing mineral traffic from the mines. After 1908, the company introduced 'market tickets' from all of its stations to Plymouth, and the same fare was charged, irrespective of which station was the starting point for the journey. In the summer of 1922, the last year before the Grouping, the passenger timetables showed five weekday trains each way, and six on Saturdays; the average journey times between Callington and Bere Alston were around 40min. At the Grouping, the PD&SWJR became part of the Southern Railway, and its three locomotives were taken into SR stock and became Nos 756/57/58. However, one thing frequently forgotten was that the PD&SWJR owned a little more than the Callington branch. The company's first stretch of line had, of course, been the section between Lydford and Plymouth, but as this had been used almost exclusively by LSWR mainline trains, the real extent of the independent PD&SWJR was often overlooked.

The Lynton & Barnstaple Railway

During the late 19th century, the neighbouring villages of Lynton and Lynmouth became well-known as beauty spots and, consequently, they came under the scrutiny of various ambitious railway promoters. Soon after the railway had arrived at Ilfracombe in 1874, a scheme had been mooted to construct a railway between Ilfracombe and Lynton, and other proposals followed.

In 1885, a completely different scheme was put forward by the Filleigh & Blackmoor Gate Railway. This involved a line which left the GWR's Taunton Barnstaple branch at Filleigh, and ran to Blackmoor Gate, some eight miles south of Lynton and in the middle of absolutely nowhere. The following year, the company received assent for an extension from Blackmoor Gate to Combe Martin and, in 1892, revised powers permitted a link with the main line at Barnstaple instead of Filleigh. Despite being reconstituted as the Barnstaple & Lynton Electric Tramroad, the hypothetical pioneer passed into oblivion without having laid an inch of track.

However, the idea was resurrected in 1895, albeit without any hint of electric traction, by the Lynton & Barnstaple Railway, and the company confounded the cynics by cutting its first sod in September 1895, just three months after receiving assent. There was strong local support for a standard gauge line to facilitate through workings from Barnstaple, but the directors knew a little about the local terrain and opted for a gauge of 1ft 11½in. The added bonus of narrower trackbeds and the consequent saving in expenditure had not been overlooked.

The contractor who was engaged to construct the line was James Nuttall of Manchester. On one hand, the L&BR's directors were rather optimistic with their estimated construction costs of £2,500 per mile, but on the other hand, Nuttall entered into the deal rather blindly. He seemed to overlook the fact that, in North Devon, there are things called hills, some of which are rather more

Below:
One of the L&BR's 2-6-2Ts is seen waiting in the narrow gauge bay of Barnstaple Town station in this early 1920s picture. The LSWR's line to Ilfracombe is seen on the right. *Lens of Sutton*

than the work of a mole with gout. Nuttall had not bargained for the extensive earthworks which would clearly be required, but he started work anyway. Part way through the work, Nuttall at last got round to estimating the real projected cost of the railway's construction, and the figure he came up with was double that of the L&BR's directors. Consequently, he took the railway company to court in an effort to recoup his additional expenditure, and the judgement went for him. The L&BR successfully appealed for a reversal of the verdict, but Nuttall considered that enough was enough, and promptly filed for bankruptcy.

This left the L&BR's directors with an uncompleted railway, no contractors and, thanks to the cost of the court cases, perilously empty coffers. Undaunted, the directors rounded up their own labour force, and it was a tribute to their determination that the railway was finished at all, let alone only a year behind schedule. On 14 March 1898, an engineers' special made the trip from Barnstaple to Lynton, and the obligatory directors' special ran on 16 March. It was 11 May before the L&BR opened its doors to the public.

While the L&BR had been having its own problems with James Nuttall, the company had inadvertently opened the old wounds between the GWR and the LSWR at Barnstaple. Neither of the big boys had been bold enough to strike out for Lynton on their own, but as soon as they had got wind that another company had done so, they had wanted to get in on the action. The GWR's plan of campaign had been, remarkably, to propose a line of its own between Filleigh and Lynton, whereas the LSWR had taken a far less alarmist course, and had offered the

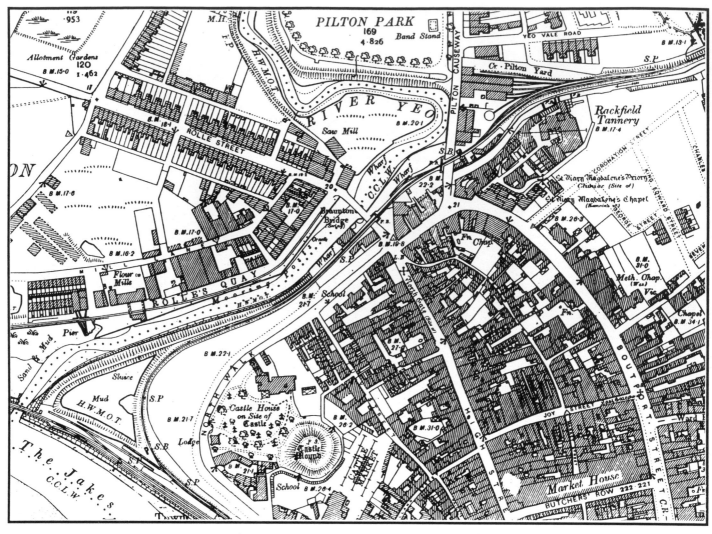

Above:
At the lower edge of this 1904 Ordnance Survey map of Barnstaple, the LSWR's line can be seen. Barnstaple Town station is only partly shown, but the route of the L&BR from the station, past Yeo Wharf and the locomotive depot at Pilton Yard, is clearly distinguishable. *Crown Copyright*

use of its facilities in Barnstaple to the L&BR. The LSWR's offer had included a new station, Barnstaple Town, to replace the older and less accessible station at Barnstaple Quay, and the L&BR had gladly accepted.

At Barnstaple Town, the L&BR used a 325ft bay platform at the rear of the LSWR's through platform, and there was a narrow gauge run-round loop and a siding. Originally, a second platform had been planned but this was never to be built. The L&BR line curved sharply northeastwards from the end of the station, and ran along the bank of the River Yeo. Just past Braunton Bridge, there was a short spur to a wharf, where vessels of up to 200 tons could be berthed; coal from South Wales was the mainstay of the wharf until World War 1, after which it fell into disuse. Just along the line from the wharf was Pilton Yard, where the L&BR had its locomotive and freight headquarters. The yard contained a twin-road engine shed and the company's only turntable, along with a three-road carriage shed.

At first, there were only four advertised intermediate stations between Barnstaple and Lynton, although an unadvertised workmen's halt at Pilton Yard remained in use until 1904. From the direction of Barnstaple, the first proper station was at Chelfham, which had a passing loop and two platforms. At the end of the down platform was a water tank, which was invaluable after the continuous climb of up to 1 in 50 from Barnstaple. Immediately before Chelfham station was the line's principal engineering feature, an impressively slender eight-arch viaduct which carried the railway 70ft above the Stoke Rivers Valley. The viaduct cost £6,500 to construct and was built with bricks from the Marland Works of the North Devon Clay Company, to the southwest of Barnstaple.

Beyond Chelfham, the next station was at Bratton Fleming which, again, had a passing loop, two platforms and a water tank. A goods siding ran from the passing loop, but when the loop was lifted in 1931, the siding was connected to the remaining line. Operations were controlled from a signal box on the main platform. The next station was at Blackmoor, which was equipped with a passing loop, two platforms, three goods sidings, a ground frame and a water tower. A hot-air pump was situated at the base of the water tower to provide the power for lifting the water. Apart from a livestock market, there were virtually no buildings, residential or commercial, in the immediate vicinity of

Blackmoor station. The reason for siting the station in an area devoid of any human inhabitants was that there were plans to use it as a major interchange point for horse-drawn coach tours of Exmoor, and so a row of stables was constructed behind one of the goods sidings.

The other intermediate station on the line was named Wooda Bay, but was rechristened Woody Bay in 1901. Whichever spelling was used, the station was, in fact, 980ft above sea level at Martinhoe Cross, some three miles from Woody Bay, and the misleading naming was in anticipation of a branch to Woody Bay itself. The branch never materialised, and in view of the local topography, it was remarkable that it had been considered in the first place. Local entrepreneurs were well aware of the scenic appeal of Woody Bay, but even in those days when environmental awareness was minimal, the residents of Woody Bay were strongly opposed to having their magnificent landscape ruined by a railway and, furthermore, they had no wish whatsoever to be subjected to hordes of visitors. Looking at the unspoilt beauty of Woody Bay today, one can fully understand why the residents were so opposed to the prospect of commercialisation. There were, however, carriage trips through the woods.

The northern terminus of the L&BR was at Lynton or, more correctly, Lynton & Lynmouth station. There was a double-fronted platform, beyond which a siding from the run-round loop continued to a substantial goods shed; another siding accommodated coal wagons. A single-road engine shed was situated at the southern end of the station yard. As the station's full title implies, it was intended to serve the village of Lynmouth as well as Lynton. The former village was surrounded by spectacularly steep hills on all sides and, without any doubt whatsoever, was a no-go area for even the most ambitious railway engineer. However, the locals in Lynton reckoned that the station provided no better service for them than it did for the res-

idents of Lynmouth. Sensibly, the L&BR had wanted to build its station in the centre of Lynton, but the company had been unable to obtain the necessary land, and so the station had had to be sited well outside the town. But it was not just the travelling public who were inconvenienced. The water supply at the station was abysmal and, during prolonged dry periods, the L&BR had to bring up additional water tanks by rail from Barnstaple.

The station building at Lynton was, in common with others on the line, in the style

of a Swiss chalet and, considering that the station was some 700ft above sea level, it was not altogether inappropriate. For trains leaving Lynton for Barnstaple, there was a continuous climb of around 1 in 50 for the three miles to Woody Bay station.

Three other stations were later opened on the L&BR. Parracombe was the largest village between Barnstaple and Lynton but, ironically, it was not treated to a station until 1899 and, even then, the facilities were virtually non-existent. In 1900, a shelter was at last provided, but the practice of purchasing

Above:
The full complement of staff pose for the photographer at Blackmoor Gate station on the L&BR. *Lens of Sutton*

Right:
This picture shows one of the L&BR 2-6-2Ts at Lynton station in pre-Grouping days. *Lens of Sutton*

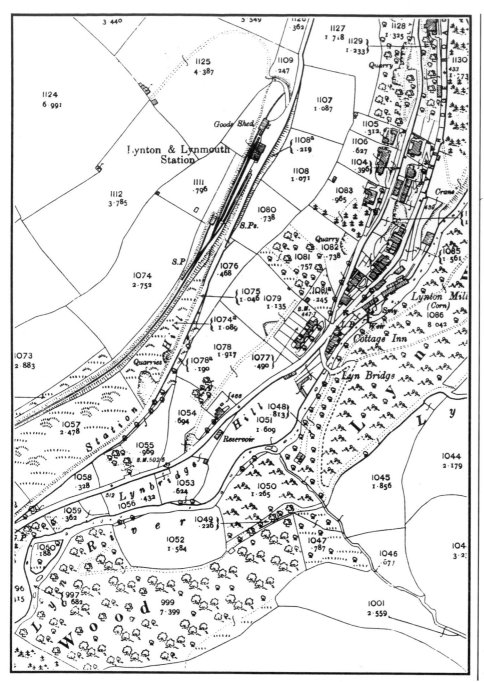

tickets from the village Post Office continued. A further halt was opened in 1903 at Snapper, three miles north of Barnstaple, to serve the village of Goodleigh and, in 1907, Caffyns halt was opened north of Woody Bay to serve a local golf course. Apart from Barnstaple Town, all of the L&BR's stations had platforms which were only about 12in high, but all of the company's passenger coaches were fitted with running boards to facilitate access.

The L&BR had taken delivery of three locomotives in 1897 in anticipation of the line's completion that year, but they had had to be stored at Barnstaple until the eventual opening in 1898. They were Manning Wardle 2-6-2Ts and carried Works Nos 1361/62/63; the L&BR named them *Yeo*, *Exe* and *Taw* respectively. They had 2ft 9in driving wheels, outside cylinders of 10½in x 16in, and they weighed 22½ tons. On the opening day of the line, the first train was hauled by *Yeo*, with *Exe* in hot pursuit with its own train. In later years, the L&BR's locomotives were often thought of as 'copies' of the Davies & Metcalf 2-6-2Ts which operated on the Vale of Rheidol Railway in Wales, but the L&BR's locomotives predated their Welsh counterparts by five years.

Even before the line opened, the L&BR's directors realised that a stud of just three locomotives would leave no leeway in case of emergency, but in the aftermath of a national engineering strike, Manning Wardle were unable to supply a fourth engine at short notice. Instead, the L&BR took the same course of action as several other railway companies elsewhere in Britain, and looked to the USA. Consequently, the Baldwin Locomotive Works of Philadelphia was given the order for the extra locomotive, and in order to speed up delivery, the L&BR agreed to a 2-4-2T instead of a 2-6-2T. It was delivered in kit form for assembly at the company's workshops in Barnstaple, and was first steamed in July 1898. Named *Lyn*, it had 2ft 9in driving wheels, 10in x 16in cylinders and weighed 22 tons. Its boiler pressure was 180lb, which was 20lb greater than that of the Manning Wardle 2-6-2Ts.

Above:
The relationship between Lynton station and the local community is seen in this well-detailed 25in Ordnance Survey map of 1904. *Crown Copyright*

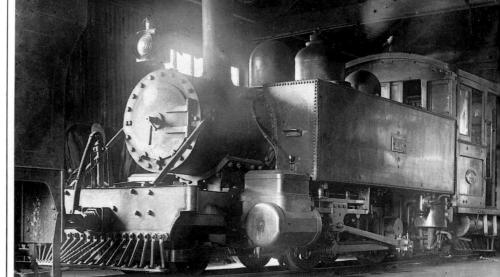

Right:
American-built 2-4-2T *Lyn* is seen inside Pilton Yard engine shed in 1927. Its subtle Southern Railway numberplate is visible on the side of the cab. *Rail Archive Stephenson*

BARNSTAPLE TOWN and LYNTON AND LYNMOUTH.—Lynton and Barnstaple. **[Commences 14th inst.**

Sec. and Man., Charles E. Drewett, Pilton Bridge, Barnstaple.

Miles	Down.	Week Days only.					Miles	Up.	Week Days only.					NOTES.
		mrn	mrn	mrn	aft	aft			mrn	mrn	aft	aft	aft	
—	Barnstaple Town......dep	6 20	3 0|10 3	4 40	5 21	....	3¼	Lynton & Lynmouth ..dep	8 15	10 51	12 17	6 20	7 H 0	H Mondays, Fridays, and Satur-
5	Chelfham	6 39	9 20|10 52	4 59	5 H 40	....	7¾	Woody Bay	8 30	11 7	12 32	6 35	7 H 15	days.
8	Bratton Fleming	6 55	9 36|11 8	5 15	5 H 46	....	11¼	Blackmoor	8 48	11 25	12 50	6 53	7 H 33	‖ Over ¼ mile to Barnstaple (G.W.).
12	Blackmoor	7 15	9 54|11 26	5 33	6 H 4	....	14¼	Bratton Fleming	9 5	11 42	1 7	7 10	7 H 50	
16	Woody Bay	7 34	10 13|11 45	5 52	6 H 34	....		Chelfham	9 19	11 57	1 22	7 25	8 H 5	
19¼	Lynton & Lynmouth ..arr	7 48	10 27|11 59	6 6	6 H 48	....	19¼	Barnstaple Town ‖ 144 arr	9 37	12 15	1 40	7 43	8 H 23	

Above:

The summer 1922 public timetable for the L&BR.

The 2-4-2T proved far less reliable than the 2-6-2Ts, and the L&BR eventually found that it was costing more in repairs than all three 2-6-2Ts combined. It demonstrated its ability to notch up repair bills when, during a routine boiler inspection in 1907, the inspector's hammer penetrated one of the plates. A new boiler had to be ordered from the Avonside Engine Co in Bristol.

Sixteen passenger carriages were delivered by the Bristol Wagon & Carriage Works in time for opening day, and a 17th was built in 1903 by Shapland & Petter of Barnstaple; they were all finished in a smart livery of lake, with white upper panels. Four first-class and four second-class carriages each had open observation sections, and the first-class vehicles had the added luxury of dog boxes. For freight, the L&BR gradually acquired a mixture of 8-ton bogie vans and four-wheeled 4-ton vans and opens.

The route between Lynton and Barnstaple was 19¼ miles, and the first timetables showed that the fastest train took 1hr 39min; the schedules were accelerated over the years, but even by 1922, the quickest trip still took 1hr 23min. The nature of the line was, of course, the biggest handicap to fast running, but the practice of operating mixed trains did not help, as the locomotives had to perform their own shunting duties at the stations *en route*. Although the L&BR is remembered as a passenger-carrying line, its freight figures were not insignificant. During the company's peak years, some 8,000 tons of freight was carried annually as well as around 100,000 passengers.

During the company's early years, the freight traffic proved to be the saviour of the line. In the early 1900s, the L&BR's passenger figures did not reach the projected levels, and this mystified the directors because, until the coming of the railway, the only scheduled public transport between Barnstaple and Lynton had been a 20-seat horse-drawn coach which had taken almost three hours for the 18-mile road journey. In 1903, the L&BR's chairman, Sir George Newnes, made an attempt to boost tourism in the area by providing a motor-bus service between

Right:

The later Southern Railway lining can be seen on the fronts of the ex-L&BR locomotive's tanks; this picture was, in fact, taken on 12 August 1935 and shows one of the 2-6-2Ts taking on water at Parracombe. *R.W. Kidner*

Blackmoor station and Ilfracombe, and it was hoped that the provision of a bus link would attract more passengers to the railway. However, the bus service was unsuccessful, and the two vehicles were soon sold to the GWR, which put them to use on the service from Helston to The Lizard. The L&BR's bus services did not impress the local constabulary, and there was constant friction between the forces of law and order and the drivers. Things fell short of becoming an Edwardian version of Smokey and the Bandit, but nevertheless, one of the drivers received a heavy fine for racing along at a death-defying speed 'in excess of the legal limit of 8 mph'.

Despite the odds which were stacked against it from the very beginning, the L&BR went on to become a modestly successful company. After the uncertainty of the early years, the company showed a small but constant profit between 1913 and 1921, and that was something which some other, more grandiose, railway companies couldn't manage. Much of the credit for the L&BR's success was due to the enthusiasm of its chairmen. After Sir George Newnes had passed away in 1910, Sir Thomas Hewitt perpetuated the spirit of enterprise. Hewitt retired in 1919, and so it fell to his successor, Colonel E. B. Jeune, to oversee the company's business during the period when the Grouping of Britain's railways was under discussion. The L&BR was actually excluded from the grouping of January 1923, but it sold out to the Southern Railway six months later.

The Bideford, Westward Ho! & Appledore Railway

The last of the three independent companies in Devon to commence operations was the Bideford, Westward Ho! & Appledore Railway. For those who combine an interest in obscure railways and English punctuation, the company was the only one in the land to have an exclamation mark in its title. The community of Westward Ho! took its name from Charles Kingsley's well-known novel. Even before the tome had been published, the Northam Burrows Hotel & Villa Co had commenced building work around the sea front near Northam, and when Kingsley's novel was introduced to the public, the developers cashed in on its popularity by naming the community after the book. Kingsley was not impressed. He had become familiar with the area, and he considered that blatant commercialisation would bring about its ruin. In later years, however, Kingsley's fears were to prove largely unfounded. Although Westward Ho! developed unashamedly as a commercial resort, it was never likely to mount a serious challenge to Ilfracombe or Bude.

The BWH&AR was not the first railway to have been proposed in the area. Almost as soon as the North Devon Railway had arrived in Bideford in 1855, a scheme had been put forward for an extension to Appledore,

Clovelly, Hartland and Bude, but this had come to nothing. The North Devon Railway, which was eventually leased by the LSWR, had its terminus on the east bank of the River Torridge in an area known locally as East-the-Water; the major problem facing any railway promoter who wished to build a line to Appledore or beyond was the crossing of the Torridge which, even at Bideford, was not the narrowest of rivers. A bout of lateral thinking in 1866 resulted in a new proposal for a railway to Appledore and Westward Ho! Its promoter considered that, rather than incur the expense of a bridge across the Torridge, there was no reason why the railway should not start from the west side of the river. The trifling matter of having a completely isolated railway seemed to be unimportant.

The promoter of this scheme was the Bideford, Appledore & Westward Ho! Railway Co. Although the necessary Act of Parliament was gained, nothing was done towards the construction of line and the company was wound up in 1870. In 1896, similar plans resurfaced but, this time, there was a slight reshuffling of the corporate title as the new promoter was the Bideford, Westward Ho! & Appledore Railway Co. The company seemed to have more enthusiasm than both of its predecessors put together, and construction work commenced in 1898. In the best traditions of Victorian railway engineering, the contractor defaulted and, furthermore, the eventual cost of construction proved to be nearly 75% more than the original projection.

While construction work was underway, the BWH&AR became a subsidiary of the British Electric Traction Group, which had extensive tramway interests, not only in this country, but also abroad. It has been suggested that the BET takeover of 1900 was a form of defence for its own plans to build a tramway from Bideford to Hartland under

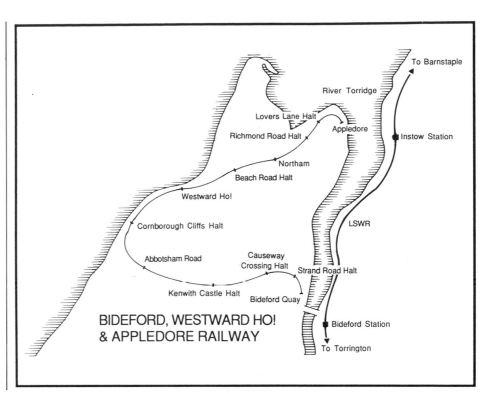

BIDEFORD, WESTWARD HO! & APPLEDORE RAILWAY

To Barnstaple

River Torridge

Lovers Lane Halt

Appledore

Instow Station

Richmond Road Halt

Northam

Beach Road Halt

Westward Ho!

LSWR

Cornborough Cliffs Halt

Abbotsham Road

Causeway Crossing Halt

Strand Road Halt

Kenwith Castle Halt

Bideford Quay

Bideford Station

To Torrington

the title of the Western Counties Light Railway, but the BWH&AR never had serious plans to extend to Hartland and, furthermore, the BET tramway was never to be constructed. The takeover by the BET had no outward effect on the day to day business of the BWH&AR, and construction work continued erratically.

The 5½-mile section of the line between Bideford Quay and Northam was eventually opened on 24 April 1901. The public timetables emphasised that 'passengers wishing to alight at any halt should inform the conductor on joining the train'. A further clause at the foot of the timetables stated that 'the published time tables...are only intended to fix the time before which the trains will not start, and the Company do not undertake that the trains shall start or arrive at the times specified in the tables'. This writer has searched through 1,430 pages of a recent British Railways timetable without finding such a disclaimer.

From the outset, the BWH&AR was at loggerheads with Bideford Town Council. The source of the Council's discontent was that the rails at Bideford Quay were laid into the road surface in true tramway fashion and, in fact, many local people expressed concern about the safety aspect of trains running along the street. Undaunted by the Council's threat of legal action, the railway company laid a much-needed run-round loop at Bideford Quay, and this was enough to prod the Council's solicitors into action. The Council was granted an injunction to compel

the BWH&AR to remove at least its run-round loop from the quay, and this was done. The railway company appealed successfully and then relaid the loop. It did not make for a happy relationship and, in later years, the Council was quick to invoke whatever bye-law it could. On one occasion, the BWH&AR was fined 40 shillings (£2) for letting one of its locomotives linger on the Quay a little too long.

The two-mile extension from Northam to Appledore was not opened until 1 May 1908. Appledore had a quay and shipyard, but there had never been any realistic anticipation that the town's commercial activities would provide substantial traffic for the railway. Nevertheless, the BWH&AR seemed unwilling even to try to promote workmen's trains, as the timetables showed no departures from Bideford until 9.30am, which was a good couple of hours too late for any self-respecting workman of the early 1900s. As for the other traffic, the peak summer season resulted in crowded trains, but the season in North Devon was shorter than that of South Devon and so the flurry of activity was all too brief. Apart from the summer season, when two-coach trains were the norm, it was rare to see anything other than single-coach trains; the railway company's staff of 28-30 men usually outnumbered the total loading of two or three off-peak trains. Freight traffic made a negligible contribution to the BWH&AR's receipts, and this is well illustrated by the company's mileage figures for the second half of 1906. In those six months, the passenger train mileage was 22,310, while the figure for 'mixed trains' was just 85 miles.

For a railway of only 7½ miles, the BWH&AR had an awful lot of stopping places. From Bideford Quay, there were halts at Strand Road (also known as The Yard), Causeway Crossing, Kenwith Castle, Abbot-

Above:
Westward Ho! station. Undated.
R. M. Casserley Collection

Below:
This photograph taken at the Pill at Bideford shows BWH&AR No 2 *Grenville* in its original lined livery. *Chris Leigh Collection*

sham Road, and Cornborough Cliffs before arriving at Westward Ho! station, where there was a crossing loop, a goods shed and a siding into a gasworks. At Westward Ho!, the BWH&AR hired a troupe of blacked-up minstrels to entertain the passengers in a small concert hall, and the company accounts for the second half of 1906 show a payment of £17/9/7d (£17.48p) for 'services of minstrels'. Between Westward Ho! and Appledore, there were intermediate stopping places at Beach Road halt, Northam, Richmond Road halt and Lovers Lane halt. The journey times were usually around 30min and, until 1908, there were over 15 trains in each direction on summer weekdays, but this was later reduced to a maximum of seven. In 1910, the third-class fare from Bideford to Appledore was 8d (3½p), but special tickets on market days could be obtained for 6d (2½p). A questionable perk was that the purchase of a normal weekday return ticket would entitle the holder to use of the Great Nassau Baths in Bideford for a discounted fee of just 4d (2p).

The BWH&AR was a standard gauge company. It had three locomotives, all of which were bought new from the Hunslet Engine Co of Leeds in 1900. They were 2-4-2Ts which had 3ft 3in diameter driving wheels, 12in x 18in outside cylinders and 140lb boilers; each locomotive weighed 27 tons. Their nominal tractive effort at 75% was 6,978lb, and this restricted them to loadings of 95

tons on the 1 in 47 gradient between Kenwith and Abbotsham. The locomotives, which were given BWH&AR Nos 1,2 and 3, bore Works Nos 713/14/15 and were named *Grenville*, *Kingsley* and *Torridge* respectively. They were fitted with side plates to cover the wheels, this being a requirement for working over the roadway at Bideford Quay and, later, cow-catchers were added below the front buffer beams. The BWH&AR had no turntable, and so when the locomotives were delivered, one was placed on the track facing Bideford and the other two facing Westward Ho! The locomotive livery was green with black and white lining and, usually, was very well maintained.

The company had six passenger carriages, all of which were built by the Bristol Carriage & Wagon Works. They were bogie vehicles which had American-style open platforms at each end and polished teak exteriors; the interiors were of mahogany and teak. The BWH&AR's fleet of goods wagons consisted of six open trucks, four covered vans and a brake van. The locomotives, carriages and freight wagons were each fitted with a single central buffer at each end, and this is believed to have been unique on Britain's standard gauge railways. The locomotives and carriages were housed in sheds at Bideford although, when the extension to Appledore was opened in 1908, it became common practice to stable one locomotive at

Appledore overnight so that the first train of the day could work from there to Bideford.

The charismatic appeal and the individuality of the BWH&AR were, however, not enough to bring in the passengers in adequate numbers. Despite the constantly increasing price of coal, the railway company dared not increase its fares because motor buses offered stiff competition between the LSWR station at East-the-Water in Bideford and Westward Ho! Admittedly, the BWH&AR operated its own buses from Bideford Quay to the LSWR station, but this presented passengers with the inconvenience of having to lug their cases twice instead of once. From the BWH&AR's point of view, the bus service across the bridge was costly to maintain, as it accounted for what was by far the largest item of traffic expenditure apart from the wages. Interestingly, one recipient of a BWH&AR salary cheque was a Mr H. Sowden, who had joined the company as traffic superintendent from his previous post of station master at Blackmoor, on the Lynton & Barnstaple Railway.

The inevitable closure of the BWH&AR was hastened by World War 1. The Government requisitioned the locomotives and the rails for the war effort, and the last trains ran on 27 March 1917. The problem of how to transfer the locomotives elsewhere was not solved until 29 July, when a temporary track was laid across Bideford Bridge to provide a

Bideford Promenade.

Left:
A two-coach BWH&AR train waits to depart from Bideford Quay c1903. *Author's collection*

Below:
BWH&AR No 3 *Torridge* **was photographed leaving Bideford for the last time on 29 July 1917, albeit by means of the temporary track which was laid across Bideford Bridge.** *Chris Leigh Collection*

connection with the LSWR. That was the first time that any of the BWH&AR's locomotives had seen the outside world since their arrival in 1900.

At least one of the BWH&AR's carriages was to finish up as a grandiose beach hut at Westward Ho!, but the eventual fate of the three locomotives has never been confirmed. They certainly became the property of the Ministry of Munitions, but that is as far as the concrete evidence goes. One report states that two of the locomotives were loaded on to the SS *Gotterdamerung*, which despite its Teutonic name was an English vessel, at Avonmouth near Bristol, and that the ship

was torpedoed and sunk near Padstow. A different, and usually impeccable, source states that only one, No 2 *Kingsley*, turned up at Avonmouth, and shows indisputably that it reappeared in 1927 as a works shunter at the nearby Imperial Smelting Co, where it lasted until 1937. That same source lists Nos 1 and 3 as going to the MoM depot at Pembrey in South Wales. Interestingly, a third source, none other than the Hunslet Engine Co, insists that all three locomotives went first to Swindon, then to Pembrey, from where all were shipped abroad. Doesn't all that provide a hint of a nice little challenge for an underworked researcher?

There was no chance whatsoever that the railway would reopen after the war, and the remaining assets were auctioned in 1921. The Saxby & Farmer signalling equipment was purchased by a certain Lt-Col Stephens, and finished up in use on the Weston, Clevedon & Portishead Light Railway in Somerset. The BWH&AR is, arguably, one of the most overlooked of Britain's long-lost railways and, quite probably, this is because of its short life. The section between Bideford and Northam had a life-span of only 16 years, but the extension from Northam to Appledore managed just nine years.

5. The Grouping and After

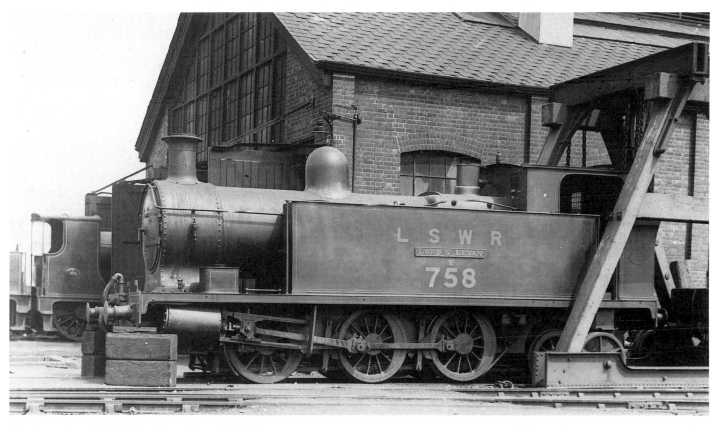

The Grouping of Britain's railways into the 'Big Four' became effective on 1 January 1923 but, in Devon, the immediate outward signs were minimal. The Great Western carried on very much as before, having taken over the Bristol & Exeter, the South Devon and the Cornwall Railways as far back as 1876. The broad gauge had become totally extinct in 1892, and so the post-Grouping GWR had only to continue the work and perpetuate the traditions of its pre-Grouping namesake. The GWR's arch-rival, the London & South Western became part of the Southern Railway but, in Devon, most of the early post-Grouping changes were purely cosmetic. The Urie olive green locomotive livery was replaced by Drummond's deeper shade of green, while the numbers of ex-LSWR locomotives were prefixed by the letter 'E'. That letter referred to the LSWR's locomotive headquarters at Eastleigh, and was used as a prefix until 1931, when the Southern at last implemented a comprehensive renumbering scheme.

The two independent companies in Devon which were still around immediately before the Grouping were the Plymouth, Devonport & South Western Junction Railway and the

Lynton & Barnstaple Railway. The PD&SWJR had been closely allied to the LSWR and, logically, was incorporated in the Southern. The L&BR was excluded from the Grouping scheme. However, the L&BR had previously been the subject of the LSWR's attentions, and it was the L&BR itself which instigated takeover negotiations with the Southern Railway early in 1923.

The Plymouth, Devonport & South Western Junction Railway had had an identity crisis. The double-track line between Devonport and Lydford had formed an integral part of the LSWR route between Exeter and Plymouth and, consequently, that section had been viewed pretty much as just another LSWR line. The section which had betrayed the PD&SWJR's independence was the branch from Bere Alston to Callington, almost all of which was on the Cornish side of the border.

At the Grouping, the PD&SWJR became

part of the Southern Railway. Its three locomotives were subsequently renumbered, Nos 3/4/5 becoming SR Nos 756/57/58 respectively, but all retained their original names. When they were renumbered, they had the 'LSWR' logo painted on their tanks, and it took a second repainting job to inscribe the word 'Southern'. The trio usually worked the Callington branch and, therefore, tended to live at Callington shed but, officially, their parent depot was Friary. In 1931, No 756 *A. S. Harris* was despatched to Eastleigh for an overhaul but, instead of being returned to Devon, it went on to do the rounds of various SR sheds. Although it was to survive until 1951, it was never to see Devon again. At first, the SR drafted in an 'O2' class 0-4-4T as a replacement on the Callington branch and, apart from visits by '0395' class 0-6-0s and an 'E1R' class 0-6-2T during the war, the 'O2s' were the only former LSWR locomotives to work regularly to Callington. During the 1920s and 1930s, there was a significant reduction in the mineral traffic on which the branch had originally depended, but an increase in market gardening in the area provided an alternative, and steady, source of traffic. Most of this

BERE ALSTON AND CALLINGTON BRANCH.

DOWN TRAINS. WEEK-DAYS.

Dist'nce (M. C.)	Station	Pass. arr. a.m.	Pass. dep. a.m.	Freight. arr. a.m.	Freight. dep. a.m.	Stone. Q arr. a.m.	Stone. Q dep. a.m.	Pass. B arr. a.m.	Pass. B dep. a.m.	Freight. N S arr. a.m.	Freight. N S dep. p.m.	Pass. S O p.m.	Pass. p.m.	Pass. WTh&SO p.m.	Pass. dep. p.m.	Freight. SOQ	Pass. p.m.	Pass. p.m.	Pass. p.m.	Pass. WTh&SO D p.m.	dep. p.m.
... ...	**Bere Alston**	...	8 15	...	9 32	...	1035	...	1048	...	12 40	12 57	...	...	3 20	...	5 22	...	7 10	... 10 11	10 5 10 13
1 66	Calstock	8 21	8 24	9 41	9 44	1043	...	1054	1057	12 50	1 0	1 3 1 42	2 16 2 18	...	3 26 3 28	5 28 5 30	7 16 7 18	10 17 10 21	10 23	10 25	10 26
4 58	Gunnislake	8 36 8 39	9 59 10 9	...	...	11X9 1110	1 16 1 40	1 16 1 19	2 30	...	3 7 3 9	3 41 3 45	4 25 4 37	7 30 7 31
5 73	Sand Hill Pk. Sdg.	C	C
5 31	Green Hill Sdg.	C
5 42	Chilsworthy	8 43 8 44	1114 1115	1 23 1 24	3 43 3 46	5 47 5 48	7 35 7 36	10 30 10 31
6 32	Hingston D Sdg.	1019	C
6 50	Latchley	8 48 8 49	1119 1120	1 28 1 29	5 50 5 51	5 52 5 53	7 40 7 41	10 35 10 36
7 69	Luckett	8 53 8 54	1124 1125	1 33 1 34	5 55 5 56	5 57 5 58	7 45 7 46	10 40 10 41
8 50	Kit Hill Siding	C
9 59	**Callington**	9 0	1131	2 18	1 40	3 35	4 2	6 4	7 52	10 47

UP TRAINS. WEEK-DAYS.

Dist'nce (M. C.)	Station	Pass. arr. a.m.	Pass. dep. a.m.	Freight. arr. a.m.	Freight. dep. a.m.	Pass. arr. a.m.	Pass. dep. a.m.	Stone. Q	Freight.	Pass. arr. a.m.	Pass. dep. a.m.	Pass. WTh&SO	Engine. SO	Pass. Q	Pass.	Pass. W Th&SO D arr. p.m.	dep. p.m.
... ...	**Callington**	...	7 13	...	7 40	...	9 47	...	...	1257	...	2 36	4 23	6 20	9 5
1 09	Kit Hill Siding	C
1 70	Luckett	7 19 7 20	C	9 53 9 54	1 3 1 4	2 42 4 29 4 30	6 26 6 27	9 11 9 12
3 09	Latchley	7 24 7 25	C	9 58 9 59	1 8 1 9	2 46 4 34 4 35	6 31 6 32	9 16 9 17
3 27	Hingston Down Siding	C	10 29
3 45	Whiterock Siding	C	10 31 11 0
4 17	Chilsworthy	7 29 7 30	10 3 10 4	1 13 1 14	2 50 4 39 4 40	6 36 6 37	9 21 9 22
5 01	Gunnislake	7 33 7 34	8 35 8X42	10 X7 10 9	11 6 11X30 1 17 1 18	2 53 4 43 4 44	6 40 6 41	9 25 9 28
5 14	Perry, Spear & Co.'s Sdg.	C
7 73	Calstock	7 48 7 50	9 0 9 10	10 21 10 23	11 5 11 52 12 2	1 30 1 31	2 47 2 48	4 56 4 58	6 53 6 54	9 38 9 39
9 59	**Bere Alston**	7 57	9 19	10 30	1114	12 11	1 38	2 55	5 5	7 1	9 46

DOWN TRAINS. SUNDAYS.

Station	Pass. arr. a.m.	Pass. dep. a.m.	Pass. arr. p.m.	Pass. dep. p.m.	Pass. C arr. p.m.	Pass. C dep. p.m.	Pass. arr. p.m.	Pass. dep. p.m.	Pass. E arr. p.m.	Pass. E dep. p.m.
Bere Alston	...	9 22	...	12 25	...	...	...	7 15	...	9 32
Calstock	9 28	9 30	12 31	12 34	3 6	3 8	7 21	7 22	9 38	9 39
Gunnislake	9 42	9 43	12 46	12 47	3 20	3 21	7 34	7 35	9 51	9 53
Chilsworthy	9 47	9 48	12 50	12 51	3 26	3 26	7 39	7 40	9 56	9 57
Latchley	9 52	9 53	12 55	12 56	3 30	3 31	7 44	7 45	10 1	10 2
Luckett	9 57	9 58	1 0	1 1	3 35	3 36	7 49	7 50	10 6	10 7
Callington	10 4	...	1 7	...	3 42	...	7 56	...	10 13	...

UP TRAINS. SUNDAYS.

Station	Pass. arr. a.m.	Pass. dep. a.m.	Pass. arr. p.m.	Pass. dep. p.m.	Pass. E arr. p.m.	Pass. E dep. p.m.	Pass. arr. p.m.	Pass. dep. p.m.	Pass. arr. p.m.	Pass. dep. p.m.
Callington	...	8 23	...	11 30	...	2 8	...	6 15	...	8 30
Luckett	8 29	8 30	11 36	11 37	2 14	2 15	6 21	6 22	8 36	8 37
Latchley	8 34	8 35	11 41	11 41½	2 19	2 20	6 26	6 27	8 41	8 42
Chilsworthy	8 39	8 40	11 45½	11 46	3 24	3 26	6 31	6 32	8 46	8 47
Gunnislake	8 43	8 44	11 49	11 50	2 28	2 29	6 35	6 36	8 50	8 51
Calstock	8 56	8 58	12 2	12 4	2 41	2 43	6 48	6 50	9 0	9 5
Bere Alston	9 5	...	12 11	...	2 50	...	6 57	...	9 12	...

B—From 18th July to 10th September, inclusive, depart Bere Alston 11.0 a.m. and run 12 minutes later than shown throughout.

C—Call when required.

D—Will not run on Wednesdays from 14th September.

E—17th July to 25th September only.

an air of quiet independence and the three locomotives all passed into British Railways ownership. It might be of interest to statisticians that there was only one other pre-Grouping railway company which could have boasted that all of its locomotives were still around at Nationalisation; that was the Cleobury Mortimer & Ditton Priors Light Railway in Shropshire. Maybe a long-winded company title was the key to the longevity of the locomotives.

In North Devon, the delightful little Lynton & Barnstaple Railway became the only narrow gauge line to come under Southern Railway ownership, but this was not a direct effect of the Grouping. In January 1923, the L&BR's much-admired former chairman Sir Thomas Hewitt died, and this seemed to knock the stuffing out of the company. Rather than face any more uphill struggles, this time without earthly guidance from its spiritual leader, the L&BR approached the Southern with a view to selling out. The sale officially took place on 1 July 1923 and the Southern had to spend no more than £39,000 to acquire the entire assets of the L&BR, right down to the last nut and bolt.

The Southern considered that, with adequate promotion of the area's scenic beauty, it could make a healthy profit from the L&BR's route, and a considerable sum was invested in the line. Rolling stock, station facilities, signalling and the lineside fencing

Left:
The SR working timetable for July 1932 showed the services on the former-PD&SWJR branch to Callington. *Author's Collection*

Below:
Manning Wardle 2-6-2T No E188 *Lew* was delivered to the Southern Railway in 1925 for work on the 1ft 11½in gauge Lynton & Barnstaple line. Here, it is seen at Pilton Yard in Barnstaple. *Lens of Sutton*

was centred on Calstock and Gunnislake stations.

During World War 2, the main line section of the old PD&SWJR was heavily used as it provided a good route into Devonport, where the Admiralty had a sizeable base. To help ease the flow of the additional traffic and to enable GWR trains to reach Cornwall if the centre of Plymouth was out of action, a connecting line between the GWR and the Southern was laid near St Budeaux and, furthermore, a number of extra sidings were built at Lydford in 1941 to act as an overflow for the yards at Plymouth, many of which had been damaged in air raids. A further extension to the siding accommodation at Lydford was undertaken in 1943, and this resulted in a new physical link between the neighbouring GWR and Southern stations. When peace was restored, the sidings at Lydford proved useful for storing the vans of garden produce which had originated on the Callington branch.

Right through to Nationalisation in 1948, the former PD&SWJR branch still retained

were all improved and much of the track was reballasted and resleepered. For the new sleepers, the Southern used its beloved concrete, but this proved unsatisfactory and so wooden sleepers were reinstated. As if to be fully prepared for an immediate rush, the Southern ordered another Manning Wardle 2-6-2T, which was to the same design as the original L&BR 2-6-2Ts of 1897/98. The new locomotive was delivered in 1925 and became No E188; it was named *Lew*. The original 2-6-2Ts, *Yeo*, *Exe* and *Taw*, had earlier become SR Nos E759/60/61 respectively, and the Baldwin 2-4-2T of 1900, *Lyn*, had become SR No E762.

Unfortunately, things did not go according to the Southern's master plan. The local road network was improved significantly in the 1920s and 1930s and, although the L&BR line was heavily used during the brief summer season, the vital year-round local traffic dwindled. However, the SR's attempts at 'improving' services on the line were little more than stabs in the dark and, if anything, they did more harm than good. For example, the freight services were revised, and an 'as required' goods train was introduced! When, in 1935, the Southern decided to call it a day, a meeting was held at Barnstaple to protest at the planned closure. However, the Southern's point was proved when most of the protesters arrived by road. The last train ran on Sunday, 29 September 1935, and two locomotives, *Yeo* and *Lew*, were required to work double-headed on a packed nine-coach train. As if to set a precedent for railway closures in future years, the total of over 300 passengers which rode on that last train far exceeded the number carried during the course of several normal working days.

The old L&BR stock was auctioned, and the five locomotives were knocked down for a total of £236. The rolling stock realised sums between £13.10s (£13.50p) for a first-class coach and £3.15s (£3.75p) for an open four-wheel truck. The turntable at Pilton Yard was sold to the Romney, Hythe & Dymchurch Railway in Kent, and the youngest locomotive, *Lew*, was retained by the scrap merchants to assist in the insulting process of cannibalising its former stomping ground. *Lew* became the only one of the five locomotives not to be cut up. In 1936, it was overhauled and modified for resale to a coffee plantation in Brazil. Of the carriages, a number finished up as rather grandiose garden sheds, but one was rescued in 1959 and transferred to the Festiniog Railway in North Wales for restoration. Another coach is at the National Railway Museum. A number of the bridges were blown up during 1939 by the Royal Engineers who wanted some practice before going abroad.

It is now almost 60 years since the L&BR line closed but, surprisingly, many parts of the route are very easy to trace today, even without the need for a machete. The line's major engineering feature, the elegant viaduct at Chelfham, still dominates the village, and the locomotive sheds at Pilton Yard in Barnstaple remain reasonably intact as part of a builders' merchant's yard. Several of the stations were bought for private or commercial use; Lynton station is now used as holiday accommodation and Blackmoor station has been extended into a sizeable tourist-orientated pub. Had the Southern kept the L&BR line open, the railway could, in later years, easily have become a major tourist attraction in the same league as the Welsh narrow gauge railways. Hindsight is, of course, a wonderful thing.

Returning to the immediate post-Grouping period, railway services throughout Britain had, more or less, recovered from the hiatus of World War 1, and the inter-company rivalries reappeared, albeit under different corporate titles. The GWR and the Southern resumed the battle for passenger traffic to Exeter and Plymouth, and each company used its newest and most powerful locomotives for the services between London and Devon. In the motive power stakes, the GWR had a distinct advantage as its 'Castle' class 4-6-0s of 1923 and 'King' class locomotives of 1927 could, when required, maintain impressive schedules non-stop to Plymouth. The Southern had its highly-satisfactory 'King Arthur' 4-6-0s and, in 1926, it intro-

Right:
This spectacular double-header was required to cope with the last day crowds on the Lynton & Barnstaple line on 29 September 1935. The train is seen crossing the elegant viaduct at Chelfham. *Lens of Sutton*

Above:
The GWR's attempts at streamlining were, to be honest, a bit of a joke when compared to the LMS's and LNER's efforts. This photograph of No 6014 *King Henry VII* wearing its dustbin lid was taken at Torquay on 24 July 1936.
E. R. Morten

duced the celebrated four-cylinder 'Lord Nelson' 4-6-0s but, although those classes recorded some excellent timings between Waterloo and Exeter, the nature of the Southern's line between Exeter and Plymouth necessitated switching to 4-4-0s. Despite the undisputed quality of Drummond's 4-4-0 designs, they were no match for the GWR's 'Castles' or 'Kings' when it came to a speedy trip from Exeter to Plymouth.

The prestigious ocean liner traffic at Plymouth had fallen to the GWR before the Grouping and, despite the growing domination of the port of Southampton, Plymouth continued to handle a reasonable amount of transatlantic trade. The peak year was 1930 when over 45,000 passengers arrived at or sailed from Plymouth, and the GWR did its best to provide an impressive after-sales service for the shipping companies. One of the best-known GWR runs was in 1924 when 'Castle' class 4-6-0 No 4078 *Pembroke Castle* hauled the mails and passengers from the SS *Mauretania* from Millbay Docks to Paddington in 3hr 57min.

At Plymouth, North Road station came into its own in the early 1920s as, gradually, a greater number of GWR main-line services

terminated there instead of at Millbay. The engine shed at Millbay closed in 1924 and its allocation was transferred to the roundhouse at Laira, but the congestion at Laira often resulted in considerable delays in dispatching light engines to North Road. Consequently, Millbay shed was reopened in 1925 as a stabling point for 10 engines, but the provision of a supplementary four-road shed and additional servicing facilities at Laira in 1931 resulted in the final demise of the old shed at Millbay.

The other GWR engine shed in Plymouth was a single-road structure between Millbay station and the Ocean Terminal; it had been opened by the South Devon Railway in 1869 and was to remain in use until the 1950s. The allocation lists for April 1936 show that the residents at Plymouth Dock shed were '1361' class 0-6-0STs Nos 1361/62. The five members of the '1361' class had been built in 1910, and their wheelbases of only 11ft made them ideal for dock duties where, usually, sharply-curved lines abounded. Normally, two or three of the '1361s' were based at one or other of the sheds in Plymouth, and No 1363 was to end its days as a Laira engine in November 1962. The SR's equivalent of the GWR's dock tanks was Adams's 'B4' 0-4-0Ts, and Friary's allocation invariably included four of the class. One of the 'B4s' which spent most of the post-Grouping period at Friary was SR No 84 (later BR No 30084), which held the distinction of being the last locomotive to have been built at Nine Elms Works before the LSWR transferred its locomotive headquarters to Eastleigh in 1908.

In the early years of the century, the railmotor services in the Plymouth area had had a significant effect, not only on railway operations, but also on the whole community. However, trams had offered stiff competition for the railmotors and, by the 1920s, the heyday of the railmotors was over. By 1930, the railmotor halts at Mount Gould & Tothill, Laira and Wingfield Villas had all closed. Also closed, on 27 October 1930, was Defiance Platform, which was built to serve the training ship, HMS *Defiance*, moored on the river; the station was probably closed when the ship was scrapped.

The only new passenger-carrying railway to be constructed in Devon after the Grouping was the 20½-mile branch between Torrington and Halwill Junction, which opened on 27 July 1925. This provided a link between two stations which had become well-established during the LSWR era but, nevertheless, the new line was worked by the Southern as a completely separate section. It was serviced by the sub-shed at Torrington, and it had intermediate stations or halts at Watergate, Yarde, Dunsbear, Petrockstow, Meeth, Hatherleigh and Hole. Although opened after Grouping, the company promoting the line, the North Devon & Cornwall Light Railway, dated from pre-1923.

Between Torrington and Dunsbear, the branch was built on the site of the Marland Railway. This was a narrow gauge industrial tramway which served a clay works; the industrial railway was subsequently realigned to connect with the branch near Dunsbear halt. There was also a clay works at Meeth and, for many years, it was clay which pro-

vided the mainstay of the new branch's freight traffic. Passenger traffic on the branch was never particularly great, the only centre of population being the market town of Hatherleigh, but the situation of the station almost two miles from the town did not exactly encourage the locals to use the railway.

For motive power on the Halwill-Torrington branch, the Southern modified a number of ex-London, Brighton & South Coast Railway 'E1' class 0-6-0Ts which, as a class, had been introduced by William Stroudley in 1874. The modification involved converting them to 0-6-2Ts and fitting them with larger bunkers and tanks. In all, 10 'E1s' were rebuilt and subsequently reclassified 'E1/R', and eight of these were drafted in for duties on the Torrington-Halwill branch. Nominally, they were allocated to Barnstaple shed, which was Torrington shed's parent depot, and five were still on Barnstaple's allocation list at the time of Nationalisation.

Elsewhere in North Devon, the Southern Railway carried out major improvements to Ilfracombe station in the late 1920s, and the double-fronted platform was extended by some 250ft. The station yard was relaid and a new engine shed, complete with a 65ft turntable, was opened beyond the south end of the station in 1929. The turntable cost £9,000 but it proved well worth it. It enabled Maunsell's 'N' class 2-6-0s to be used on the line and these locomotives were far superior to the 4-4-0s on the steeply-graded sections around Mortehoe. The advantages of the 'Ns' for mixed traffic duties had first been seen on

the Barnstaple-Exeter section in 1925. The branch to Holsworthy and Bude also benefited from the attentions of the 'Ns' but, most frequently, it was Drummond 4-4-0s of the 'K10', 'L11' and 'S11' classes which dominated on that branch's heavier passenger duties.

The former Bristol & Exeter Railway station at St Davids in Exeter had been rebuilt twice since its opening in 1844. On top of the hill above St Davids was the ex-LSWR station at Queen Street which, by complete contrast, had received little more than the occasional lick of paint since its opening in 1860. Even

during the 19th century, Queen Street station had been described as 'spartan' – and that had been one of the more polite adjectives – but the LSWR had procrastinated furiously about spending money on the place. Consequently, it fell to the Southern Railway to fork out the much-needed pennies.

The modernisation of Queen Street was done in two stages, both rather protracted. In 1925, work started on the first stage, which included the lengthening of the platforms, the new up platform being 1,210ft long and partially double-faced (one side was effectively a bay platform); the goods yard on the north side of the station was rearranged and, furthermore, the entire station was completely resignalled, this resulting in two older boxes being replaced by one new box at the east end of the station. The second stage in the rebuilding of Queen Street station was completed in 1933. This included the provision of a bay at the rear of the down platform and, with new slip crossings at the east end of the station, the down and the up bays both became accessible for arriving and departing trains. Given the number of branch services to Exmouth and the practice of running local trains on the main line as far as Yeovil, the provision of two highly-usable bay platforms was a godsend. The major change in the 1930s rebuilding was, however, the demolition of the old entrance buildings and the construction of a smart new frontage. As if to emphasise the complete revitalisation of the station, it was renamed Exeter Central in time for the ceremonial reopening on 1 July 1933.

While the first phase of Queen Street's transformation was under way, the locomotive depot at Exmouth Junction was completely rebuilt. By the 1920s, the framework and corrugated iron roof of the shed had acquired a severe dose of rust, and many of the roofing panels had already fallen off. The walls had disintegrated to such a degree that most of the windows had fallen out in sympathy. The remains of the old structure were completely dismantled and the replacement

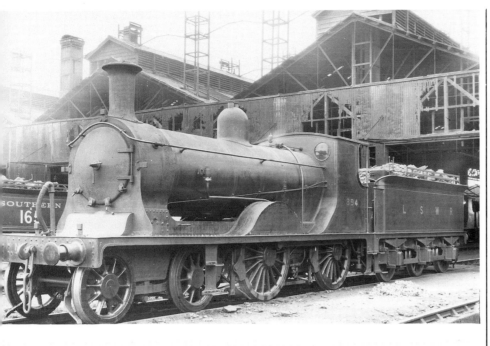

shed was built in the Southern's new-found medium of ferro-concrete. Although the Southern Railway actually had its own concrete works adjacent to Exmouth Junction shed, the sheer size of the new locomotive depot necessitated much of the construction work being put out to contract.

The new shed was operational in 1927 but the repair shops were not completed until 1929. The shed had 13 roads, each 270ft long, and was equipped with an electrically-operated 65ft turntable; a large mechanical coaling plant could extract the contents from 20-ton wagons and coal two locomotives simultaneously. The shed had a staff of over 400, including 120 pairs of drivers/firemen. The allocation lists for 1933 show that Exmouth Junction shed was home for 109 locomotives, ranging from a pair of ex-London, Brighton & South Coast Railway 'D1' class 0-4-2Ts to a stud of nine 'King Arthur' 4-6-0s; the most numerous class was the 'N' class 2-6-0s, 30 of which were allocated to the shed. At the heavyweight end of the scale, there was 'Z' class 0-8-0T No 954, known to local crews as 'Dolly', which was used, primarily, for banking duties on the ferocious incline between St Davids and Central stations in Exeter. Nevertheless, 'Dolly' was also used on transfer traffic between the two stations, and when performing solo, she had an official loading limit of 200 tons on the 1 in 37 bank. This could be compared to the 140 ton limit of 'M7' 0-4-4Ts and 'T9' 4-4-0s; even the 'U' class 2-6-0s were restricted to 165 tons. By the time of Nationalisation in 1948, Exmouth Junction's allocation was 125 locomotives, all but 36 of which were 0-4-4Ts, 2-6-0s or Bulleid Pacifics.

The Southern's admirable activity in transforming its facilities and services in Exeter in the 1920s and 1930s did not go unnoticed by the GWR. Between 1938 and 1940, St Davids station was improved once again. The work involved extending the buildings on the main down platform, and enlarging the station entrance area so that a new booking hall and divisional offices could be accommodated. The final stages of the work included the construction of new parcels and telegraph offices. During the 1930s the proposals for the St Davids area included the construction of an independent high level line for SR trains, with a bridge carrying the tracks from Central station over the GWR lines. From St Davids the SR would have been provided with separate lines to Cowley Bridge Junction. This development, which would have significantly reduced the traffic congestion in St Davids, was not progressed due to the high costs involved.

At Exmouth, the Southern's station was rebuilt with two platforms, each of which was some 600ft long and double-faced; work was completed by 1927. In that year, the original engine shed at Exmouth was replaced by a concrete structure and, as the branch duties were monopolised by 'O2', 'M7' or 'T1' class 0-4-4Ts, the turntable was deemed superfluous and was subsequently removed. The improvements at Exmouth were in keeping with the town's rapidly-growing commuter traffic to and from Exeter, and a side-effect of the branch's

SIDMOUTH JUNCTION, SIDMOUTH, and EXMOUTH.

Miles	Down.	mrn	mrn	mrn	mrn	mrn		mrn	mrn		mrn		aft		aft		aft		aft		aft		aft
		Week Days only.																					
	Sidmouth Junction.dep.	6 30	..	8 1	8 30	..	..	9 25	..	..	1110	..	1 9	..	2 15	..	3 30	..	5 10	..	6 35	..	8 30
2¼	Ottery St. Mary..........	6 37	..	8 8	8 36	8 57	..	9 31	..	..	1115	..	1 14	..	2 20	..	3 40	..	5 15	..	6 40	..	8 35
5	Tipton St. John's....arr.	6 42	..	8 13	8 41	9 1	..	9 36	..	..	1120	..	1 19	..	2 25	..	3 44	..	5 20	..	6 45	..	8 40
—	Tipton St. John's..dep.	6 43	..	8 14	8 43	9 2	..	9 47	1036	..	1122	..	1 20	..	2 27	..	3 46	..	5 21	..	6 47	..	8 44
8¼	Sidmouth..........arr.	6 53	..	8 23	8 52	9 11	..	9 55	1044	..	1132	..	1 29	..	2 38	..	3 55	..	5 30	..	6 58	..	8 52
—	Tipton St John's....dep.	..	7 45	..	9 10	..	..	9 42	..	..	1132	..	..	..	2 40	..	4 45	..	..	..	6 55	..	8 53
6¼	Newton Poppleford.....	..	7 48	..	9 12	..	..	9 46	..	..	1134	..	..	..	2 43	..	4 48	..	..	..	6 58	..	8 56
9¼	East Budleigh............	..	7 53	..	9 18	..	..	9 52	..	..	1139	..	..	..	2 48	..	4 52	..	..	..	7 3	..	9 2
11½	Budleigh Salterton { arr.	..	7 58	..	9 23	..	..	9 58	..	..	1144	..	..	..	2 53	..	4 57	..	..	..	7 8	..	9 8
	dep.	..	8 0	..	9 24	..	..	10 3	..	..	1145	..	..	..	2 54	..	5 0	..	..	..	7 9	..	9 9
14¼	Littleham..................	..	8 7	..	9 32	..	..	1014	..	..	1152	..	..	..	3 2	..	5 8	..	..	—	7 17	..	9 16
16¼	Exmouth .....arr.	..	8 12	..	9 37	..	..	1019	..	..	12 0	..	..	..	3 7	..	5 13	..	..	..	7 22	..	9 21

Miles	Up.	mrn		mrn	mrn	mrn		mrn		mrn		aft	aft		aft		aft	aft	aft	aft	aft	aft	aft
		Week Days only.																					
	Exmouth ....dep.	6 55	..	8 30	..	..	..	9 50	..	..	..	..	..	..	1 35	..	..	4 13	..	6 20	..	8 14	..
1¾	Littleham................	6 59	..	8 35	..	..	..	9 55	..	..	..	..	..	..	1 39	..	..	4 17	..	6 24	..	8 18	..
4¾	Budleigh Salterton { arr.	7 6	..	8 43	..	..	..	10 3	..	..	..	..	..	..	1 46	..	..	4 24	..	6 31	..	8 25	..
	dep.	7 7	..	8 44	..	..	..	10 4	..	..	..	..	..	..	1 49	..	..	4 25	..	6 32	..	8 26	..
7	East Budleigh............	7 12	..	8 48	..	..	..	10 9	..	..	..	..	..	..	1 54	..	..	4 29	..	6 35	..	8 31	..
10	Newton Poppleford.....	7 18	..	8 54	..	..	..	1015	..	..	..	..	..	..	2 0	..	..	4 35	..	6 41	..	8 37	..
11¾	Tipton St. John's...arr.	7 22	..	8 58	..	..	..	1019	..	..	..	..	..	..	2 4	..	..	4 39	..	6 45	..	8 42	..
—	Mls Sidmouth........dep	7 20	..	8 35	9 20	9 33	..	1020	..	1114	..	1225	1 0	..	..	..	3 24	4 36	5 42	..	7 45	..	9 15
—	3¼ Tipton St. John's arr.	7 27	..	8 42	9 27	9 40	..	1028	..	1121	..	1233	1 7	..	..	..	3 31	4 43	5 49	..	7 52	..	9 22
—	Tipton St. John's....dep.	7 28	..	8 43	..	9 42	..	1030	..	..	..	1235	1 8	..	..	..	3 32	4 45	5 50	..	7 53	..	9 23
13¼	Ottery St. Mary	7 33	..	8 49	..	9 47	..	1036	..	..	..	1241	1 13	..	..	..	3 37	4 50	5 55	..	7 58	..	9 28
16¼	Sidmouth Jn. arr.	7 41	..	..	..	9 55	..	1045	..	..	..	1250	1 23	..	..	..	3 45	4 58	6 3	..	8 6	..	9 36

Above:
Bradshaw's, March 1940. A combination of wartime economies and the off-peak season explains the sparsity of services between Sidmouth Junction and Exmouth. *Author's collection*

upgrading was that Exmouth became even more of a focal point for other branch sevices in the immediate area.

On the other East Devon branches, the engine shed at Sidmouth had closed by 1930 and its seldom-used turntable was removed. It is known that 'L11' 4-4-0s made the occasional foray to Sidmouth but, by the 1930s, most of the services were looked after by 'M7' 0-4-4Ts. Just along the coast, the Seaton branch saw a change of motive power in 1930 when ex-LBSCR 'D1' class 0-4-2Ts were transferred from the Central Section of the Southern, complete with Brighton two-coach motor sets; the 'D1s' carried Nos B214/B256, and had been displaced from their traditional territory by the spread of electrification. The station at Seaton was completely rebuilt in 1937 and a new engine shed was provided.

On the Lyme Regis branch, the Adams 4-4-2Ts were feeling their age by the end of the 1920s, and so ex-LBSCR 'D1' 0-4-2T No B612 and former SECR 'P' class 0-6-0T No A558 were given chances to show their wares. The 0-4-2T looked promising and, along with three classmates, was modified in order to reduce its weight. The intruders took over completely on Lyme Regis duties, and one of the Adams 4-4-2Ts was scrapped and the other two were put in storage to await a similar fate. It looked like the end for the Adams Radial Tanks but, in 1930, two of the 0-4-2Ts were sidelined because of leaking tanks, and this coincided with one of the remaining two 0-4-2Ts being away for repair. Fortunately, the two stored Radial Tanks had not yet been sent for cutting up, and so they were taken out of mothballs and despatched to Eastleigh Works for extensive rebuilding. They were both returned to active duties on the Lyme Regis branch by August 1930.

At the time, the two rebuilt Radial Tanks were the only members of their class left in service on the Southern, but a third, which had been sold for Government service in 1917, had subsequently been purchased by the East Kent Light Railway. When an extra locomotive became necessary on the Lyme Regis branch in 1946, the Southern bought the East Kent locomotive for £120. That price reflected the locomotive's derelict condition, but the sum of £1,638 was spent transforming the rusting hulk to full work-

Below:
Despite having been numbered in the LSWR's duplicate list in 1904, Adams '395' class 0-6-0 No 029 was to survive until 1958. Here, it is seen outside the 'new' concrete shed at Okehampton on 3 August 1928. *H. C. Casserley*

ing order, and it returned to traffic in November 1946. At Nationalisation in 1948, the trio of Radial Tanks took BR Nos 30582/83/84 and, by then, they had outlived any of their classmates by 20 years. Happily, they still had 13 years' work ahead of them.

Back on the GWR, the company's station at Newton Abbot had been little altered since 1861, at which time the town's population had been just 6,000, but by the mid-1920s the population had risen to 15,000, and so the provision of more modern station facilities were considered long-overdue. The rebuilding of Newton Abbot station was completed in April 1927 and the new layout incorporated two main-line island platforms, each around 1,500ft long, and an isolated platform for branch trains to Moretonhampstead. The main-line platform roads were equipped with crossovers, so that Plymouth-bound trains which had through carriages for Torbay could be easily divided. Consequently, each of the four platform faces was treated not as one, but two separate platforms. The bill for the work came to £247,100. Three years previously, the locomotive repair shop at Newton Abbot had been extended and modernised.

The vast improvement at Newton Abbot station did no harm at all to the Moretonhampstead branch. The GWR astutely realised that Moretonhampstead was a good base for visitors to Dartmoor, and the company did much to promote, not just the town, but the entire branch. There was even a visitors' book in the waiting room at Lustleigh station. In 1928, halts were opened

Above:
This interesting view of the approach to Kingswear was taken in June 1936. The locomotive is a 'King' class 4-6-0 and the coaches are 'Torbay Limited' stock.
Rail Archive Stephenson

at Brimley and Hawkmoor (renamed Pullabrook in 1955) and, in 1929, the GWR opened the Manor House Hotel at Moreton-hampstead, which was one of the earliest hotels to be owned by the GWR. Mindful of courting up-market clientele, the GWR advertised the hotel as 'select', and proudly announced that the establishment had an 18-hole golf course and grounds of some 200 acres.

In July 1929, the British Pullman Co introduced the 'Torquay Pullman', a luxury eight-coach train which was scheduled to cover the 199¾ miles from Paddington to Torquay in 3hr 40min. But for once, the company's marketing bods had miscalculated and the GWR itself proved less than wholly co-operative. The general public was quite happy with the GWR's own 'Torbay Limited' express service which was not only 10min faster, but did not require the payment of a Pullman fare supplement. The Pullman service was taken off in September 1930 and, simultaneously, the other GWR Pullman service was also withdrawn. This was the 'Ocean Liner Express' from Paddington to Plymouth (Millbay Docks), which had been introduced in May 1929. The withdrawal of the latter service was unpopular amongst its rich clientele and the GWR was forced to introduce its own Pullman-style service to placate them.

In Torbay, work was undertaken in 1930 to improve the station at Paignton and also to build a new goods depot in the town. At the same time, the long-standing problem of empty stock storage in the Torbay area was cracked by the laying of extensive carriage sidings. The main line was doubled southwards from Paignton in the late 1930s, but only as far as Goodrington Sands halt, which had opened in 1928. An additional halt was opened at Broadsands, south of Goodrington, in July 1928 for excursion traffic but it closed in September 1929 without having appeared in any public timetables.

Throughout the 1920s and 1930s, the GWR brought increasing numbers of holidaymakers to South Devon and it was not only the main lines which benefited. The Ashburton, Brixham, Kingsbridge and, particularly, the Moretonhampstead branches all saw sharp and continuing upturns in their traffic figures during the summer months. Even the branch between Exeter and Heathfield did reasonably well and, in 1928, it was treated to additional halts at Alphington, Dunsford and Chudleigh Knighton. In the late 19th century, the GWR had come to regard the Heathfield branch as an emergency alternative to the main line, and this was to prove wise in 1938. In August that year, heavy storms caused considerable damage in the area, and the main line at Teignmouth was one of several sections of track which had to be closed to traffic.

The growth in holiday traffic during the 1920s and 1930s was also noticeable in the Plymouth area, and this resulted in several new halts being constructed. On the GWR's Launceston branch, Clearbrook halt opened in 1928 and Liddaton halt in 1938 while, on the Princetown branch, three new halts were provided. One was at Burrator and it opened in 1924 primarily as a tourist-orientated interchange point for GWR buses; King Tor halt opened in 1928 to serve a cluster of quarrymen's cottages and Ingra Tor halt opened in 1936. The last-named was princi-pally for Dartmoor-bound hikers and ramblers, and as an acknowledgement that it was likely to be used mainly by non-locals, the GWR erected a conspicuous sign which warned 'Beware of Snakes'. Adders are plentiful on Dartmoor.

Despite the GWR's healthy traffic figures in most parts of South Devon, there was one branch line which bucked the trend. In July 1930, the GWR branch to Yealmpton closed to passengers. The new residential developments which had grown up around Plymouth in the early 19th century had not

Right:
The GWR published a series of booklets called *Through the Window*, and each described the delights of one particular main line route. This extract is from the 1939 Paddington-Plymouth edition.
Author's collection

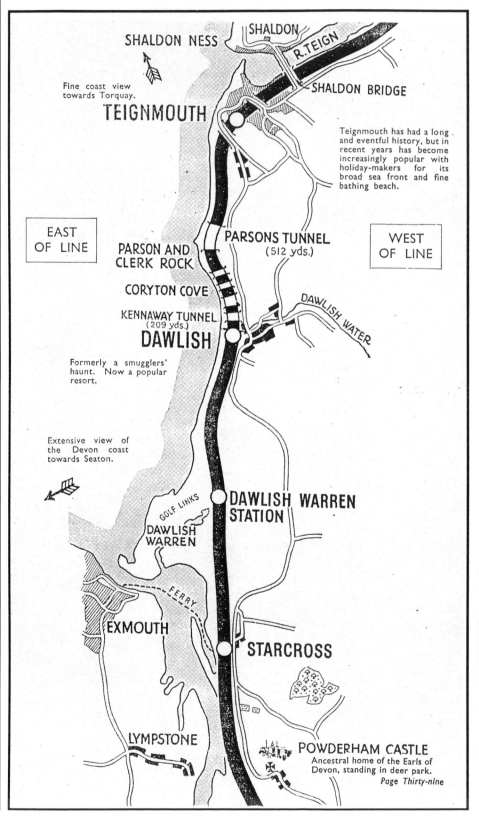

SHALDON NESS

SHALDON

R. TEIGN

SHALDON BRIDGE

Fine coast view towards Torquay.

TEIGNMOUTH

Teignmouth has had a long and eventful history, but in recent years has become increasingly popular with holiday-makers for its broad sea front and fine bathing beach.

EAST OF LINE

WEST OF LINE

PARSON AND CLERK ROCK

PARSONS TUNNEL (512 yds.)

CORYTON COVE

KENNAWAY TUNNEL (209 yds.)

DAWLISH

DAWLISH WATER

Formerly a smugglers' haunt. Now a popular resort.

Extensive view of the Devon coast towards Seaton.

GOLF LINKS

DAWLISH WARREN

DAWLISH WARREN STATION

FERRY

EXMOUTH

STARCROSS

LYMPSTONE

POWDERHAM CASTLE
Ancestral home of the Earls of Devon, standing in deer park.
Page Thirty-nine

reached Yealmpton and, furthermore, that enclave of the South Devon coast had seen little increase in the holiday trade. The Yealmpton branch had not been opened until 1898, and so the closure provided a very early illustration of the railway adage of 'last in, first out'. The branch reopened in 1941 to provide a service for Plymothians who had been evacuated to the country during the war, but the line was operated by the Southern Railway from the terminus at Friary. The Yealmpton branch finally closed its doors to passengers on 7 October 1947.

Elsewhere in the Plymouth area, Mutley station, on the main line to the east of North Road station, closed in 1939 and, two years later, Millbay station closed to passengers. Since its opening, Millbay had suffered from inadequate platform length and, by the 1930s, it was by-passed by most main line trains to Cornwall; the bombing of the adjacent goods depot in 1941 meant that Millbay's passenger facilities had to be used for goods, and the station was never to return to passenger usage.

Returning to the 1920s, the whole country was affected by the General Strike of

Table 5.1: Summary of stations and halts opened 1923-1947

Name	Opened	Co	Location
Alphington Halt	June 1928	GWR	Heathfield branch
Bolham Halt	June 1928	GWR	Exe Valley branch
Brimley Halt	June 1928	GWR	Moretonhampstead branch
Broadsands Halt	July 1928	GWR	Torbay main line
Burn (Up Exe) Halt	Mar 1929	GWR	Exe Valley branch
Burrator Halt	Feb 1924	GWR	Princetown branch
Chudleigh Knighton Halt	June 1928	GWR	Heathfield branch
Clearbrook Halt	Oct 1928	GWR	Tavistock branch
Coldharbour Halt	Mar 1929	GWR	Hemyock branch
Cove Halt	1923	GWR	Exe Valley branch
Dunsbear Halt *	July 1925	SR	Halwill-Torrington branch
Dunsford Halt	June 1928	GWR	Heathfield branch
Goodrington Sands Halt	June 1928	GWR	Torbay main line
Halberton Halt	June 1928	GWR	Tiverton branch
Hatherleigh *	July 1925	SR	Halwill-Torrington branch
Hawkmoor Halt†	1928	GWR	Moretonhampstead branch
Hole *	July 1925	SR	Halwill-Torrington branch
Ingra Tor Halt	Mar 1936	GWR	Princetown branch
King Tor Halt	June 1928	GWR	Princetown branch
Liddaton Halt	Apr 1938	GWR	Launceston branch
Maddaford Moor Halt	July 1926	SR	Okehampton-Halwill main line
Meeth Halt *	July 1925	SR	Halwill-Torrington branch
Morebath Junction Halt	1928	GWR	Exe Valley branch
Petrockstow *	July 1925	SR	Halwill-Torrington branch
Sampford Peverell Halt	June 1928	GWR	Exeter-Taunton main line
Watergate Halt	Sept 1926	SR	Halwill-Torrington branch
West Exe Halt	June 1928	GWR	Exe Valley branch
Whitehall Halt	1932	GWR	Hemyock branch
Yarde Halt	July 1926	SR	Halwill-Torrington branch

* Opened with new line.　　†Renamed Pullabrook Halt, June 1955.

Below:
Apart from the lettering on the locomotive and the wagons, this picture is almost timeless. The '2721' class locomotives were originally built as saddle tanks, but were later converted to panniers. In their day, they were the most powerful shunting 0-6-0Ts on the GWR and were usually to be found in South Wales. This unidentified member of the class, however, was one of the few escapees, and it was photographed at Totnes in the early 1930s. *Lens of Sutton*

1926. Although the major effects were felt in industrialised areas, Devon was not immune, and the dock railways at Plymouth became extremely congested due to the non-movement of freight trains. During the period of the strike, 20 incoming ocean liners were diverted to Plymouth Docks, and this placed the GWR in the position of having to transport over the cluttered dock lines some 3,000 extra passengers at short notice, in addition to the normal ocean liner services. The GWR admirably demonstrated its ability not to make a drama out of a crisis, and even provided the train services for three transatlantic departures from Plymouth during the same period.

After the General Strike came a period of severe recession throughout Britain, with consequent high unemployment. One of the Government's methods to combat the unemployment was to offer cheap loans to large companies for the purpose of encouraging building work or general expansion, thereby creating jobs. The GWR knew a good thing when it saw one, and instigated a number of major improvement schemes which qualified for financial assistance under the Loans Act.

One scheme involved Tiverton Junction, where the station was completely rebuilt in 1932 in order to accommodate two through lines between the platform roads. In addition, the old B&E engine shed was replaced by a brick-built structure at the down end of the station; the new building perpetuated the tradition of housing the locomotives for the Tiverton and Hemyock branches which, after 1932, were almost invariably '48xx' or '58xx' class 0-4-2Ts. The allocation lists for January 1934 show that the residents at Tiverton Junction shed were, indeed, Nos 4808 and 5812. On the Hemyock branch, halts were

opened at Coldharbour and at Whitehall in 1929 and 1932 respectively. At Culmstock, a run-round loop was installed in 1932 as some trains ran only as far as that station and, as part of the general improvements of that year, Hemyock lost its engine shed and had the layout of its small goods yard altered by the extending of two sidings into the adjacent milk factory. In later years, the provision of a rail link to the factory was to prove the saviour of the branch.

The quadrupling of the tracks through Tiverton Junction and the necessary station modifications were repeated almost simultaneously at Cullompton and Stoke Canon,

Above:
GWR '44xx' class 2-6-2T No 4403 was photographed shunting 'foreign' wagons at Princetown on 15 June 1926.
H. C. Casserley

Below:
If the GWR could conjure up almost timeless pictures, the Southern wasn't to be left out. Adams 'O2' class 0-4-4T No 207 shows off its motor-train equipment at Seaton Junction in the 1930s. *Real Photographs/Ian Allan Library*

		a.m.	a.m.	a.m.	p.m.	p.m.	p.m.	p.m.
Plymouth (Friary) (S.R.)	dep.	7 0	9 0	10 33	1 14	2 50	5 20	6 40
Lucas Terrace Halt	„	7 2	9 2	10 35	1 16	2 52	5 22	6 42
Plymstock	„	7 6	9 6	10 39	1 20	2 56	5 26	6 46
Billacombe	„	7 9	9 9	10 42	1 23	2 59	5 29	6 49
Elburton Cross	„	7 13	9 13	10 46	1 27	3 3	5 33	6 53
Brixton Road	„	7 17	9 17	10 50	1 31	3 7	5 37	6 57
Steer Point	„	7 21	9 21	10 54	1 35	3 11	5 41	7 1
Yealmpton	arr.	7 27	9 27	11 0	1 41	3 17	5 47	7 7

		a.m.	a.m.	a.m.	p.m.	p.m.	p.m.	p.m.
Yealmpton	dep.	7 40	9 35	11 17	1 55	3 30	5 55	7 15
Steer Point	„	7 46	9 41	11 23	2 1	3 36	6 1	7 21
Brixton Road	„	7 50	9 45	11 27	2 5	3 40	6 5	7 25
Elburton Cross	„	7 54	9 49	11 31	2 9	3 44	6 9	7 29
Billacombe	„	7 57	9 52	11 34	2 12	3 47	6 12	7 32
Plymstock	„	8 2	9 57	11 39	2 17	3 52	6 17	7 37
Lucas Terrace Halt	„	8 5	10 0	11 42	2 20	3 55	6 20	7 40
Plymouth (Friary) (S.R.)	arr.	8 7	10 2	11 44	2 22	3 57	6 22	7 42

Above:
The summer 1943 services on the Yealmpton branch were detailed in the GWR public timetable, although the line was worked by the Southern. *Author's collection*

Right:
The Southern Railway followed the LSWR's example and avoided double-heading as much as possible. Therefore, the sight of 'S11' 4-4-0 No 403 piloting 'T9' 4-4-0 No 721 on the approach to Devonport Tunnel on 6 August 1928 was something of a rarity. *H. C. Casserley*

while the tracks through Sampford Peverell halt, 1¾ miles to the north of Tiverton Junction, were also quadrupled. Sampford Peverell halt had opened in 1928 and, the same year, halts had appeared in the area at Halberton, on the main Tiverton branch, and at West Exe, Bolham and Morebath Junction, all on the Exe Valley branch to Dulverton. Cove halt, also on the Exe Valley branch, had opened in 1923 complete with the distinctive GWR pagoda-style platform building, and Burn halt, on the same branch, was added in 1929.

One scheme that was not progressed, however, was that for a Dawlish avoiding line. The scheme, which appeared in the 1930s, would have enabled more stopping trains to call at Dawlish & Teignmouth on summer Saturdays. The lack of track capacity at this point meant that the sheer number of through trains was so great that there were no diagrams available for local services!

Between 1904 and 1927, the GWR had held the distinction of operating the world's longest non-stop service. This was between Paddington and Plymouth, and the 1920s schedules for the 225¾-mile trip to North Road allowed 4hr 7min. This was reduced to four hours exactly at the end of 1927. The non-stop trains to Plymouth were, usually, to continue their journeys to Penzance but a change of locomotive was necessary at Plymouth. On peak summer Saturdays in the 1920s, the congestion at Plymouth was such that locomotives on the 'Cornish Riviera Express' were sometimes changed at Devonport Junction instead of North Road station and so, on a technicality, the non-stop run was actually ½-mile longer than the distance which was officially credited.

The 'Cornish Riviera' or, as it had previously been known, the '10.30 Limited', was one of the GWR's prestige services and, for the company's centenary in 1935, new coaching stock was introduced specially for the service. The coaches were 60ft long and

9ft 7in wide, that width being possible because of the wider loading gauges which had resulted from the conversion from the broad gauge in 1892. Due to their 'Red Triangle' loading gauge restriction, the 'Centenary' coaches were limited in the routes they could be used on – effectively to the old broad gauge network. Withdrawn from service on the 'Cornish Riviera' by 1941, the coaches were used on a variety of services post-1945 but not the 'Riviera'. A train of 13 of the new coaches weighed in at 420 tons tare, and could seat 84 first- and 336 third-class passengers, with dining car accommodation for a further 88 passengers.

The naming of trains on the GWR was not exclusive to passenger services. Since the broad gauge days, railwaymen had regularly dreamed up nicknames for certain scheduled freight services and, in 1929, the GWR decided to adopt many of the names officially. This resulted in some titles which could have caused confusion had they ever appeared in the public timetables. Among the named freight trains which operated to or from Devon, there was the 'Flying Pig' (the 4pm Exeter to Old Oak), the 'Rasher' (the 3.50pm Swindon to Tavistock Junction), the 'Pasty' (the 7.20pm Penzance to Plymouth) and the 'Biscuit' (the 10.30pm Reading to Laira).

The late 1920s were certainly boom years for the GWR and, in the eyes of the public, the company could do little wrong. In 1929, the Government granted permission for railway companies to operate their own air services and, typically, the GWR was the first to make use of the new legislation. On 12 April 1931, it inaugurated an air service between Cardiff and Haldon (near Exeter) which took just 50min; the fares were £3 single and £5 return. The service was run in conjunction with Imperial Airways which supplied the plane and, considerately, did not object to it being painted in GWR chocolate and cream. Very shortly, the air service was extended to Roborough Aerodrome, on the outskirts of Plymouth.

In the early 1920s, the GWR had hogged the limelight with its fast train services to Plymouth, but the Southern was not prepared to sit back and be ignored. Of the three major companies which had been grouped into the Southern Railway in 1923, the LSWR had been the only one not to have operated a named train. In 1925, the Southern considered that the lack of a named train on its Western Section should be rectified and, rather than do things by halves, it proposed naming three West Country expresses. The 10am train from Waterloo to Bude and Padstow was to be christened the 'North Cornwall Express', and the 12noon ex-Waterloo for Seaton, Sidmouth and Exmouth was designated the 'East Devon Express'. However, no name sprang to mind for the

11.00am from Waterloo to Exeter and Plymouth which had through carriages for, among other places, Ilfracombe. In the best traditions of staff relations, the Southern announced an in-house competition to find a suitable name for the train.

The winning name was the 'Atlantic Coast Express' and, for the record, it was entered by a guard at Waterloo who won 3 guineas (£3.15p) for his ingenuity. The three runners-up each received a paperweight in the shape of a 'King Arthur' class 4-6-0. The 11.00am service from Waterloo to Exeter and beyond had operated since the late 1890s,

but the inaugural run with the new title took place on 19 July 1926. By then, it had been decided to abandon the two other proposed named trains from Waterloo and, instead, to run the 'ACE' in two portions.

The first portion of the 'ACE' left Waterloo at 11.00am and arrived at Exeter Queen Street at 2.16pm, having had a four-minute stop at Salisbury for a change of locomotive. At Queen Street the train was divided, and the front section left at 2.25pm stopping at Exeter St Davids and, by prior arrangement only, at Portsmouth Arms on its journey to Barnstaple. Here, the train was divided once

Right:

In those blissful pre-Premier League days of 1933, the GWR announced cheap return fares to coincide with home matches at Exeter, Plymouth and Torquay.

Above:
Ex-ROD 2-8-0 No 3029 was photographed on the sea wall near Teignmouth in charge of a down goods.
E. Bruton

Right:
The ex-LSWR station at Devonport photographed on 30 August 1945. The once-distinctive roof was removed after receiving bomb damage during the war.
H. C. Casserley

Below right:
This extract is from the GWR rule book of 1936.

again. One section continued to Torrington, with a stop at every station except Fremington, before finishing its journey at 4.12pm; the other section ran on an 'all stations' basis to Ilfracombe, where it arrived at 4.24pm. At Exeter, meanwhile, the rear section of the train from Waterloo restarted at 2.33pm on its journey to Plymouth Friary, where it arrived at 4.29pm; the intermediate stops were at Exeter St.Davids, Okehampton, Tavistock, Devonport, North Road and Mutley.

The second portion of the 'ACE' was timed to leave Waterloo at 11.10am and had four stops before arriving in Exeter at 2.43pm. One of those stops was at Yeovil Junction where the coaches for Sidmouth and Exmouth were detached. From Queen Street, the train resumed its journey westwards and arrived at Halwill Junction at 3.56pm, where a coach was detached for a scheduled 4.42pm arrival at Bude. The remaining section of the train then continued to Padstow.

WORKING OF ENGINES IN STEAM COUPLED TOGETHER.—page 142.

The instruction under heading "(B) **Over Royal Albert Bridge, Saltash**" to be cancelled and the following substituted:

(1) The maximum speed of all engines passing over the structure is 15 m.p.h.

(2) Two engines of the "red" classification must not run coupled.

(3) The following "red" engines may be assisted by any of the "blue" engines shown:

"Red"	Assisting Engine "Blue"
4-6-0 "Castle"	4-6-0 78XX.
49XX, 68XX,	4-4-0 33XX, 34XX.
"1000" Class	2-6-0 43XX.
29XX, 39XX,	2-6-2T 41XX, 51XX,
40XX.	61XX, 81XX.

and also by engines of the "yellow" and "uncoloured" classes.

Assisting tender engines with a leading bogie may be coupled either in front of the train engine or between the train engine and the train. In all other respects the general instructions for assisting or double heading of trains apply.

(G.A. 18. 11/47. E. 78000/42H.)
(26—F.)

In the up direction, the 12.04pm and 12.32pm departures from Exeter provided the two portions of the eastbound 'ACE'. The front-runner had the coaches from Padstow and Bude while the later train contained the coaches from Ilfracombe, Torrington and Plymouth. The respective arrival times at Waterloo were 3.44pm and 4.29pm. During the peak summer season, it was often necessary to run the train in four parts from Waterloo but, unlike some other named trains elsewhere in Britain, the 'ACE' was intended to operate all-year round. Indeed, the Sunday 'ACE' which was introduced for the summer of 1932 was actually retained throughout the winter of 1933/34. The weekday schedules during the winter had slight variations, one being an extra stop at Sidmouth Junction for the separation of the Sidmouth and Exmouth carriages.

The carriages used on the 'ACE' were standard Southern stock and, in the eyes of passengers who were accustomed to the luxury of the GWR, these left a little to be desired. The Southern was not prepared to order a complete set of new coaching stock but, as a compromise, it introduced brand new restaurant cars in 1928. As for motive power, the 'ACE' used almost the whole gamut of the Western Section's range at one part or other of its journey. Between Waterloo and Salisbury, the 'Lord Nelsons' dominated after their introduction in 1926 whereas, between Salisbury and Exeter, the slightly more modest 'King Arthurs' were the usual steeds. Westwards from Exeter, the Plymouth portions of the 'ACE' were usually entrusted to 'T9' 4-4-0s, although 'U1' 2-6-0s took over during the late 1930s; 'M7' 0-4-4Ts often hauled the Bude portion while the 'E1/R' 0-6-2Ts took care of the Torrington coaches. Throughout Britain, there were precious few instances of named expresses turning up at their destinations behind veteran tank locomotives.

Inevitably, the war years caused considerable disruption throughout the country but, although many parts of rural Devon were comparatively unaffected, Plymouth became a prime target for enemy raids. The city suffered appallingly during the war. The important naval base at Devonport was attacked time and time again and, of course, the commercial docks were another focal point for bombing raids. Throughout all this, the railways were worked to maximum capacity to provide the necessary back-up for the war effort, and shunting activities on the harbour branch lines in Plymouth became a round-the-clock affair. There was considerable bomb damage to a number of railway installations in the Plymouth area but, in the spirit of the day, things were soon patched up for a return to business as usual. The only long-term casualty among Plymouth's stations was Ford halt, which closed in November 1941 after being bombed. At the Southern's station at Devonport, the distinctive overall roof received bomb damage and was subsequently removed as a safety precaution. Ironically, one of the more significant disruptions to the main line during the war was caused, not by enemy action, but a landslip. In December 1942, a major slip occurred on the main line near Saltash, just over the border in Cornwall, and all GWR trains for

Cornwall had to be diverted via the Southern's route through Launceston, the very line which the GWR had so strongly opposed in 1890.

Apart from the 'Atlantic Coast Express', which had been formally inaugurated in 1926, the only other named train to be operated by the Southern Railway in Devon was the 'Devon Belle'. However, this did not make its debut until 20 June 1947, a little over six months before Nationalisation. The 'Devon Belle' was an all-Pullman train which carried, at its rear, a 27-seat observation car; two mothballed Pullman cars had been converted to 'observation saloons' in preparation for the new service. The train operated between Waterloo and Exeter, where the sections for Plymouth and Ilfracombe were divided, but it ran only on Fridays, Saturdays, Sundays and Mondays. Although there was a supplementary charge for the luxury service, there was no premium for the seating in the observation cars, although you were expected to buy a drink from the bar! However, the sheer discomfort of those seats meant that only the pluckiest of passengers were prepared to hog them for any length of time.

By 1947, Bulleid's lightweight Pacifics had come into their own on West Country routes, and they were the ideal engines for hauling each section of the 'Devon Belle' westwards from Exeter. The Plymouth section of the train usually consisted of four coaches, but the Ilfracombe section normally comprised eight to 10. On the banks around Mortehoe, even a Pacific couldn't handle that little lot unaided and so banking assistance was provided by 'N' class 2-6-0s or 'M7' 0-4-4Ts, sometimes in multiple. At Ilfracombe, the 'Devon Belle's' observation car was turned on the locomotive turntable.

Oliver Bulleid's Pacifics may have been controversial but, nevertheless, they were absolutely ideal for duties westwards from Exeter. As soon as Bulleid had become the Southern Railway's Chief Mechanical Engineer in 1937, he had seemed to forget the wealth of practical experience which he had amassed as Nigel Gresley's principal assistant on the LNER. Instead, Bulleid's attitude seemed, to at least one eminent observer of the day, as if he were 'trying to re-invent the steam locomotive'. A number of innovative features were incorporated in the Bulleid Pacifics but, externally, the most controversial feature by far was the 'air-smoothed' casing which, much to Bulleid's disgust, was usually referred to as 'streamlining'. This gave rise to the nickname of the 'Spam Cans'. A further departure from tradition was the numbering of the Pacifics. For some mysterious reason, Bulleid incorporated the Continental system of wheel notation in the Pacifics' numbers and, therefore, the first batch of 70 'West Countries', introduced in 1945, became Nos 21C101-21C170 (the earlier 'Merchant Navies' were number 21C1 onwards). Further members of the class were built after Nationalisation. Prior to the appearance of the Pacifics, even the 'King Arthurs' had been barred west of Exeter and, consequently, services over the steeply-graded and, in some parts, lightly-built lines in mid- and North Devon had had to be entrusted to 4-4-0s or 2-6-0s. Despite the controversy, the design for a Pacific locomotive which could work on those difficult lines was a considerable achievement.

And then came Nationalisation. On 1 January 1948, virtually all of Britain's public railways were placed in the gentle, caring hands of British Railways. In many cases, a century or more of tradition disappeared overnight, and the railways of Devon were to be no less affected than their counterparts elsewhere in Britain. The 1950s were to prove traumatic for the traditionalists, as British Railways proved to be ill-prepared to match the challenge of the private motor car. As if the decline of the 1950s was not bad enough, the following decade saw the emergence of one Dr Beeching. The story of how Devon's railway network fared under State ownership is not for the faint-hearted.

CHEAP TICKETS

On Tuesdays, Wednesdays, Thursdays & Fridays
Commencing October 1st, 1947, and until further notice
CHEAP DAY TICKETS WILL BE ISSUED TO
EXETER
(ST. THOMAS or ST. DAVID'S)

FROM	Return Fares 1st Class	Return Fares 3rd Class	FROM	Return Fares 1st Class	Return Fares 3rd Class
	s. d.	s. d.		s. d.	s. d.
Alphington Halt	—	- 6	Ide Halt	—	- 9
Ashton	—	2 4	Kingskerswell	7 9	4 8
Bampton	—	4 6	Longdown	—	1 4
Bolham Halt	—	3 4	Lustleigh Via Newton A.	—	5 11
Bovey Via Newton Abbot	—	5 4	Via Ide	—	4 6
Via Ide	—	4 2	Morebath Jct Halt	—	4 9
Brampford Speke Halt	—	- 11	Moretonhampstead		
Brimley Halt Via Newton A.	—	5 4	Via Newton Abbot	—	6 7
Via Ide	—	3 11	Via Ide	—	5 4
Burlescombe	6 7	4 2	Newton Abbot	7 1	4 3
Burn Halt	—	1 11	Norton Fitzwarren	9 11	5 11
Cadeleigh	—	2 2	Paignton	9 10	5 10
Christow	—	2 1	Sampford Peverell	5 5	3 3
Chudleigh	—	3 1	Silverton	2 7	1 7
Chudleigh K. Halt	—	3 3	Starcross	3 0	1 10
Coldharbour Halt	—	3 7	Stoke Canon	1 4	- 9
Cove Halt	—	4 2	Taunton	10 7	6 4
Cullompton	4 6	2 9	Teigngrace Via Newton A.	—	4 8
Culmstock	—	4 2	Via Ide	—	3 9
Dawlish	4 5	2 7	Teignmouth	5 2	3 1
Dawlish Warren	3 9	2 4	Thorverton	—	1 5
Dulverton	—	5 2	Tiverton	—	3 0
Dunsford Halt	—	1 7	Tiverton Junction	5 0	3 0
Exminster	1 10	1 0	Torquay	9 1	5 5
Halberton Halt	—	3 0	Torre	8 8	5 4
Hawkmoor Halt			Trusham	—	2 9
Via Newton Abbot	—	5 8	Up Exe Halt	—	1 5
Via Ide	—	4 5	Uffculme	—	3 7
Heathfield Via Newton A.	—	4 11	Wellington (Som.)	8 2	4 11
Via Ide	—	3 7	West Exe Halt	—	2 10
Hele & Bradninch	3 0	1 10	Whitehall Halt	—	4 6
Hemyock	—	4 8			

AVAILABILITY OF TICKETS:
Tickets are available for travel by ANY TRAIN provided the return journey is commenced the same day as the outward journey.

Break of journey is not allowed ; but on Tuesdays, Wednesdays and Thursdays passengers holding Cheap Day tickets are allowed to alight at a station short of destination in either direction on surrender of ticket and to return from any intermediate station. This concession is not permitted in respect of Cheap Day Tickets, advertised above, issued on Fridays for Market purposes.

Children under 3 years of age, free ; 3 and under 14 years of age, half-fare.

NOTICE AS TO CONDITIONS.—These tickets are issued subject to the conditions of issue of ordinary passenger tickets where applicable and also to the special conditions as set out in the Ticket, etc., Regulations, By-Laws and General Notices. Luggage allowances are as set out in these general notices.

For further information apply at any of the Company's Stations and Offices, or to Mr. H. A. G. WORTH, Divisional Superintendent, Exeter (St. David's) (Telephone—Exeter 2281, Extension 301); or Mr. GILBERT MATTHEWS, Superintendent of the Line, Paddington Station, W.2.

Paddington Station, September 1947.
457B—Royal 8vo.—E9—46—5,000.

JAMES MILNE,
General Manager.

Left:
In the last year of its independent existence, the GWR promoted cheap day tickets to Exeter. The prices make for very interesting reading. *Author's collection*

6. Contraction

The era of Nationalised railways dawned on 1 January 1948 and, from that date, the Western and Southern Regions of British Railways took over where the GWR and the Southern Railway had left off. In amateur and professional circles alike, there was considerable apprehension about how the railways would fare under state ownership, but in Devon, one event of the early months of Nationalisation created undeniable interest.

In May 1948, BR conducted a series of locomotive exchanges in order to evaluate various types. The Western Region was given a pair of ex-LNER 'A4' Pacifics and two ex-LMS locomotives, a 'Coronation' 4-6-2 and a 'Royal Scot' 4-6-0, and it was instructed to test them on the Paddington-Plymouth route. The Southern Region tried out similar locomotives between Waterloo and Exeter. One of the 'A4s' was none other than

No 60022 *Mallard* but, much to the disappointment of Exeter's railway enthusiasts, these trials lasted only for a short period, although others involving mixed traffic locomotives also took place.

The exchange trials did not result in any permanent transfers. The regular ex-GWR and former SR classes continued to dominate the workings in Devon after Nationalisation, but the new BR 'Britannia' 4-6-2s started to appear on WR expresses in 1951. However, a hint of more radical change was seen at

Below:
The stranger on the shore near Teignmouth on 3 July 1954 was LMR '8F' 2-8-0 No 48424. The working was from Tavistock to Rogerstone, and owed nothing to the locomotive exchanges of earlier years. *S. Creer*

Exeter Central in October 1951. In that month, English Electric Type 3 diesel locomotive No 10202 appeared on workings between Waterloo and Exeter, and classmate No 10201 joined in five months later. The more-powerful variant, Type 4 No 10203, appeared in 1954 and it too did its share of Waterloo-Exeter duties, including the 'Atlantic Coast Express'.

The 'ACE' had been formally inaugurated in 1926 and had become a West Country tradition, but the other SR named train in Devon, the all-Pullman 'Devon Belle', had a comparatively brief life. The 'Devon Belle' had first appeared in 1947, but as early as 1950, the Plymouth portion of the train had been discontinued. Nevertheless, the Ilfracombe portion remained well-patronised for a few years, but the service was discontinued completely in 1954. The last 'Devon Belle' to

Right:
'Merchant Navy' class 4-6-2 No 35025 *Brocklebank Line* was photographed leaving Exeter with the up 'ACE' on 7 August 1952. *A. Dixon*

Below:
'King' class No 6007 *King William III* was photographed passing Laira at the head of an up express on 16 July 1953. Deceased auto coaches are stored in the sidings and, in the extreme foreground, the boarded crossing is that used by the horse-operated Lee Moor Tramway, more of which in Chapter Seven. *E. R. Morten*

operate was the up train on Sunday 19 September 1954. One of the observation cars was transferred to Scotland where it spent much time on the Kyle of Lochalsh line, but was eventually brought back to Devon for use on the preserved Paignton-Kingswear line.

During the early 1950s, most of the express workings between Exeter Central and Waterloo were looked after by 'Merchant Navy' class 4-6-2s but, in April 1953, a serious axle failure on one of the class resulted in all Bulleid Pacifics being rushed into the

workshops for examination. This might have prompted a few 'told you so' remarks among those who disliked the locomotives' unorthodox features, but its effect was a serious depletion of the SR's motive power stock. However, in the post-Nationalisation spirit of enforced camaraderie, the other regions lent locomotives to help ease the SR's crisis. The WR and LMR supplied 'Britannia' class 4-6-2s, but the NER came up with six of Gresley's 'V2' class 2-6-2s. Usually, it fell to the 'Britannias' to work the Exeter expresses, but the 'V2s' were known to materialise at

Exeter Central on occasions. By this time, the late Sir Nigel Gresley was gaining quite a fan club in Exeter.

Other 'foreign' visitors to Exeter Central during the early 1950s included ex-LMS Type 3 diesel-electrics Nos 10000/01, but their appearances in Devon were not a consequence of the problems with the Bulleid Pacifics. In many circles, the SR's wish to evaluate the ex-LMS diesels was seen as a further example of its enthusiasm for the alternative form of motive power, but Nos 10000/01 were soon returned to the

TORBAY EXPRESS
REFRESHMENT CAR SERVICE

LONDON (Paddington), EXETER, TORQUAY, PAIGNTON and KINGSWEAR

WEEK DAYS and SUNDAYS

	E	S	SUNS.		E	S	SUNS.
London (Paddington) dep	noon 12A0	noon 12A0	noon 12A0	Kingswear .. dep	am 11A25	am 11B20	am 11A25
				Churston (for Brixham) „	11A35	11B32	11A35
Exeter (St. David's) arr	pm 2 55	..	..	Paignton .. „	11A48	11B45	11A48
Torquay .. „	3 35	pm 3 50	pm 4 7				
				Torquay .. „	noon ·12A0	noon 12B 0	noon 12A0
Paignton ... „	3 48	4 8	4 25	Exeter (St. David's) „	p.m. 12 40	..	..
Churston (for Brixham) „	4 .0	4 23	4 35	London (Paddington) arr	3 35	pm 4 10	pm 4 5
Kingswear .. „	4 10	4 35	4 46				

A—Seats can be reserved in advance on payment of a fee of 1s. 0d. per seat (see page 26).

B—Passengers for London travelling by this train are required to hold reserved seat tickets which can be obtained in advance without charge on prior application upon production of a valid rail ticket at any Station or Ticket Agency, or, if within three weeks of date of travel by this train, at the Station from which the journey is to be made.

E—Except Saturdays.   **S**—Saturdays only.

LMR and, furthermore, the SR's own diesel trio, Nos 10201/02/03, eventually followed. Internal combustion was not yet ready to mount a serious challenge to steam traction in Devon.

The early 1950s saw another boom in Devon's holiday trade, but this time there were signs of change. The larger resorts which had main line stations became used to the sight of jam-packed trains on summer Saturdays, but fewer holidaymakers ventured on to the branch lines. The era of widespread car ownership was really under way, and the less commercialised corners of the county were, usually, more accessible by road. Throughout the country, the railways were often slow to react to the threat of the car, but in South Devon, at least the Western Region tried.

By the mid-1950s, services over the WR's branches in South Devon were, in most cases, more frequent than they ever had been. A comparison can be drawn from the summer timetables for 1922, 1948 and those for summer 1955.

NUMBER OF SATURDAY TRAINS

	1922	1948	1955
Moretonhampstead branch	8	8	9
Kingsbridge branch	6	7	11
Brixham branch	17	15	17
Ashburton branch	6	8	8
Princetown branch	6	5	6
Launceston branch	4	5	6

Despite the WR's valiant rearguard action, passenger figures continued their steady decline. More alarmingly, many of the services ran almost empty during the winter months, and this emphasised that the locals were defecting to the roads.

The writing was on the wall but, nevertheless, there were only two line closures during the early and mid-1950s. On 2 July 1951, the SR's Turnchapel branch in Plymouth was closed temporarily because of the fuel crisis, but its reopening was to be extremely brief. Passenger services were irreversibly withdrawn on 10 September that year, but the line was kept open for freight until October 1961. The other closure was that of the Princetown branch; services were withdrawn between Yelverton and Princetown on 3 March 1956, and a double-headed train of six coaches had to be laid on to cope with the 'last day' crowds. Printable photographs taken on the last day are scarce, however, as a full-blooded Dartmoor mist reduced the visibility to virtually nil.

In the early 1950s, an economy was made at Launceston, just over the border in Cornwall, which saw the end of the duplication of passenger stations. In 1943, a connecting spur had been laid between the GWR and the Southern lines in the town, and British Railways made full use of this by diverting WR passenger trains into the SR station from 1 July 1952. The WR station was kept open until February 1966 for goods only. The old LSWR engine shed at Launceston had closed in October 1943 and, since then, the GWR shed had served both railways. Even in the pre-Nationalisation era, things had been very cosy at the shed; the GWR and the Southern had each had two resident engine crews, and it had not been unknown for firemen to have an unofficial stint on the opposition's locomotives. The year before the closure of Launceston's WR station to passengers, both stations in the town had been retitled, the WR one having become Launceston North, and the SR establishment Launceston South. At nearby Tavistock, the SR station had been retitled Tavistock North in September 1949, the town's ex-GWR station having always been known as Tavistock South.

In North Devon, trains on the WR's Taunton-Barnstaple branch worked through to Ilfracombe (a daily service from Paddington had started in the 1930s with a slip coach for Tiverton), and a number of the summer Saturday services contained through carriages for places such as Cardiff, Wolverhampton and Manchester. Not to be outdone, the SR proved to be no slouch in providing its own services to Ilfracombe and, during the summer of 1952, 17 SR trains were advertised to work to Ilfracombe on Saturdays. At Barnstaple, the WR engine shed at Victoria Road was closed in January 1951, and the locomotives and staff were transferred to the SR shed at Barnstaple Junction. However, the fraternisation between ex-GWR and ex-LSWR locomotives at the shed was interrupted by the arrival of ex-LMS Ivatt '2MT' 2-6-2Ts in 1953, and the allocation

Above:
Departmental 'G6' class 0-6-0T No DS3152 is seen with a quarryman's coach at Meldon in 1959. *J. H. Aston*

Right:
By the mid-1950s, the WR's summer services to Barnstaple and Ilfracombe were very frequent. This page is from the WR timetable for summer 1955.
Author's collection

lists show that, five years later, Nos 41294/95/97/99 and 41314 were all resident at Barnstaple. On 13 June 1960, the WR station at Victoria Road was closed, and all railway activities in the town were subsequently centred on the former Southern Railway stations.

Elsewhere in North Devon, more and more passenger traffic was lost to the roads during the 1950s, but freight figures remained surprisingly steady. Agricultural produce provided the mainstay, but there was also a considerable amount of granite transported from Meldon Quarry, near Okehampton. The quarry had been extended on several occasions since its opening in 1897, and had been modernised in 1933; a 2ft-gauge tramway had operated within the quarry until the late 1940s, which, for some years, had been worked by four-wheeled petrol or diesel shunters.

Much of the stone extracted at Meldon was used for ballast, for which the SR was the prime customer, and so the SR was happy to provide an Engineer's Department locomotive for transfer duties at Meldon. By November 1949, Meldon's departmental 0-6-0T, an ex-SE&CR locomotive of 1890, was considered well past its sell-by date, and

Table 84 — **TAUNTON, DULVERTON, BARNSTAPLE and ILFRACOMBE (Week Days only)**

Miles		Mondays to Fridays								Saturdays only											
		night	am	am	am	pm	pm	pm	pm	night T	night D	night T	am T	am	am T	pm	am K	pm W	pm T	pm	pm
	61 London (Pad.) 62..dep	11d50	5 30	9R30	11R30	1R30	..	3R30	5R30	11F50	11F50	11F50	..	5H30	9 35	..	1130	12R5	1R35	3R30	5R30
—	**Taunton** .... dep	8a 3	10 13	12p15	2p44	4 35	5 45	6 17	8 25	5a20	6a20	7a15	8 30	1025	12p50	1 48	2 25	3 35	4 35	6 17	8 35
2	Norton Fitzwarren	..	10 19	12 19	..	4 39	5 49	..	..	..	..	7 19	8 34	1029	..	1 54	..	..	..	6 22	..
6¼	Milverton	8 17	10 28	12 27	2 57	4 47	5 57	6 31	8 37	....	....	7 28	8 43	1037	1 3	2 2	....	....	4 47	6 30	8 47
9½	Wiveliscombe	8 25	10 35	12 34	3 4	4 54	6 4	6 38	8 44	5 40	6 40	7 36	8 51	1046	1 12	2 10	2 44	..	4 54	6 37	8 54
14¼	Venn Cross	8 36	10 46	12 45	3 15	5 5	6 15	6 49	8 55	....	....	7 47	9 4	1058	1 24	2 22	....	....	5 5	6 48	9 5
17¾	Morebath	8 42	10 52	12 51	3 21	5 10	6 21	6 55	9 1	..	..	7 55	9 10	11 4	1 30	2 28	..	..	5 10	6 54	9 11
19¼	Morebath Junction Halt ..	8 47	10 57	12 56	3 29	5 16	6 26	....	9 6	....	....	....	9 15	1110	....	2 33	....	....	5 16	6 59	9 16
21	Dulverton	8 53	11 3	1 2	3 35	5 22	6 30	7 5	9 12	6 5	7 5	8 5	9 21	1118	1 43	2 39	3 15	4 23	5 25	7 5	9 24
24¾	East Anstey	9 3	11 13	1 11	3 44	5 31	....	7 14	9 21	....	....	8 14	9 30	1128	1 54	2 48	....	....	5 34	7 14	9 35
26½	Yeo Mill Halt	9 8	11 18	1 15	3 49	5 36	..	7 18	9 26	..	..	..	9 35	1133	1 59	..	..	..	5 39	7 18	9 40
30	Bishop's Nympton and	9 14	11 24	1 21	3 55	5 42	....	7 27	9 34	....	7 25	8 26	9 41	1139	2 5	2 58	....	....	5 47	7 26	9 46
34¼	South Molton ...[Molland	9 23	11 33	1 29	4 3	5 50	..	7 34	9 43	6 30	7 34	8 35	9 49	1147	2 13	3 7	3 43	4 50	5 55	7 34	9 54
37½	Filleigh	9 32	11 42	1 38	4 12	6 0	....	7 43	9 52	....	....	8 44	9 58	1156	2 22	3 17	....	....	6 5	7 43	10 3
40¾	Swimbridge	9 39	11 49	1 45	4 20	6 7	..	7 50	9 59	..	..	8 51	10 5	12 5	2 30	3 24	..	..	6 14	7 50	1010
44¾	**Barnstaple Victoria Road** .. arr	9 46	11 56	1 52	4 28	6 14	....	7 57	10 6	6 52	7 55	8 58	1012	1212	2 38	3 31	4 10	5 11	6 22	7 57	1017
	Barnstaple Victoria Road .. dep	9 51	12 4	2 0	4 34	6 19	..	8 4	..	7 10	8 4	9 4	1030	1220	2 54	3 46	4 19	5 15	6 36	8 4	..
45¾	**Barnstaple Junction** arr	9 57	12 10	2 5	4 40	6 25	....	8 10	....	7 16	8 10	9 10	1035	1226	3 0	3 50	4 25	5 22	6 42	8 15	....
60¾	**Ilfracombe** .. .. „	10 52	1 48	3 40	5 56	7 17	..	9 4	..	8 12	9 5	9 58	1122	2A 5	3 56	..	5 10	6 16	7 37	9 4	..

Miles		Mondays to Fridays									Saturdays only												
		am	am	am	pm	pm	pm	pm	pm	pm	am	am	am M	am N	am D	am P	noon	pm	pm	pm	pm B	pm B	pm W
—	**Ilfracombe** .. .. dep	..	..	8 55	1220	..	3 0	.	.	5 45	..	6 42	8 25	9 25	1012	1055	12 0	..	2 55	..	5 10	6 30	8 0
15	**Barnstaple Junction** „	....	....	10 0	1 10	2 25	3 58	....	....	6 40	....	7 45	9 10	1016	11 3	1142	1242	2 5	3 55	4 55	5 53	7 15	8 43
16	**Barnstaple Victoria Road** .. arr	..	..	10 5	1 16	2 30	4 3	.	.	6 45	..	7 50	9 17	1023	1110	1150	1248	2 10	4 0	5 0	6 0	7 22	8 50
	Barnstaple Victoria Road .. dep	6 55	8 20	1010	1 20	2 35	4 12	525	....	6 54	6 55	7 56	9 25	1027	1120	1155	1253	2 20	4 10	5 14	6 5	7 25	8 54
20	Swimbridge	7 2	8 27	1018	1 29	..	4 20	532	.	7 2	7 2	8 3	..	1035	1130	..	1 1	2 30	4 18	..	6 14	7 34	..
23½	Filleigh	7 9	8 34	1025	1 38	....	4 28	541	....	7 9	7 9	8 10	....	1043	1138	....	1 8	....	4 26	....	6 22	7 43	....
26½	South Molton ...[Molland	7 17	8 42	1033	1 47	2 55	4 37	552	.	7 17	7 17	8 18	9 50	1051	1150	1218	1 16	2 46	4 34	5 38	6 31	7 52	9 16
30¾	Bishop's Nympton and	7 25	8 50	1041	1 55	....	4 46	6 3	....	7 25	7 25	8 26	....	1059	1158	....	1 24	2 57	4 44	5 46	6 39	8 1	....
34¼	Yeo Mill Halt	7 32	8 57	1048	2 2	..	4 53	.	.	7 32	7 32	8 33	..	11 6	12 5	..	1 30	..	4 51	..	6 46	8 8	..
36	East Anstey	7 37	9 3	1053	2 7	....	4 58	617	....	7 37	7 37	8 38	....	1111	1211	....	1 35	....	4 57	....	6 51	8 13	....
39¾	Dulverton	7 45	9 15	11 2	2 15	3 20	5 9	630	7 5	7 45	7 45	8 47	1016	1120	1220	1245	1 43	3 17	5 8	6 8	7 3	8 26	9 44
41½	Morebath Junction Halt ..	7 51	9 20	11 8	2 22	....	5 14	....	7 9	7 51	7 51	8 52	....	1126	1225	....	1 49	....	5 14	....	7 9	8 31	....
43	Morebath	7 54	9 24	1110	2 25	..	5 18	641	712	7 55	7 54	8 55	..	1130	1229	..	1 53	..	5 18	..	7 12	8 35	..
46½	Venn Cross	8 2	9 32	1119	2 33	....	5 26	655	720	8 3	8 2	9 3	....	1138	1237	....	2 1	....	5 26	....	7 20	8 43	....
51¼	Wiveliscombe	8 11	9 41	1129	2 42	3 45	5 36	7 8	732	8 12	8 11	9 12	1045	1148	1247	1 12	2 10	3 42	5 36	6 36	7 32	8 55	1010
54¼	Milverton	8 17	9 47	1135	2 47	....	5 42	715	738	8 18	8 17	9 18	....	1154	1253	....	2 16	....	5 42	....	7 38	9 2	....
58¾	Norton Fitzwarren	8 25	9 55	..	..	..	5 50	.	746	8 26	8 25	9 26	..	12 2	1 1	..	2 24	..	5 50	..	7 46	9 10	..
60¾	**Taunton** .... arr	8 30	10 1	1148	3 0	4 3	5 55	728	751	8 31	8 30	9 31	11 3	1210	1 6	1 30	2 31	3 57	5 55	6 55	7 51	9 18	1030
203¾	61 London (Pad.) 62.. arr	12R10	1R30	2R50	6 15	7R10	9R 0	.	.	..	12R15	1V35	2 40	..	..	5R15	6 25	7U15	9R 5	..	..	..	5a 0

A On Saturdays 2nd July to 13th August arr 1 27 pm
a am
B Through Train Ilfracombe to Taunton
D Through Train between Taunton and Ilfracombe. Runs 16th July to 27th August inclusive only
d Sunday to Thursday nights
F Friday nights only
G Change at Bristol (T.M.); limited accommodation from Bristol. Refreshment Car available
H On Saturdays from 25th June to 20th August inclusive dep 7 0 am. Refreshment Car to Taunton.
K Through Carriages London to Ilfracombe
M Through Train Ilfracombe to Bristol (T.M.). Commencing 2nd July extended to Manchester (Ex.), arr 6 48 pm (Table 168)
N Through Train Ilfracombe to Cardiff (Tables 61 and 104)
P Through Carriages Ilfracombe to Wolverhampton (L.L.) (Tables 61 and 169)
p pm
R Refreshment Car between Paddington and Taunton
T Through Train Taunton to Ilfracombe
U Refreshment Car available 25th June to 20th August inclusive only
V Refreshment Car Train. From 2nd July to 10th September passengers can arr 1 20 pm without Refreshment Car
W Through Train between Taunton and Ilfracombe. Runs 18th June to 10th September inclusive only

A Road Motor Service is operated by the Southern National Omnibus Company between Barnstaple Junction and Chelfham Cross, Bratton Fleming, Blackmoor Gate, Parracombe, Woody Bay Cross and Lynton.

For OTHER TRAINS between Taunton and Norton Fitzwarren, see Tables 81 and 82—Morebath Junction Halt and Dulverton, Table 87.

so a replacement was sought. This was found in the form of an ex-LSWR 'G6' class 0-6-0T, which had yet to receive its designated BR number of 30272; it was taken into departmental stock in June 1950, renumbered DS3152, and dispatched to Meldon. It worked there until its withdrawal in August 1960, and its successor was another 'G6', ex-No 30238, which had become departmental No DS682. The latter locomotive was succeeded in December 1962 by No DS234, a 'USA' class 0-6-0T which had previously carried BR No 30062; on withdrawal of the 'USA' in 1967, 'Class 08' diesel shunters took over. Elsewhere in Devon, another arm of the Engineer's Department was the sleeper depot at Broad Clyst, which was worked by a diminutive 0-4-0 diesel shunter, No DS1169, from 1959 to 1964.

While most of Devon's secondary and branch lines suffered during the 1950s, the SR's Exmouth branch defied the trend. In 1957, the number of tickets collected at Exmouth was over 486,000; by comparison, 530,000 were collected at Exeter Central dur-

Left:
The first regular service locomotive at Meldon Quarry was a Manning Wardle 0-4-0ST which had started life with the South Eastern Railway in 1881. It worked at the quarry between March 1927 and July 1938, this picture being taken on 3 August 1928. *H. C. Casserley*

Right:
Drummond 'M7' 0-4-4T No 30021 and auto set No 381 are seen leaving Colyton for Seaton Junction with an evening local on 1 August 1959.
D. Fereday Glenn

Below:
The Exmouth signalman prepares to take the token as '3MT' 2-6-2T No 82023 enters with the 4pm from Exeter Central on 12 October 1959.
R. C. Riley

ing the same year. Ex-LMS Ivatt '2MT' 2-6-2Ts had started to appear on the Exmouth branch in the early 1950s and, soon after, BR Standard 2-6-2Ts and 2-6-4Ts had been drafted in.

For many years, the Budleigh Salterton and Sidmouth branches had been worked in conjunction with the Exmouth branch and, consequently, they too received the attentions of the same types of BR and ex-LMS locomotives. During the 1950s, there were two sightings of Bulleid Pacifics on the Sidmouth branch, which proved the versatility of those locomotives beyond all doubt. One of those occasions was in August 1959, when a 'West Country' class 4-6-2 hauled a nine-coach special from Plymouth to Sidmouth and back, without requiring any assistance on the 1 in 45 bank near Tipton St Johns. Along the coast at Seaton, push-pull fitted 'M7' 0-4-4Ts tended to hold their own during the 1950s, but Exmouth Junction's Standard '3MT' 2-6-2T No 82040 is known to have made a number of appearances.

The Lyme Regis branch continued to provide a headache for the operating department. It was appreciated that even the veteran Adams Radial Tanks would not last for ever, but the list of suitable replacements was pretty scanty. In 1958, ex-GWR '14xx' class 0-4-2T No 1462 was tried on the branch, but proved to be about as consistent as the away form of Torquay United, and was subsequently returned to Exeter shed in disgrace. In 1959, some sections of track on the branch were renewed and two curves were marginally straightened so that Ivatt '2MT' 2-6-2Ts could be tried, and No 41297 was put to the test in September 1960. Although it performed well, there were still doubts about using such a heavy locomotive on the line. However, the worsening condition of the Radial Tanks necessitated a 'flexible' attitude in the operating department, and the 2-6-2Ts were reluctantly given the official blessing.

The lines of the former Southern Railway west of Exeter had been transferred to the

Table 58   **AXMINSTER and LYME REGIS**

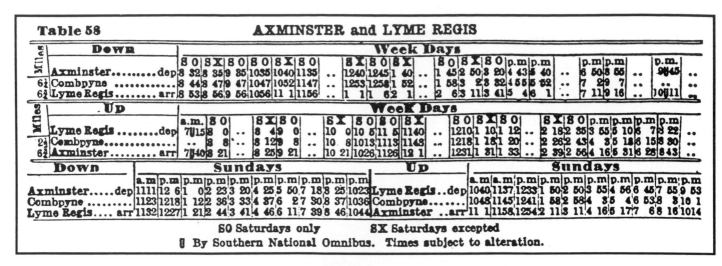

Miles	Down	Week Days																				
		SO	SX	SO	SO	SX	SO		SX	SO	SX		SO	SX	SO	p.m	p.m		p.m	p.m		p.m
	Axminster....dep	8 32	8 35	9 35	1035	1040	1135	..	1240	1245	1 40	..	1 45	2 50	3 20	4 43	5 40	..	6 50	8 55	..	9 45
6¼	Combpyne.......	8 44	8 47	9 47	1047	1052	1147	..	1253	1258	1 52	..	1 58	3 2	3 32	4 55	5 52	..	7 29	7	..	..
6¾	Lyme Regis....arr	8 53	8 56	9 56	1056	11 1	1156	..	1 1	1 62	1	..	2 6	3 11	3 41	5 4	6 1	..	7 11	9 16	..	1011

Miles	Up	Week Days																			
		a.m	SO		SX	SO		SX	SO	SO	SX		SO	SX	SO	p.m	p.m	p.m	p.m	
	Lyme Regis....dep	7 15	8 0	..	8 49	9 0	..	10 0	1011	5 11	1140	..	1210	1 10	1 12	..	2 18	3 55	3 55	10 6	7 22
2¼	Combpyne.......	..	8 8	..	8 129	9 8	..	10 8	1013	1113	1148	..	1218	1 18	1 20	..	2 26	4 3	4 3	5 18	6 15
6¾	Axminster....arr	7 40	8 21	..	8 25	9 21	..	10 21	1026	1126	12 1	..	1231	1 31	1 33	..	2 39	2 56	4 16	5 31	6 28

Down	Sundays											Up	Sundays								
	a.m	p.m	p.m	p.m	p.m	p.m	p.m	p.m	p.m	p.m			a.m	a.m	p.m	p.m	p.m	p.m	p.m	p.m	p.m
Axminster....dep	1111	12 6	1 0	2 23	3 20	4 25	5 50	7 18	8 25	1023		Lyme Regis..dep	1040	1137	1233	1 50	2 50	3 55	4 56	6 45	7 55	9 53
Combpyne.........	1123	1218	1 12	2 36	3 33	4 37	6 2	7 30	8 37	1036		Combpyne.......	1048	1145	1241	1 58	2 58	4 3	5 4	6 53	8 10	1
Lyme Regis....arr	1132	1227	1 21	2 44	3 41	4 46	6 11	7 39	8 46	1044		Axminster....arr	11 1	1156	1254	2 11	3 11	4 16	5 17	7 6	8 16	1014

SO Saturdays only   **SX** Saturdays excepted

Ⓤ By Southern National Omnibus. Times subject to alteration.

Above:
This extract from the SR timetable for the summer of 1952 shows the services on the Lyme Regis branch. *Author's collection*

Left:
Standard Class 4 460 No 75026 is seen piloting 'Castle' class No 5071 *Spitfire* at Exeter St Davids on 22 July 1955. *S. Creer*

Western Region of British Railways in 1950, but another bout of regional boundary changes in 1958 resulted in those lines passing back to the SR. This lasted only until 1963, when further boundary alterations passed all SR lines west of Wilton, in Wiltshire, to the WR. In Devon, the word 'shuttlecock' became frequently used. However, the period of status quo between 1958 and 1963 saw the first signs of what would become of Devon's railways during the next 10 years or so.

On 17 February 1958, the WR unveiled its new diesel-hydraulic A1A-A1A Type 4 No D600 *Active*, and the following month, No D601 *Ark Royal* entered service. On 16 June, No D601 was at the head of the first diesel-hauled 'Cornish Riviera', and an irreversible change was underway. The original Type 4s were to number only five and, much to the amusement of steam enthusiasts, were to prove spectacularly unreliable. Consequently, they spent much of their lives based at Laira, from where they could be kept out of harm's way on the Plymouth-Penzance section, and were all withdrawn at the end of 1967. However, during the same year as their debut, the first of the Swindon-built B-B Type 4s had appeared, and these were altogether superior machines.

The Type 4s were later designated Classes 42 and 43 under the TOPS coding but, of course, they were better known as the 'Warships'; they soon dominated express duties throughout the Western Region. In 1959, the Class 22 B-B diesel-hydraulics were introduced, primarily for secondary and local duties, and most were divided between Newton Abbot and Laira sheds. The introduction of the powerful Class 52 diesels for express services in 1961 resulted in some of the 'Warships' being displaced, and subsequently becoming available for secondary duties. For branch work, there were the ubiquitous diesel multiple-units.

The emergence of diesel traction in the late 1950s was not the only change afoot in Devon. The traffic figures on many branch lines were still dwindling, and it became inevitable that closures would result. The first to go in the late 1950s was the Exeter-Heathfield branch, which was closed to passengers on 9 June 1958. Although it had never been a heavily-used line, it had provided a useful, albeit lightweight, alternative route if the main line via Dawlish had had to close, but after Nationalisation, the old LSWR line via Okehampton had become available as a better alternative. During the final years of the Heathfield branch, its lowly

status was well and truly emphasised; if holiday traffic were causing congestion at St Davids station, the branch trains were often booked to terminate at Alphington Road halt, and the passengers were left to fend for themselves from there onwards, although a bus service was provided. The Christow-Heathfield section of the branch remained open for freight, and was used by three trains a week until 30 September 1960, when floods severed the line. Total closure followed.

At Heathfield, the line from Exeter joined the Moretonhampstead branch, and the latter had its passenger services withdrawn on 2 March 1959. Since the closure of the engine shed at Moretonhampstead in November 1947, the branch had been serviced by Newton Abbot shed, with '45xx' class 2-6-2Ts being the usual steeds. Nevertheless, the Moretonhampstead branch remained open for freight until 1964 and, at the time of writing, the section between Newton Abbot and Heathfield is still in use; its purpose is to provide access to the Oil Terminal at Heathfield Trading Estate, some ¾-mile beyond the site of Heathfield station. During 1992, five or six trains, each comprising eleven 100-tonne tank wagons from the Gulf Oil refinery at Milford Haven, usually worked to the terminal each month. Class 37s were the usual locomotives.

Between the closures of the Heathfield and the Moretonhampstead branches, the Ashburton branch met its demise. It lost its passenger services on 3 November 1958 but remained open for freight until September 1962. Officially, the largest locomotives permitted on the Ashburton branch were '44xx' class 2-6-2Ts, but in October 1947, 'Castle' class No 5094 *Tretower Castle* boldly went where no 'Castle' had gone before, and found

Above:
'Grange' class No 6802 *Bampton Grange* is seen emerging from the lifting shop at Exeter St Davids shed on 4 September 1956. *E. H. Sawford*

Below:
On 4 September 1965, the 7.50am Paddington-Paignton working was performed by Type 4 'Warship' No D859 *Vanquisher*. Here, it is seen passing Gasworks Siding between Torquay and Paignton. *A. N. Yeates*

its way to a point between Totnes and Staverton. That was no ordinary working, however, as the locomotive was in charge of a Royal train which was stabled on the branch for two nights, and the engine was required to provide overnight steam heating for the carriages. Royal toes and Devon autumns are not always compatible. During the early 1950s, the regular locomotives on the Ashburton branch were '44xx' class 2-6-2Ts Nos 4405/06, but both were withdrawn in September 1955. Their singular replacement was, usually, '14xx' class 0-4-2T No 1429, but '16xx' class 0-6-0PT No 1608 was occasionally seconded from Newton Abbot shed to assist. Happily, the Totnes-Buckfastleigh section of the Ashburton branch was later reopened by preservationists.

In Plymouth, the old LSWR station at Friary closed to passengers on 15 September 1958. This was part of a rationalisation of workings in the city, the main object of which was to centralise all passenger workings at North Road station. Rebuilding work had started at North Road in 1938, but had been interrupted by the war. Work did not recommence until 1956, and it was 1962 before the new station, complete with its seven through platform faces and three bays, was officially unveiled. Friary station subsequently became Plymouth's main goods depot and, with the closure of the former-PD&SWJR station at Devonport in 1964, North Road was retitled, more simply, 'Plymouth'.

Back on the branches, the WR's Plymouth-Launceston line was scheduled for closure on 29 December 1962. It proved to be a case of bad timing, as that month saw the start of one of the worst winters in the

Above:
A 'King' and a 'Pannier' provide ample evidence that this picture was taken in former-GWR territory. The 'King' is No 6013 *King Henry VIII*, and it is seen leaving Newton Abbot with a service for Cornwall on 3 July 1959. *S. Creer*

Right:
With evidence of the continuing work of rebuilding the station visible above the platform canopy, Plymouth North Road station was reconstructed over a six-year period from 1956 until 1962. This view, taken on 14 August 1961, shows the construction of the ten-story office block built to accommodate the staff of BR's Plymouth Division. *British Railways*

West Country for many years. The last two trains on the branch each comprised four corridor coaches, and although they managed to leave on time, both trains became marooned in snowdrifts. The first was headed by '45xx' class 2-6-2T No 4591, which had been a regular locomotive on the branch for many years, and it did not complete its journey until 30 December. The second train, hauled by 2-6-2T No 5568, surfaced the following day and, consequently, the record books show that the official closure to passengers was on 31 December. The branch was kept open for freight traffic and the usual form of motive power were the Class 22 diesel-hydraulics, but steam was to have one final fling on 15 May 1964, when ex-LMS 2-6-2T No 41308 hauled an inspection train over the branch prior to the line's complete closure.

And so, by the end of 1962, six of Devon's branch lines had closed to the fare-paying public. However, all of those which survived were to come under very close scrutiny in the Government document which was published on 27 March 1963. Innocuously entitled *The Reshaping of Britain's Railways*, it

was better known as the 'Beeching Report', and it was intended to transform British Railways into supreme financial health. Thirty years on, we're still waiting. Despite ferocious opposition, most of Beeching's proposed cuts were eventually implemented, and so the rest of the 1960s saw a catalogue of line closures.

The two-mile long Brixham branch closed on 13 May 1963 but, admittedly, that closure had been on the cards even before Beeching had spoken. The first Beeching-inspired closure in Devon was that of the Tiverton Junction-Hemyock branch, which hosted its last passenger train on 7 September 1963. However, the line was left intact for the daily milk trains from the factory at Hemyock, and these continued until September 1965. Until

the cessation of passenger services on the Hemyock branch, the little '14xx' class 0-4-2Ts had enjoyed a long-standing monopoly, but haulage of the milk trains eventually passed to lightweight diesel shunters.

The Exe Valley branch, which ran from Stoke Canon to Dulverton via Tiverton, closed on 7 October 1963 and, somewhat insultingly, the last train was diesel-operated. The inability to muster a steam locomotive stemmed largely from the impending demise of Exeter shed, which was due to close to steam on 14 October, just seven days after services ceased on the Exe Valley branch, and Exeter's locomotives had been either withdrawn or transferred in the preceding weeks. One of those which had been

earmarked for retirement was '14xx' class 0-4-2T No 1471 which, arguably, would have been the most suitable candidate for the last rites on the Exe Valley line.

Exeter shed was reinstated as a service depot for diesel shunters, but it soon fell into decay and the roof was removed as a safety precaution. When the shed had been closed to steam, its sub-shed at Tiverton Junction had become a subsidiary of Taunton, and was kept open until 5 October 1964 to house the locomotive engaged on the branch service to Tiverton, but with the closure of the branch on that date, the sub-shed became redundant. Although the milk trains from Hemyock continued operating for another 11 months, the diesel locomotive was supplied by Taunton and stabled in the yard of Tiverton Junction station. The last major change in the area was the construction of Tiverton Parkway (built on the site of the closed Sampford Peverell halt), which was formally opened in May 1986.

In South Devon, the last train ran on the Kingsbridge branch on 14 September 1963; the engine shed at Kingsbridge had succumbed two years previously. Although a popular spot with tourists, Kingsbridge had never been developed into a full-blooded holiday resort, and the vast majority of locals were, most sensibly, very happy with that situation. The loss of a railway was a small price to pay for having largely evaded the trippers.

Apart from the closure of the Tiverton branch in 1964, it was 1965 before the real slaughter of the Beeching era commenced. The Southern Railway's branch between Torrington and Halwill had been the last new line to have been built in Devon, but this claim to fame cut no ice with the authorities. It was closed to passengers on 1 March 1965, still awaiting its 40th birthday. On 4 October that year, when the last real traces of the holiday season had disappeared, the line

between Barnstaple and Torrington had its passenger services withdrawn, thereby removing the important town of Bideford from the public timetables. The day before the official closure, '4MT' No 80039 worked to Torrington with a portion of the specially-chartered 'Exeter Flyer' from Waterloo.

At Torrington, the small engine shed had been closed in 1959, and the locomotives for the Halwill branch had been sent from Barnstaple shed on a day-to-day basis. In the final year of the Halwill branch, a 65-seat single-car diesel unit had been used, but even this

Above:
A northbound IC125 is seen preparing to leave Tiverton Parkway on 30 October 1992. The haze in the background is due, in part, to smoke from a nearby Little Chef service station which was on fire (honest!) *Author*

Left:
Class 55xx 2-6-2T No 5551 is pictured near Kingsbridge station with a Permanent Way train in 1956. The ex-Great Western branch from Brent was to close to passenger services on 16 September 1963. *D. A. Bosomworth*

Above:

The Torrington portion of the special working of Sunday 3 October 1965, the 'Exeter Flyer', was hauled by '4MT' 2-6-4T No 80039. Despite the general decline of services in the area, this picture shows that the station and yard at Torrington were still well-maintained. *Ron Fisher*

Right:

Having arrived from Meeth, diesel-hydraulic No D6334 is seen being coupled up to its train at Petrockstow on 14 October 1965 in readiness for its onward journey to Torrington. *Ian Allan Library*

had not brought about the necessary economies. Despite the loss of passenger services beyond Barnstaple in 1965, the line was kept open as far as Meeth for outwards clay traffic, but this came to an end on 13 September 1982. Some of the clay from the Meeth area was exported through Fremington Quay until its closure in 1969. By then, however, Fremington's peak handling figures of 20,000 tons p.a. were very much a thing of the past. The very last passenger train to Torrington was a special working from Bristol which ran on 6 November 1982; promoted by British Rail itself, it was hauled by Class 31 diesels Nos 31158/74.

The Lyme Regis branch closed on 29 November 1965. The three celebrated Radial Tanks, Nos 30582/83/84, had all been retired in 1961 and had been replaced by ex-LMS '2MT' 2-6-2Ts. In November 1963, two-car DMUs were introduced and this brought about the redundancy of Lyme Regis engine shed. The '2MTs' made a brief return in 1964 but, in February 1965, GWR '14xx' class 0-4-2Ts Nos 1442/50 were transferred from Yeovil Town to Exmouth Junction shed for duties on the Lyme Regis and Seaton branches. As a result of the track improvements which had been undertaken for the '2MTs', the '14xxs' behaved much better this time but, nevertheless, their stay was short lived. They were replaced by single-car diesel units in March 1965, and these were used until the closure of the branch.

Just along the coast from Lyme Regis was Seaton, which saw its last train on 7 March 1966. When the Seaton branch had been transferred to the Western Region in 1963, the traditional 'M7' 0-4-4Ts had been replaced by push-pull fitted ex-GWR '64xx' class 0-6-0PTs, but DMUs were introduced on 4 November of that year. That spelt the end for the engine shed at Seaton. Early in 1965, a spate of DMU failures resulted in '14xx' class 0-4-2Ts being drafted in for temporary duties, but the diesels were reinstated and subsequently worked the branch until its closure. With the demise of the branch, Seaton Junction station on the main line was closed to passengers. There was a degree of irony about the closure of the Seaton branch. During the late 1950s and early 1960s, the traffic figures had not been at all bad, and over 1,000 passengers had used Seaton station on summer Saturdays. Nevertheless, the anti-closure lobby was far from vociferous and, in complete contrast to other closures of the period, the last train on 7 March 1966 carried only 11 passengers.

In North Devon, the ex-GWR Taunton-Barnstaple branch was closed to passengers on 3 October 1966. Although Barnstaple was the commercial centre of North Devon, the luxury of two railways into the town had been considered superfluous, and it had been decided that the better line was the old Southern Railway route from Exeter. Further closures in the area followed on 5 October 1970, when services on the Ilfracombe extension ceased. On that same date, the line from Exeter to Barnstaple was truncated at Barnstaple Junction, and the station at Barnstaple Town was closed completely. Since 1963, the regular services on the Exeter-Ilfracombe line had been worked by diesels, with multiple-units looking after the local services, and Class 22 and Class 42 locomotives handling the through workings. The last recorded steam working to Barnstaple was on 3 October 1965, when '4MT' 2-6-4T No 80043 hauled a four-coach portion of a special working from Waterloo. At Ilfracombe, dieselisation rendered the engine shed redundant and it was closed in 1964, but locomotives occasionally used the station's sidings as an unofficial stabling point until the line's closure.

The most drastic closure of 1966 occurred on 3 October. From that date, passenger services were withdrawn from the former Southern Railway line westwards from Meldon Junction, near Okehampton. This included the main line into Cornwall through Launceston, and also the branch between Halwill and Bude. On the Bude branch, the BR Standard 2-6-2Ts and 2-6-4Ts had gradually taken over in the late 1950s and early 1960s, but were replaced by DMUs in 1964. By then, the branch had come under WR control, and the official policy of that year was the extinction of steam haulage west of Exeter. Predictably, the engine shed at Bude was closed with the cessation of steam workings. Steam had a final fling on 5 September 1965, when Ivatt 2-6-2T No 41283 hauled an enthusiasts' special from Launceston to Okehampton.

In the Plymouth area, the former lines of the once-independent Plymouth, Devonport & South Western Junction Railway had mixed fortunes in the Beeching era. The main line section between St Budeaux and Bere Alston, and the branch section as far as Gunnislake both defied the trend of the day and remained open. However, from 7 September 1964, main line services were diverted on to the ex-GWR line at St Budeaux by means of the connection which had been laid during the war and, therefore, the trains were routed via Keyham into North Road station. Consequently, the ex-SR stations at Ford and Devonport were closed. The section of the branch between Gunnislake and Callington closed to all traffic on 5 November 1966; the introduction of DMUs in 1964 had

resulted in the closure of the engine shed at Callington in September of that year.

In 1952, ex-LMS 2-6-2Ts had started to appear on the Callington branch, and this had been bad news for the ex-PD&SWJR locomotives. One of the three PD&SWJR locomotives, SR No 756 *A.S.Harris*, had been transferred out of the area as early as 1931 and had been withdrawn in 1951 as BR No 30756, but the other two had remained active in their traditional area. At Nationalisation in 1948, those two had become BR Nos 30757/58 and had still carried their respective names of *Earl of Mount Edgcumbe* and *Lord St Levan* but, after 1954, their appearances on the Callington branch had been few and far between. In the early summer of 1956, both had been sent to Eastleigh for minor repairs, but instead of returning to Devon, had been retained as works shunters. No 30758 had been withdrawn in December 1956, and No 30757 had followed suit one year later.

Back in East Devon, passenger services were withdrawn from the Sidmouth branch on 6 March 1967, and Sidmouth Junction was closed simultaneously. The ex-LMS and BR Standard 2-6-2Ts and 2-6-4Ts had been ousted by DMUs on regular services in November 1963, and through workings from

Waterloo to Sidmouth on summer Saturdays had usually been entrusted to Class 22 or Class 35 diesel locomotives. The secondary branch, that from Tipton St Johns to Exmouth via Budleigh Salterton, closed to passengers on the same day as the Sidmouth branch. At the site of Sidmouth Junction, the singling of the main line on 11 June 1967 resulted in the severing of the connection with the branches, and the subsequent routeing of lifting trains via Exmouth. However, this presented a problem in 1968 when heavy flooding breached the remains of both branches, and left a train of disused wagons stranded at Tipton St Johns. Consequently, the rescue of the wagons and the remainder of the lifting work were undertaken by road. On a happier note, Sidmouth Junction station was reopened for commuter trains on 3 May 1971 under its original name of Feniton.

In contrast to the other East Devon branches, the Exeter-Exmouth line remained in a healthy position. Traffic figures were good, and even freight made a significant contribution. The docks at Exmouth provided the main source of freight and, over the years, the locomotives which had been used on dock shunting duties had ranged from the diminutive 'B4' class 0-4-0Ts to the sturdy 'G6' 0-6-0Ts. Passenger services on the Exmouth branch had, since the mid-1950s, been dominated by ex-LMS and BR Standard 2-6-2Ts and 2-6-4Ts, but the passing of the branch to the Western Region in 1963 resulted in '64xx' class 0-6-0PTs making the occasional guest appearances. The inevitable change to DMUs took place on 9 September 1963, and the engine shed at Exmouth was closed two months later.

The dieselisation of the Exmouth branch resulted in a number of the services being extended to St Davids station in Exeter but during the commuter periods, the majority of branch passengers used Central station which was far better situated for the hub of

Below:
Seen pulling out of Plymouth station, the 12.05 Newquay-Nottingham working on 1 September 1973 was in the care of Class 45 No 112. In spring of the following year, the station was remodelled with five through platform faces, one bay and four loading docks.
Philip D. Hawkins

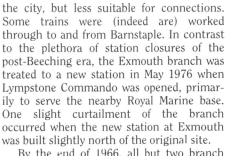
the city, but less suitable for connections. Some trains were (indeed are) worked through to and from Barnstaple. In contrast to the plethora of station closures of the post-Beeching era, the Exmouth branch was treated to a new station in May 1976 when Lympstone Commando was opened, primarily to serve the nearby Royal Marine base. One slight curtailment of the branch occurred when the new station at Exmouth was built slightly north of the original site.

By the end of 1966, all but two branch lines in Devon had closed and, furthermore, the former Southern Railway main line to Cornwall had not met, but had been removed from, its Waterloo. It seemed as if there were little left to close, but that was not to be the case. On 6 June 1968, passenger services were withdrawn on the Okehampton-Tavistock-Plymouth line, and the section between Yeoford and Okehampton suffered a similar fate on 5 June 1972. The engine shed at Okehampton had been demolished in 1966 following the closure of the Cornwall line. The last regular steam workings in the Okehampton area had been the stone trains from Meldon Quarry which had, for many years, been entrusted to 'N' class 2-6-0s. An unadvertised stopping place, Meldon Quarry halt, had opened for the benefit of railway workmen and their families as far back as 1890 and remained in use until May 1968, the month before the withdrawal of passenger services beyond Okehampton.

Below:
**The 'Britannia' 4-6-2s were infrequent
visitors to Kingswear, and the visit of
No 70024** *Vulcan* **on 28 July 1957 was,
it is believed, the class's only
appearance on the line that year. This
picture was taken between Churston
and Kingswear.** *D. S. Fish*

As for Meldon Quarry itself, its future was secured in 1982 when new machinery was installed and, by 1985, over 750,000 tonnes of rock were being processed at the quarry annually. Some 450,000 tonnes of that took the form of ballast, the SR and WR taking about half each, while various by-products were sold to private customers, principally in the construction industry. After the extinction of steam haulage, Class 33 diesels were, for many years, the usual locomotives to work the trains from Meldon Quarry, but Class 37s eventually took over.

Even in the 1970s, Devon's railway network was not immune from closures. The ex-LSWR line to Stonehouse Pool in Plymouth, which had once been looked on as a major source of Ocean Liner traffic, faded away unnoticed in 1970; it had seen no traffic whatsoever since 1966. Elsewhere in the dock areas of Plymouth, the almost disused spurs to Millbay and Sutton Harbour were officially closed in July 1971 and December 1973 respectively. The only former dock line at Plymouth to remain in use today is the Cattedown spur but, with the recent cessation of rail traffic to and from the Conoco Oil depot at Cattedown, only its bitumen traffic remains. Along with docks and harbours all over Britain, Plymouth's maritime trade has diminished significantly in the last few decades. As recently as 1962, Millbay docks recorded the handling of 1,401 vessels and over 177,000 tons of goods while, during the same year, Cattedown Wharves handled over 1,000,000 tons of imports and exports. The story at Exeter was similar. In 1962, the Canal Basin handled 54,762 tons of freight, of which 53,066 tons was classified as 'motor spirit', but trade dropped and the need for rail connections consequently lessened. Exeter's City Basin goods branch closed in September 1965, leaving little more than a private siding into the Texaco oil depot.

4-6-2 No 35013 *Blue Funnel* in charge from
Exeter. The 'ACE' itself was abruptly discontinued from 5 September 1964 as a consequence of the down-grading of the Waterloo-
Exeter route, but the final down train on
4 September was, most appropriately, steam-
hauled.

The demise of steam traction in Devon
resulted in the redundancy of the engine
shed at Exmouth Junction. The depot had
passed to the Western Region in 1963, and
had become recoded as 83D, still with its
sub-sheds at Bude, Callington, Exmouth,
Launceston, Lyme Regis, Okehampton and
Seaton. At the end of 1963, Exmouth Junction shed had a healthy allocation which
included 29 lightweight Bulleid Pacifics,
seven 'Merchant Navy' 4-6-2s and 24 'N' class
2-6-0s but, nevertheless, the new administration's policy of 'no steam west of Exeter'
meant that the future of Exmouth Junction
shed looked pretty grim. Official closure did
not take place until March 1967 and, by then,
the buildings were in an abysmal state of
repair. At Plymouth, the WR earmarked Friary shed for complete closure in May 1963,
and the remaining locomotives and staff
were transferred to Laira. Laira shed itself
had been recoded as 84A in September 1963,
by which time its allocation of steam locomotives was almost nil, and the inevitable
closure to steam ensued in April 1964.

On what was left of Devon's railway network, the diesel locomotives and, later, the
IC 125s perpetuated some of the traditional
train names which either headed for or
passed through the county. The 'Cornish
Riviera', the 'Night Riviera' and the 'Torbay
Express' from Paddington all continued to
appear in the timetables as did the 'Devonian' from Leeds (although not all have been
IC 125 operated). The 'Golden Hind' was
added in 1964, originally with a Class 52 at
the head of a seven-coach train, but it was
later given Pullman status with timings from
Paddington of 2hr 5min to Exeter and 3hr
5min to Plymouth. Later introductions were
the 'Mayflower' between Paddington and Plymouth and the 'Armada' between Leeds and
Plymouth. More recent innovations have
been the introduction of the 'Cornish Scot'
and the 'Devon Scot' from Glasgow and
Aberdeen respectively.

Throughout the history of Britain's railways, the general adage has been 'last in, first
out'. The first railways to be built were, on
the whole, between important towns and
cities where the long-term prospects for
traffic were reasonably good, and the railways which arrived later were, usually, not as
vital as their predecessors. Consequently, the
lines which have tended to escape closure are
those which arrived first. This is particularly
true in Devon, where the main-line flag is
kept flying by the route from Paddington,
through Exeter and Plymouth, and into

On the main lines in Devon, the Newton
Abbot-Kingswear line was truncated at
Paignton in January 1973, but preservationists stepped in straightaway to purchase the
Paignton-Kingswear section from BR and
subsequently reopen it with steam-hauled
services. On BR metals in Devon, locomotives started to give way to the IC 125s in the
autumn of 1979 and, within a few years,
locomotive-hauled passenger trains were
becoming candidates for the list of endangered species. The Exeter-Waterloo line
became the last bastion of regular locomotive haulage; in the late 1960s, the Class 42
'Warships' were used on most services on
that route, but they were superseded by
Class 33s and, later, Class 50s. At the time of
writing, locomotive-hauled trains are still

the norm on the Exeter-Waterloo route, but
plans are afoot to introduce Class 159 units.
Between 1972 and 1977, a Saturdays-only
Brighton-Exeter through working brought
Class 201 Hastings DEMUs to Exeter, but
that service reverted to locomotive haulage.
The ex-Southern Railway route was, for
many years, the Cinderella service to the
west and suffered in comparison with the ex-
GWR route. Although electrification was
considered, most recently, by Network
SouthEast, plans have never been progressed. The new Class 159s will, however,
bring modern rolling stock to the line.

The crack service on the Waterloo-Exeter
run was the 'Atlantic Coast Express'. The last
steam-hauled 'ACE' in the up direction ran
on 14 August 1964 with 'Merchant Navy'

Table 6.1: British Railways Shed Codes

A) November 1950 (Southern Region)

72A	Exmouth Junction. Sub-sheds: Bude, Callington, Exmouth, Lyme Regis, Okehampton, Seaton.
72D	Plymouth Friary.
72E	Barnstaple Junction. Sub-sheds: Ilfracombe, Torrington.

November 1950 (Western Region)

83A	Newton Abbot. Sub-sheds: Ashburton, Kingsbridge.
83B	Taunton (Somerset). Sub-shed: Barnstaple.
83C	Exeter. Sub-shed: Tiverton Junction.
83D	Plymouth Laira. Sub-shed: Launceston.

B) November 1963 (Western Region)

83A	Newton Abbot.
83B	Taunton (Somerset). Sub-shed: Tiverton Junction.
83D	Exmouth Junction. Sub-sheds: Bude, Callington, Okehampton, Seaton.
83F	Barnstaple Junction. Sub-shed: Ilfracombe.
84A	Plymouth Laira.

Cornwall. As for the branches, the Beeching programme saw off countless rural lines which had long since struggled to compete with the motor car, and the proliferation of country branches in Devon more or less ensured the reduction in the county's railway network. Today, the only surviving Devon branches are those from Exeter to Exmouth, Exeter to Barnstaple, and from Plymouth to Gunnislake via Bere Alston.

Ironically, two of the most charismatic railway lines in Devon were closed when Dr.Beeching was a mere youngster. The Bideford, Westward Ho! & Appledore Railway closed in 1917, and the Southern Railway gave up on its narrow gauge Lynton & Barnstaple line in 1935.

Below:
Two members of Exmouth Junction's heavy brigade were 'Z' class 0-8-0Ts Nos 30952/57, and they were photographed at Exeter Central in August 1959. *Horace H. Bleads*

Above:
Class 50 No 50010 *Monarch* and Class 47 No 47503 were caught snuggling alongside each other for warmth at Laira depot on 17 November 1987. *Brian Morrison*

Left:
Two-car Class 158 No 158871 stands at Tiverton Parkway on 30 October 1992 with the 09.55 ex-Cardiff service to Paignton. *Author*

Above:
Exeter St Davids is one of the most recognisable stations in the country. Here it is playing host to Class 47 No 47498 on the 13.30 Paddington-Penzance service on 21 July 1977. *Brian Morrison*

Left:
As part of the West of England Resignalling Scheme, a new power box was constructed at Exeter to replace the existing signalboxes. It is seen here under construction on 6 August 1984. Amongst those boxes made redundant by the construction of this new box was Exeter West, which has been preserved and is now reconstructed at the Crewe Heritage Centre. *C. G. Maggs*

Bottom left:
For many years the Class 50s were regularly to be seen in the West Country. Now all withdrawn from normal service, the type's happier days are recalled by this view of No 50032 climbing Dainton Bank on 12 January 1978 with the 10.30 Paddington-Plymouth service. *Mark S. Wilkins*

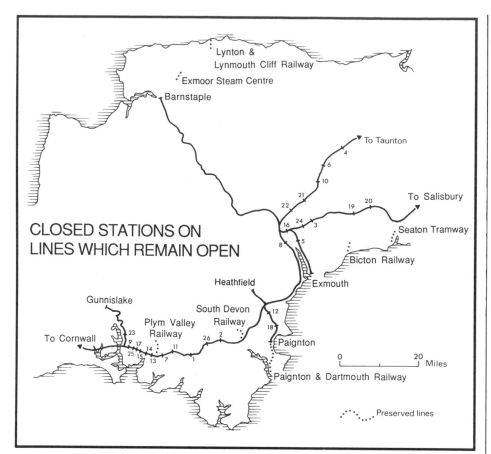

CLOSED STATIONS ON LINES WHICH REMAIN OPEN

Above:
Closed stations on lines which remain open to passengers.

Below:
Aller Junction is the point where the branch to Paignton diverges from the main line to Cornwall. An IC125 set, headed by No 43044, heads towards Newton Abbot with the 13.32 Penzance-Paddington service on 8 July 1980 passed the ex-GWR signalbox. Aller Junction box was another casualty of the West of England Resignalling Scheme, being closed in early 1987.
Brian Morrison

7. The Industrials

Throughout Britain, many of the earliest railways were descendants of horse-operated freight tramways. This was particularly true in heavily industrialised areas, and it goes part of the way to explain why the northeast of England was one of the first entrants into the railway stakes. During the early 1800s, the prime source of fuel was coal; consequently, heavy industry tended to be centred around mining areas, and tramways were found to provide an effective means of transportation, not only for the coal, but also for other raw materials. In Devon, coal deposits were negligible, and so it might seem strange that industrial tramways appeared there as early as 1756, but the first tramways in the county were constructed to transport something completely different. That commodity was stone.

The Early Non-mechanical Tramways

In 1756, a timber-railed tramway was used by John Smeaton during the reconstruction of the Eddystone Lighthouse. The old lighthouse had burned down in 1755, and Smeaton was under strict instructions to build a stone replacement as quickly as possible. As the Eddystone Rocks were not exactly the ideal place for intricate stonemasonry, Smeaton ingeniously took to having a 'dry run' with each layer of stones at Plymouth before transporting the stones to the site, and his wooden tramway was used for bringing the stones to the trial assembly point at Plymouth. This was the first known tramway in Devon. Another very early 'railway' in the county was the 3ft 6in gauge plateway which opened at Oreston in August 1812. This was used by the civil engineer, John Rennie, who was in charge of constructing the breakwater in Plymouth Sound. The plateway was used for the transportation of the foundation stones from the quarry to the pier at Oreston, from where a fleet of 10 boats operated a form of 'roll on/roll off' shuttle service to the site of the breakwater. The tracks in the quarry survived for many years and, interestingly for industrial archaeologists with access to a boat, rails can still be seen today in the surface of the breakwater itself.

Both of those early horse-operated tramways were constructed for use with specific civil engineering contracts and, consequently, they have often tended to be over-looked. By default, the distinction of Devon's first tramway is more usually credited to the Haytor Tramway. This 7-mile line opened on 16 September 1820 to connect the quarries at Haytor Rock to the Stover Canal at Teigngrace. The traffic to be carried was granite. Apart from the debatable claim of being the first 'railway' in Devon, the line's other main distinction was that its tracks were made, not from iron, but granite blocks. The blocks were about 1ft 3in wide but their lengths varied between 4ft and 8ft; they were laid end-to-end without joints. The gauge was 4ft 3in, and in contrast to later railway practice, it narrowed on the curves; this no doubt explains why some sources refer to 'the 4ft gauge Haytor Tramway'. The line was worked exclusively by horses, although the 1,300ft climb with the empties back from Teigngrace to Haytor must have presented Neddy with a fair old challenge.

During the 1850s, quarries elsewhere found that they could extract and transport granite more cheaply, and so the workings around Haytor went into decline. The tramway was abandoned in 1858, but the durability of the granite tracks was such that many sections can still be clearly seen today. Some of the stone used in the construction of the National Gallery, the British Museum and London Bridge came from the quarries at Haytor and, therefore, will have been conveyed over Devon's pioneering 'railway'.

Above:
In this undated photograph, one of Devonport Dockyard's 'Planet' shunters, Yard No 4858, is seen at the exchange sidings. The BR locomotive in the picture, 0-6-0PT No 9711, was a Laira engine for much of its life. *Hugh Davies*

The Haytor Granite Co, which owned the tramway, also had a small quarry at Dewerstone Rock on the south western edge of Dartmoor, and a tramway was built there in 1858. It was horse-operated, and the original intention had been to link up with the South Devon Railway's branch to Tavistock, which was due to open the following year. However, the connection with the branch was never made, and the tramway was to be used only sporadically.

Whereas the Haytor Tramway and Smeaton's Eddystone Lighthouse tramway in Plymouth compete with each other for the title of Devon's first real 'railway', there is little dispute about the line which acted as the first carrier of public goods in the county. This was the Plymouth & Dartmoor Railway, which opened its 4ft 6in gauge horse-operated system between King's Tor, near Princetown, and Sutton Harbour at Plymouth on 26 September 1823.

As soon as its line opened, the P&DR found itself in a catch-22 situation. An extension into Princetown itself was essential for the survival of the railway, but the company had no funds left for its construction. The saviours who financed the building of the extension were the Johnson brothers who, as the major quarry owners at King's Tor, needed the Princetown section for their own business. However, constant wranglings between the Johnsons and the P&DR hampered the growth of what should have been, in theory, a highly-useful railway. Apart from transporting granite from the numerous quarries in the Princetown area to Sutton Harbour, the railway also had traffic on the return journey to Princetown in the form of lime, coal and timber. Although the prison at Princetown had started taking in French prisoners of war in 1809, the end of the Napoleonic Wars in 1815 had reduced the number of inmates from 5,000 to nil, and so the railway rather missed the boat regarding the transportation of prison supplies and unfortunate Frenchmen. Throughout the 22-mile route of the P&DR, its most famous feature was the 620yd tunnel at Leigham which, according to the railway company at least, was the first tunnel on a public railway anywhere in the world.

The P&DR stumbled along keeping only a short step away from insolvency. In the early 1870s, the company spent what little money it had on relaying the line but, by then, there was no chance of a reversal of fortunes. This was mainly due to the opening of the broad gauge locomotive-operated Tavistock branch in 1859 which offered a far superior means of transportation between Plymouth and Yelverton. The Tavistock branch was worked by the South Devon Railway, and that company had muscled in on the P&DR in previous years. In 1853, the SDR had added a broad gauge rail to the section of the P&DR between Laira Junction and Sutton Harbour, although the Sutton Harbour branch was later relaid as two separate, but parallel, tracks one to the P&DR's gauge, and the other to that of the SDR.

Despite the widespread use of steam traction elsewhere, the P&DR struggled on in its non-mechanical state. Predictably, the traffic on the P&DR's section between Yelverton and Plymouth grew more and more erratic after the opening of the Tavistock branch, and the final nail in the company's coffin came with the proposal of a standard gauge passenger-carrying branch from Yelverton to Princetown. The branch was promoted by the Princetown Railway, but that company was little more than a subsidiary of the GWR, and the P&DR happily sold the Princetown section of the tramway to the railway company. The branch opened in 1883. Nevertheless, the P&DR remained open for business between Yelverton and Plymouth until 1900, when the section above Crabtree was finally abandoned. The rails were lifted in 1916.

There were several other tramways in Devon which did not graduate to mechanical traction, and a number of these were on the western edge of Dartmoor, where there were extensive mineral deposits. The earliest was the 3ft gauge plateway at Wheal Friendship, near Mary Tavy, which opened in 1826 and was used until the mine's closure in 1873. A few miles to the south of Mary Tavy was the 4½-mile long Tavistock canal, the basin of which was linked by a rope-worked edge-rail incline to Morwellham Quay on the River Tamar. From the basin, the canal ran through a 1½-mile tunnel to Buctor, and then on to Mill Hill. The Buctor-Mill Hill section of the canal was replaced by a tramway in 1846, but it soon fell into decline and was out of use by 1860.

Other horse-operated lines in South Devon included the wooden-railed Zeal Tor Tramway of 1847, which linked the peat workings at Redlake to Shipley Bridge, above South Brent on the River Avon. It is believed to have fallen into disuse in the early 1880s. At Bulkamore, north of Rattery, an iron mine was linked by means of a tramway to the Ashburton branch between Staverton and Buckfastleigh, but the mine and the tramway were operational only for a short period in the mid-1870s. The standard gauge Rattlebrook Tramway was opened in 1879 to serve a peat works over 1,000ft up on the western slopes of Amicombe Hill; it connected with the LSWR just to the north of Bridestowe station, and was operational until 1930. To the north of Bridestowe, the Fatherford Tramway linked a quarry near Belstone to the main line near Okehampton station; it is believed that the tramway opened in the 1890s, but its later history is uncertain.

In North Devon, a horse-operated narrow gauge tramway system was opened by the New Florence Mining Co in 1874. It linked the iron mines near South Radworthy to the GWR's Taunton-Barnstaple branch near South Molton, but fell into disuse after mining ceased in 1894. Elsewhere in the county, horse-worked tramways were used by the Grand Western Canal Co to serve the quarries at Ponds Green, Westleigh and Whipcott in the Tiverton area.

The horse-operated tramways in Devon were, with one notable exception, fairly localised affairs, and in view of their spheres of operation, it was unsurprising that they did not convert to locomotive haulage. That exception was the Plymouth & Dartmoor Railway which was, from the outset, a carrier of public goods. Considering that the P&DR was severely affected by competing locomotive-operated railways, it is quite remarkable that the company remained active until 1900. By then, steam was the usual form of traction for, not only main and branch line railways, but also many industrial lines, and the rest of this chapter deals with the private and industrial railways of Devon which progressed beyond four-legged traction.

Plymouth

The main private user of locomotives in Plymouth, and for that matter all of Devon, was the Ministry of Defence. The naval base at Devonport dates back to 1691, and despite MoD cutbacks, Plymouth is still a major centre for operations; at the time of writing, at least, there are also armament depots at Bullpoint and Ernesettle, just to the north of Devonport. A short tramway opened in the dockyard in 1857, but this did little more than provide a connection through the tunnel which linked North and South Yards. In 1867, the first real railway opened in the dockyard, and the system grew as the dockyard expanded; by 1907, the two extremities of the dockyard railway were some two miles apart. The majority of the system was standard gauge from the off, but it is known that there were interchange facilities with the broad gauge spur from the Cornwall Railway's main line which was laid into the dockyard in April 1869. The broad gauge line into the dockyard ran, nominally at least, to Keyham Admiralty platform where a regular, but unadvertised, passenger service operated until 1954.

Such was the extent of Devonport Dockyard that an internal passenger service was introduced in 1900; it ran every 30min during working hours. The coach bodies, which were mounted on secondhand frames, were constructed in the dockyard's workshops; the custom building was not so much out of grandeur, but primarily because the bore of the 856yd tunnel between North and South Yards precluded the use of conventional-size rolling stock. The Navy was not the least class-conscious of organisations, and so the carriages were designed to offer six classes of accommodation, the official titles of which were:
1) Admiral Superintendent and Principal Dockyard Officers.
2) Superior and Commissioned Officers.
3) Subordinate Officers.
4) Chief Petty Officers and Petty Officers.
5) Chargemen and Recorders.
6) Dockyard Workmen.

Only the first three classes were treated to padded seats and gas lamps; the rest owed more than a little to the 'Parliamentary' style which had appeared on Britain's main line railways in the 1840s.

There were six recognised stopping places for the dockyard passenger trains but none had even a raised platform; they were known as Extension, Cantilever, North Yard, Central Office, Morice Yard and South Yard. The passenger service operated until 13 May 1966, when road improvements allowed the use of buses, thereby giving greater flexibility to transport within the dockyard area.

The first locomotive to be used in Devonport Dockyard was an Aveling & Porter geared 0-4-0T, Works No 450, which was delivered in 1866. Between 1898 and 1950, a succession of 0-4-0STs were purchased for dockyard duties, the majority being supplied new by either Hawthorn Leslie or Andrew Barclay. There were two secondhand acquisitions; one was a 0-4-0ST of 1882 which was purchased in 1907 from the contractor, Sir John Jackson, and the other was a Barclay 0-4-0ST of 1915 which spent a short time at the Naval depot at Rosyth before arriving at Devonport. Diesel shunters started to appear in 1955, and all but one of Devonport's stud were 150hp 'Planet' locomotives from the works of F. C. Hibberd. The exception was a Strachan & Henshaw Ro-Rail diesel which was delivered in 1967 but, much to the delight of the staff, dispensed with in 1969.

Most of the steam locomotives were

retired in the mid-1950s, but four remained in action until the withdrawal of the passenger services in 1966. Two of these were eventually purchased by preservationists. One was a Barclay locomotive of 1946, which was acquired by the Dowty Preservation Society at Ashchurch in March 1968 before being transferred to its present home at Norchard in the Forest of Dean, and the other was a Bagnall engine of 1950, which went to the Great Western Society at Bodmin in February 1969 and now performs very happily indeed on the Bodmin & Wenford Railway. The locomotives were nominally based at the engine shed in North Yard, which was a three-road structure with a corrugated iron front and a stone rear, but some of the diesels were, in later years, regularly out-stationed at South Yard. At the time of writing, two Planet diesel locomotives, Yard Nos 4858/60, remain in action at Devonport, and a third, Yard No 5199, is still on site but out of use.

Between 1896 and 1907, Devonport Dockyard was treated to another bout of major extensions, and the main civil engineering contractor was Sir John Jackson. Jackson had a fleet of locomotives of his own, and over 20 different engines were known to have been used on his Devonport contracts at one time or another. Of these, most were 0-4-0STs or 0-6-0STs which were built either by Manning Wardle or Andrew Barclay, and many had previously seen service on the construction work of the Manchester Ship Canal.

Just to the north of Devonport Dockyard, an armaments depot opened at Bullpoint in 1916 with a standard gauge connection to the GWR just beyond the southern end of St Budeaux station. An internal 1ft 6in gauge railway system was established at Bullpoint, and the tiny locomotives were, at first, four-wheeled battery electric machines built by Wingrove & Rogers of Kirkby, but these were

Above:
One of Devonport Dockyard's 'Planet' diesel shunters is seen at the head of the internal passenger train. *Hugh Davies*

Left:
Devonport Dockyard's Barclay 0-4-0ST No 18 of 1942 was photographed in March 1956. Note how its livery differs from that of the locomotives shown in the other pictures. *Frank Jones*

Table 7.1: Devonport Dockyard Steam Locomotives

No	Type	Builder	W/No	Date	Wheels	Cyls	Weight	Withdrawn
—	0-4-0T	Aveling Porter	450	1869	3ft 0in	7¾x10	9¾t	?
1	0-4-0ST	Hawthorn Leslie	2399	1898	3ft 0½in	12x18	20t	1948
2	0-4-0ST	Hawthorn Leslie	2400	1898	3ft 0½in	12x18	20t	1949
3*	0-4-0ST	reb.J.Jackson 1903	?	1882	2ft 9in	10x16	15¾t	1935
6	0-4-0T	Hawthorn Leslie	2599	1904	2ft 10in	12x15	34t	1955
7	0-4-0ST	Hawthorn Leslie	2820	1910	3ft 0½in	12x18	21t	1957
8	0-4-0ST	Hawthorn Leslie	2821	1910	3ft 0½in	12x18	21t	1955
9*	0-4-0ST	Andrew Barclay	1406	1915	3ft 5in	14x22	28t	1957
10	0-4-0ST	Andrew Barclay	1379	1914	3ft 2in	12x20	22t	1957
11	0-4-0ST	Andrew Barclay	1380	1914	3ft 2in	12x20	22t	1957
12	0-4-0ST	Avonside	1690	1915	3ft 3in	14x20	25t	1959
13	0-4-0ST	Andrew Barclay	1397	1915	3ft 5in	14x22	28t	1959
14	0-4-0ST	Hawthorn Leslie	3200	1916	3ft 6in	14x22	27t	1957
15	0-4-0ST	Hawthorn Leslie	3201	1916	3ft 6in	14x22	27t	1957
16	0-4-0ST	Andrew Barclay	1516	1919	3ft 5in	14x22	28t	1955
17	0-4-0ST	Andrew Barclay	2071	1939	3ft 2in	12x20	22t	1968
18	0-4-0ST	Andrew Barclay	2137	1942	3ft 2in	12x20	22t	1968
19†	0-4-0ST	Andrew Barclay	2221	1946	3ft 2in	12x20	22t	1968 P
19	0-4-0ST	William Bagnall	2962	1950	3ft 6in	14½x22	27t	1969 P

* Secondhand acquisitions: No 3 purchased 1907; No 9 obtained 1915.
† Became No 2 in 1950.
P Locomotive preserved.

Below:
This impressive turnout of Devonport Dockyard motive power was photographed during the mid-1950s.
Hugh Davies

Above:
Escombe Lambert's 18-ton Planet diesel of 1948, Works No 3281, is seen on duty at Victoria Wharf on 9 May 1991. *M. G. East*

eventually ousted by small Ruston & Hornsby diesels. The locomotives were replaced by road tractors in 1958. Some of the disused track from the standard gauge siding to St Budeaux was donated in 1988 to the Plym Valley Railway for relaying at its Marsh Mills site.

The third naval establishment in Plymouth was the armaments depot at Ernesettle, on the northern outskirts of the city. A standard gauge siding connected with the LSWR's Plymouth-Tavistock line south of Tamerton Foliot station, and a 2ft 6in gauge internal system, complete with a line to a jetty on the River Tamar, was built in 1938 in anticipation of increased production as the possibility of war became more and more likely. A succession of diesel shunters was used, all but one being four-wheeled machines. The last new diesel to be acquired was a Hunslet locomotive which appeared in 1967, and from 1972, it was the only survivor at Ernesettle. That locomotive was eventually replaced by a pair of 'Unimogs', vehicles which were equipped to work on either rails or roads.

For transfer duties at Ernesettle's interchange sidings, the MoD based a standard gauge diesel locomotive at the site as early as 1945. The use of diesel traction in an armaments depot might seem an obvious safety precaution but, until the early 1960s, the goods wagons arriving at or departing from the exchange sidings were invariably hauled by a steam locomotive. Even the lightweight Bulleid Pacifics were known to have been used for hauling goods to and from Ernesettle, and the sight of one of those blowing

sparks so close to a depot where explosives were handled must have alarmed even the strongest-hearted individuals.

Elsewhere in Plymouth, the LSWR opened a freight spur from Laira Bridge to Cattewater in 1880, and extended it to Cattedown in 1888. At the end of the ¾-mile line at Cattedown, the shipowning firm of Powell & Hough (later part of Coast Lines and now Escombe Lambert) had its own standard gauge sidings to serve Victoria Wharf. The sidings terminated in a headshunt which was situated inside a short tunnel underneath Queen Anne's Place, and the tunnel also acted as the engine shed. Unfortunately, details of the locomotives used at the wharf are sparse, but it is known that a 0-6-0ST named *Alicia* was used and, sometime during the locomotive's life, it was converted to a 0-4-0ST. A pair of four-wheeled Planet locomotives were also used at Victoria Wharf, one being a 60hp petrol machine of 1933, and the other a diesel locomotive of 1948. A further petrol locomotive, which had been supplied by Howards of Bedford, is believed to have seen service at the wharf. The steam locomotive was scrapped in 1935 and the Planet petrol locomotive met its demise in 1956 but, at the time of writing, the Planet diesel remains on site in full working order, although its last reported use was in 1991. Along the rest of the Cattedown branch, the Plymouth Tar Distilleries made only a brief venture into the world of industrial locomotives. It acquired a 22-year old Planet diesel shunter from Weston-super-Mare Gasworks in 1968, but the machine was sold to preservationists in 1971.

At Plymstock, just to the east of Plymouth, the Associated Portland Cement Co opened a standard gauge siding into its works in 1963, and a new Thomas Hill 0-4-0 diesel locomotive was purchased for shunting between the works and the interchange point on the site of Plymstock station. Rail

traffic to the works ceased in 1988, and the locomotive was passed to the Plym Valley Railway for preservation. The only other recorded use of industrial locomotives in the Plymouth area was at Hooe Lake Quarry, near Oreston, where four-wheeled Simplex diesel shunters were introduced on the 2ft gauge internal system in the mid-1930s. The US Army took over the quarry during World War 2, and the last locomotive was sold in 1949.

South Devon

Earlier in this chapter, the story of the horse-operated Plymouth & Dartmoor Railway was told, and one of the company's quarry branches was from Crabtree to Cann Quarry. In September 1858, the Lee Moor Tramway opened its 8½-mile line from Plym Bridge, on the P&DR's Cann Quarry branch, to the clay pits at Lee Moor. The Lee Moor Tramway was a completely separate undertaking but, as it had to rely on its physical connection with the P&DR, it was also built to the 4ft 6in gauge and was horse-operated. The LMT had intended to commence operations before 1858, but its line had been so poorly constructed that it had had to be partially rebuilt even before it had opened. The line had two rope-worked inclines, one at Cann Wood and the other at Torycombe. Unlike the P&DR, the Lee Moor Tramway eventually decided to upgrade part of its line for locomotive haulage; the section of the LMT to be modernised was the 2½-mile stretch between the inclines at Cann Wood and Torycombe, but horse-power was retained for the remaining parts of the tramway.

For its locomotive-operated section, the LMT purchased two 0-4-0STs from Pecketts of Bristol; they were 4ft 6in gauge versions of the maker's standard 'M4' class with 2ft 6in wheels and 10in x 14in outside cylinders.

Right:
**The passing place at Plym Bridge
Incline, on the Lee Moor Tramway, was
photographed in 1933.** *R. W. Kidner*

Below:
**Peckett-built 0-4-0ST *Lee Moor No 2*
was photographed near the level
crossing at Torycombe in 1931. On the
Lee Moor Tramway, both locomotives
always faced towards Cann Wood.**
R. C. Sambourne

They carried Peckett's Works Nos 783/84 and
were christened, most imaginatively, *Lee
Moor Nos 1/2*. Changes in the method of clay
production caused the upper section of the
LMT to fall into disuse early this century, but
the section southwards from Torycombe
remained in regular use until World War 2.
Traffic resumed after the war, albeit very
intermittently, but after 1947, the only activity on the tramway was the occasional
haulage of a truck of sand from Marsh Mills
to Plymouth, and this was done mainly to
preserve the status of a right of way. By 1954,
the line, the locomotives and the wagons had
become derelict.

In 1960, it was decided to lay a pipeline
for carrying liquid clay from the Lee Moor
area, and the old trackbed between
Torycombe and Marsh Mills was used for its
route. The last of the tramway rails in the
Laira and Cattewater areas of Plymouth were
lifted in June 1962, but the LMT's story does
not end there. In 1964, a preservation society
was formed, and the two derelict Peckett
locomotives and the old engine shed at
Torycombe were acquired for restoration. At
Marsh Mills, the clay drying works had perpetuated the tradition of industrial locomotives as early as 1948, when it had acquired
its own diesel shunter. This was replaced by a
fireless 0-4-0 in 1957, and a second locomotive, a Vulcan 0-4-0 diesel shunter, was purchased in 1970. The last privately-owned
shunter at the Marsh Mills site was ex-BR
Class 08 No 08 801 which, with its new name
of *Annabel*, was transferred to the ECC plant
at Blackpool on 24 January 1991. Since then,
shunting has been carried out by BR under
contract, and up to five trains of loaded 'CDA'
wagons leave the works behind a Class 37
each weekday.

Left:
**A train of wagons loaded with clay is
seen being drawn by a pair of horses on
the Lee Moor Tramway on 23 August
1933. The tracks being crossed were,
in fact, the main Plymouth-Exeter line
at Laira.** *R. W. Kidner*

The Lee Moor Tramway had opened its horse-operated line in September 1858 and, just seven miles or so to the west, another mineral railway opened in November 1859. However, while the LMT took 41 years to convert to locomotive haulage, the newcomer had no hesitation about using steam traction from the outset. The new arrival was a standard gauge railway built specifically to transport the copper from the Devon Great Consolidated Mining Co's workings north of Chilsworthy. Mining for copper and arsenic had started in the area in 1844 and, in its heyday, Devon Great Consols, as it became known, was one of the largest sources of copper in the world with its five separate mines covering an area of 167 acres. The railway started from Wheal Anna Maria, on the edge of Blanchdown Wood, and took a circuitous 4½-mile route via other mines before reaching a point overlooking Morwellham Quay. The final leg to the quay was by means of a ½-mile long cable-worked incline.

Prior to the opening of the Devon Great Consols's railway in 1859, two outside-cylindered 0-4-0Ts had been ordered from Gilkes Wilson & Co, and this dynamic duo went on to handle all the line's traffic for 23 years. They were eventually replaced by 0-4-0STs which were built by John Spittle of Newport, one being named *Hugo*, and the other *Ada*. The first of those arrived in 1882 and the other in 1896, and their respective works numbers of 3 and 5 emphasised that Mr Spittle was hardly the most prolific locomotive builder in the land. By the end of the century, the mining was very much in decline, and Devon Great Consols Ltd went into vol-

untary liquidation in December 1901; the railway was therefore closed. At that time, *Hugo* was under repair at Newport but, although *Ada* was also set for a return to South Wales, it was used instead on the construction of the PD&SWJR's standard gauge Bere Alston-Callington branch. It was later earmarked for similar construction tasks for a railway between the GWR's Princetown branch and Merrivale quarries, but that line was never to be completed. *Ada* was sold to the Belgian Government in 1915, and saw out her days at Flanders.

Mention was made of the PD&SWJR's Callington branch. This had started life as a 3ft 6in gauge locomotive-operated railway in 1872 under the ownership of the East Cornwall Mineral Railway, and the tale of the ECMR is related along with the story of the PD&SWJR in Chapter Four.

Elsewhere in South Devon, the impecunious Teign Valley Railway opened its GWR-worked branch from Heathfield to Ashton in 1882, and the line was extended to Exeter in 1903. One object of the branch was to provide transportation for the area's mineral deposits, and privately-owned railways were established by three of the local mining and quarrying companies. One was a 1½-mile line from Christow station to a barytes quarry near Bridford, the last section being by means of a rope-worked incline. Two 0-4-0STs were used at different times, until the quarry's closure in 1932. A quarry near Trusham was connected to Christow station by means of an aerial ropeway, from the end of which a 2ft gauge tramway ran to the quarry itself. Small diesel locomotives were used on the tramway until it was dismantled in 1953. Another quarry near Trusham had a

Right:

Morwellham Quay, on the banks of the River Tamar, was the terminus of both the Devon Great Consols railway and the Tavistock Canal. This extract is from the 25in Ordnance Survey map of 1885 and shows the approach of the DGC's self-acting incline to the quay. In the 60 years that the DGC's mines were working, some 700,000 tons of copper and 72,000 tons of arsenic were extracted, and most was transported to Morwellham by means of the railway. At one time, over 200 people lived and worked at Morwellham and the hotel shown on the map (marked 'P.H.'), the Ship Inn, was usually full with visiting mine agents, ships' captains and other interested industrialists. Almost parallel with the railway in the upper part of the map can be seen the site of the Tavistock Canal's edge-rail incline. The canal basin, which was 237ft above Morwellham, is just off the map, but the canal dock on the River Tamar can be clearly seen near the school. The canal had been abandoned some 25 years before this map was made, but it continued to provide a major source of water power until Morwellham fell into decline early this century. The water was directed downhill by means of purpose-built leats to power a series of wheels, these being used not only to drive hauling winches but also to grind manganese ore. *Crown Copyright*

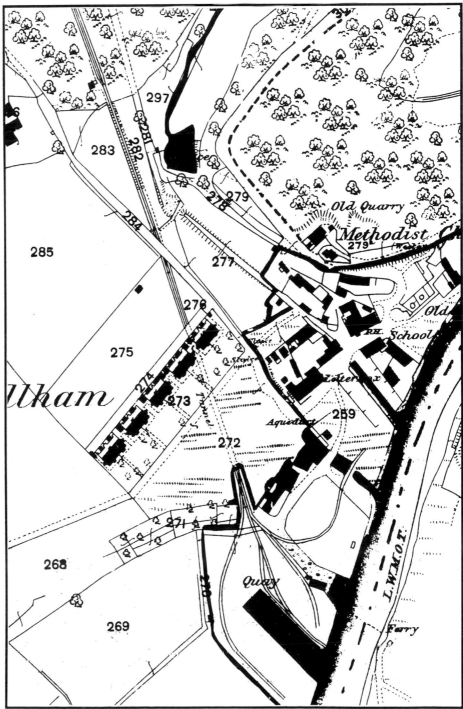

standard gauge siding which connected with the Teign Valley branch near Christow and, between 1911 and 1917, it was worked by an Avonside 0-4-0ST named *Finetta*.

To the north of Newton Abbot, a 2ft gauge tramway served a clay pit at Preston, and diminutive four-wheeled petrol shunters were in use between 1920 and 1954. Just to the south of Preston, a small mining complex was started in 1963, and a battery-electric locomotive was used on the 2ft 6in gauge internal system. The expansive limestone quarry at Stoneycombe, to the south of Newton Abbot near Dainton, used locomotives on its 2ft gauge system from 1932, the first being a Kerr Stuart 0-4-0ST, and the second a four-wheeled Simplex diesel. Road vehicles took over in the early 1950s, by which time one of the quarry's major products was ballast for the Western Region of British Railways. At Hennock, near Bovey Tracey, a haematite mine had been operational since 1902, but did not convert to locomotive traction until 1957. Gauges of 1ft 6in and 2ft were used on alternate levels, and small battery-electric locomotives were used until the company ceased trading in 1969.

Further south, the 3ft gauge Redlake Tramway opened on 11 September 1911 to connect the china clay works at Brown Heath, almost in the middle of Dartmoor and 1,400ft above sea level, to the GWR line between Ivybridge and Bittaford. From the GWR line, a 600ft cable-worked incline provided access to the tramway, which then started its 7½-mile journey across the moors. From the outset, the tramway was worked by locomotives, and the engine which was delivered in 1911 was Kerr Stuart 0-4-2T *C. A. Hanson*, Works No 1228, which had 2ft 2in driving wheels and 9½in x 15in outside cylinders. Another Kerr Stuart locomotive, 0-4-2ST *Dartmoor*, Works No 1146, was purchased in 1912, and this had 2ft driving wheels and outside cylinders of 7in x 12in. The purpose of the tramway was not to transport clay from the works, as a pipeline was used for that purpose. Instead, it carried coal to the works and sand from it, and workmen were accommodated in both directions.

The Rediake Tramway's first locomotive, *C. A. Hanson*, was scrapped in 1921, but a replacement did not appear until 1928. The new arrival was a four-wheeled vertical-boilered tank engine which had been built by the Atkinson Walker Wagon Works of Preston in Lancashire. Apart from one short break in production, the works continued operating until 1932. Its closure in that year rendered the tramway redundant; the two remaining locomotives were sold for scrap in 1933, and the rails were lifted in 1935. Records show that a 2ft gauge Kerr Stuart 0-4-0ST, Works No 1190, was delivered to the line in 1911, and it is generally assumed that this locomotive was used during the construction of the tramway; it was returned to the manufacturer in part-exchange for the 3ft gauge 0-4-2ST *Dartmoor* in 1912.

At Pitts Cleave Quarry, near Tavistock, a standard gauge siding connected with the Tavistock-Launceston branch, and was worked by a diesel shunter from 1927; there

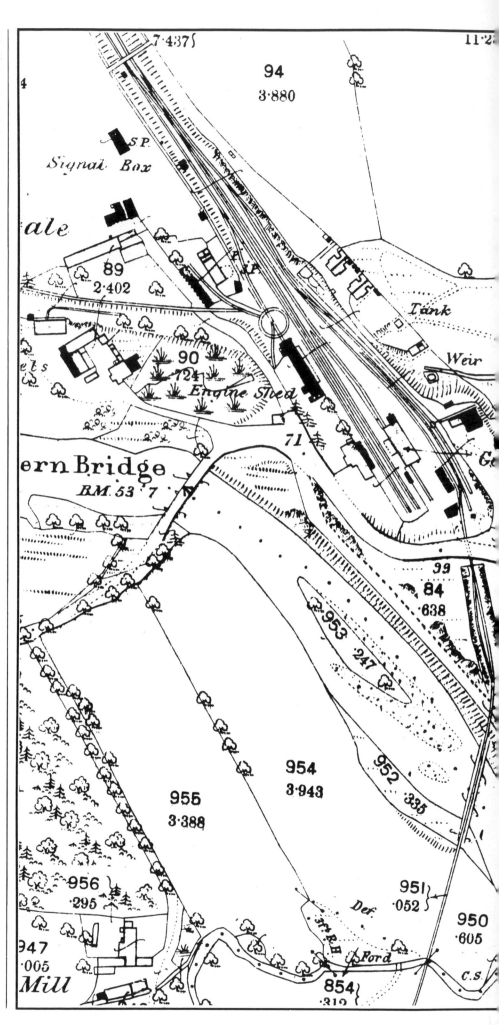

Left:
This 25in Ordnance Survey map of Torrington dates to 1887 and, therefore, the track to the south of the station is the 3ft gauge line to Peters Marland clay works. The standard gauge Torrington-Halwill branch did not materialise until 1925. *Crown Copyright*

Right:
This former London tram was converted for carrying workers on the Peters Marland 3ft gauge system. The picture was taken at the clay works on 5 July 1912. *LCGB/Ken Nunn Collection*

Below:
A Bagnall 0-6-0T was bought new in 1883 for work at Peters Marland, where it was given No 2 and named *Marland*. This picture of the locomotive on site is undated, but must have been taken before 1925 as the machine was scrapped that year. *Ian Allan Library*

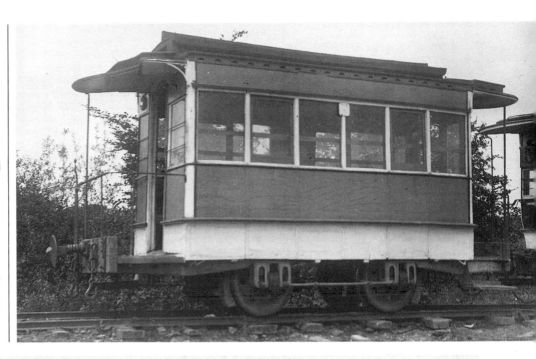

was a locomotive-worked 2ft gauge tramway in the quarry itself. The standard and narrow gauge operations ceased in 1963, the year before BR closed the Tavistock branch completely. Another quarry near Tavistock, that of the South Devon Granite Co, used a petrol shunter on its 2ft gauge tramway between 1928 and 1935.

North Devon

One of the most expansive industrial railways in the whole of Devon is the system which once served the North Devon Clay Co's works at Merton and Peters Marland, to the south of Torrington. North Devon was one of the three largest sources of heavy ball clay in Britain, and the industrial revolution of the mid-1800s enabled the clay to be extracted at a previously unseen rate. The move to rail haulage was a logical progression.

The clay company opened the 3ft gauge Marland Light Railway in 1880, ostensibly for the purpose of transporting the clay to Torrington where the LSWR had arrived in 1872, but the narrow gauge line also carried workmen to and from the clay pits. For the passengers, the railway operated a pair of converted single-deck London tramcars, which must surely have been among the most unusual railway carriages anywhere in Britain. In its entirety, the line stretched for eight miles. It left the station yard at Torrington and crossed the River Torridge on a spindly 40ft-high timber viaduct; from there, it passed through Watergate and continued up a 1 in 45 bank near Yarde on its way to the mining complex. At Peters Marland, the railway was routed via several drying sheds and a number of pits before terminating adjacent to the Merton-Petrockstow road.

Steam traction was used from the outset, and the first locomotive was a 0-6-0ST which was purchased new from Black Hawthorn in 1880. By 1908, the motive power fleet comprised eight locomotives, some of which had been bought new and others secondhand. Among the secondhand machines was a trio of Fletcher Jennings 0-4-0STs of 1873-75 vintage which had previously been used on the construction of the breakwater at Jersey Harbour. The three were rebuilt as 0-4-0Ts between 1910 and 1915, two receiving surgery on site at Peters Marland, and one of those became the last steam locomotive to remain in action at the clayworks. It was retired in March 1952. However, the demise of steam did not mean the end of the railway; diesel locomotives had started to appear in 1947, and six new diesel shunters made their debuts between then and 1965.

In 1925, the Southern Railway opened the new standard gauge branch line between Torrington and Halwill, and much of the 5¾-mile section between Torrington and Dunsbear was built on the trackbed of the Marland Light Railway. Consequently, a standard gauge exchange siding had to be provided at

Table 7.2: 3ft 0in Gauge Locomotives of the Marland Light Railway

No	Name	Type	Builder	Date	Wheels	Cyls	Acquired	Withdrawn
1	*Mary*	0-6-0ST	Black Hawthorn	1880	1ft 8in	7x10	1880	1925
2	*Marland*	0-6-0T	Bagnall	1883	?	7½x10	1883	1925
3	*Peter*	0-4-0T	Stephen Lewin	1871	1ft 9in	?	?	1925
11	*Avonside*	0-6-0ST	Avonside	1901	1ft 8in	7x10	1901	1925
—	*Jersey I*	0-4-0T	Fletcher Jennings	1873	2ft 9in	9x16	1908	1949
—	*Jersey II*	0-4-0T	Fletcher Jennings	1874	2ft 9in	9x16	1908	1952
4	*Merton*	0-4-0T	Fletcher Jennings	1875	2ft 9in	9x16	1908	1949
—	*Forward*	4w diesel	Fowler	1947	2ft 0in	(40HP)	1947	1970
—	*Advance*	4w diesel	Fowler	1949	2ft 0in	(40HP)	1949	1970
—	*Efficiency*	4w diesel	Fowler	1951	2ft 0in	(40HP)	1951	1974
98	—	4w diesel	Ruston Hornsby	1959	2ft 0in		1959	1972
93	—	4w diesel	Ruston Hornsby	1961	2ft 0in		1961	1971
87	—	4w diesel	Ruston Hornsby	1965	2ft 0in		1965	1971

NB: A Vertical-boilered 0-4-0T was also used in the early 1900s, but further details are unknown. A Bagnall 0-4-0ST named *Tudor* was hired for a brief period in 1883, and a secondhand Ruston & Hornsby diesel was bought in 1965 for cannibalisation.

Table 7.3: Standard Gauge Locomotives Used at Peters Marland

No	Name	Type	Builder	Date	Wheels	Cyls	Acquired	Withdrawn
—	*Mersey*	0-4-0ST	Black Hawthorn	1892	3ft 3in	12x19	1925	1950
79	—	0-6-0ST	Manning Wardle	1888	3ft 0in	12x17	1925	1945
—	*Progress*	0-4-0diesel	Fowler	1945	3ft 0in	(80HP)	1945	1982
—	*Peter*	0-4-0diesel	Fowler	1940	3ft 0in	(80HP)	1950	1982
—	—	4w diesel	Ruston Hornsby	1960			1975	1982

Peters Marland and the clay company bought
two secondhand standard gauge locomotives
in 1925. One was a Manning Wardle 0-6-0ST
of 1888, and the other a Black Hawthorn
0-4-0ST of 1892. These were replaced by
Fowler 0-4-0 diesel shunters in 1945 and
1950 respectively.

By 1960, much of the narrow gauge system had fallen into disuse, although some
40,000 tons of clay was still being produced
annually. About half was for export, and ship-
ments to Europe were usually handled at
Fremington Quay. During the 1960s, open-
cast workings gradually replaced many of the
remaining mine shafts, and this enabled an
internal road system to be developed to connect the workings to the transhipment
sheds. The last load of clay to be transported
over the narrow gauge system made its journey in November 1970 and the six remaining
3ft gauge diesel shunters were either
scrapped or sold. The standard gauge sidings
survived until BR's total closure of the
remaining section of the Torrington-Halwill
line in 1982, and three of the clay company's
diesel locomotives lasted until the end.

The opening of the Southern Railway's
Torrington-Halwill line in 1925 not only pro-

vided a better means of transportation for the ball clay works at Peters Marland, but also prompted the opening of a new works at Meeth. This was operated by the Meeth Clay Co, which later became part of the ECC empire, and there was a 2ft gauge tramway system which connected the clay workings. The first locomotive, bought in 1925, was a seven-year-old Hudswell Clarke 0-6-0WT named *Western Lea*, which was purchased from the contractor who had constructed the Torrington-Halwill line. A pair of small Muir Hill petrol shunters arrived later in 1925, and two Ruston Hornsby diesels were purchased new in 1945/48. The narrow gauge operations at Meeth continued until 1969, and the four remaining locomotives were sold the following year.

At East Yelland, between Bideford and Barnstaple, a large power station was opened by the CEGB in 1953 but, although it was normal practice to bring in the coal by sea, a diesel locomotive was occasionally kept on site for shunting on the standard gauge sidings. The only year when there there was any significant rail movement was 1971, when 14,000 tonnes of the power station's diet of 340,000 tonnes of coal were brought in by rail. During the construction of the power station, two of the contractors had used steam locomotives, and Taylor Woodrow's representative had been an ex-SR 'B4' class 0-4-0T. The contractor had purchased two 'B4s' for £750 apiece in 1949, and ex-SR No 101 (which would have become BR No 30101) was the one to be used at East Yel-land. After its duties in Devon were over, it was taken back to Taylor Woodrow's main depot at Southall and was scrapped in 1952.

Exeter and East Devon

In East Devon, the need for industrial railways was less than elsewhere in the county. Mineral deposits were sparse in that area, and the only significant quarry line was that at Westleigh, some 18 miles northeast of Exeter, where limestone was extracted.

A 3ft gauge tramway was laid between Westleigh Quarries and Burlescombe station in March 1875, and the provider of the line was none other than the Bristol & Exeter Railway. The B&E had obtained a 25-year lease on the quarries in 1873 and thoughts had turned to locomotive traction. Two 0-4-0WTs were constructed at the company's own works in Bristol, and carried Nos 112/13 in the conventional B&E stock list; they had 2ft wheels, and outside cylinders of 8in x 12in. When the B&E was absorbed by the GWR in 1876, the locomotives became GWR Nos 1381/82.

Although the quarry line was only ¾-mile long, it included a 80ft iron bridge over the Grand Western Canal; travelling from Burlescombe towards the quarry, there was a drop of 1 in 40 and then a climb of 1 in 50. The GWR inherited the B&E's lease of the quarries, and when the lease expired in 1898, the quarry company decided to work the line itself. Consequently, the spur was relaid to the standard gauge and Vignoles rails, which were spiked direct to the sleepers, were used. Those antiquated rails were to survive until the 1950s. The two ex-B&E locomotives were sold, and it is known that one, GWR No 1382 (ex-B&E No 113), was used by Manchester Corporation before being scrapped in 1914.

The Westleigh Quarry Co acquired its first standard gauge locomotive in 1900. It was a seven year-old Manning Wardle 0-6-0ST named *Cantreff* which had been purchased from Cardiff Corporation; it worked at Westleigh until 1926, when it was part-exchanged for a new Peckett 'R2' class 0-6-0ST. The locomotive was housed in a timber-built shed on the west side of the canal and, in later years, the post of engine driver required an ability to act as fireman, shunter and permanent way engineer. Between all those duties, a bout of weeding of the tracks was occasionally required. The other side of the coin was that the driver did not have far to go to work each morning. He was given a house only a few yards from the shed.

In the quarries, a new 3ft gauge internal system was eventually laid, and this was worked by four-wheeled petrol or diesel shunters from 1931. In 1950, the internal system and the standard gauge connection to Burlescombe station were abandoned in favour of road transport; the Peckett 0-6-0ST and two of the 3ft gauge diesels were scrapped in 1954, and the other two diesels were sold to a firm of contractors in Doncaster in the same year.

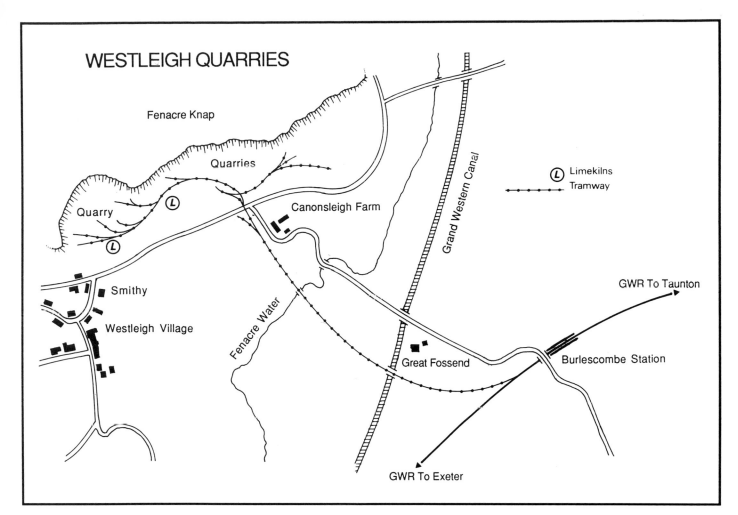

WESTLEIGH QUARRIES

Fenacre Knap

Quarries

Quarry

Ⓛ

Canonsleigh Farm

Smithy

Westleigh Village

Fenacre Water

Grand Western Canal

Ⓛ Limekilns
••••• Tramway

GWR To Taunton

Great Fossend

Burlescombe Station

GWR To Exeter

Above:
The railways of Westleigh Quarries.

Left:
Westerleigh Quarries' Peckett 0-6-0ST (works No 1717 of April 1926) was photographed at the head of a stone train in 1948.
Bernard Roberts/Courtesy of J. A. Peden

The Westleigh Quarry line had opened in 1875, complete with locomotives, but it was 1903 before the next privately-owned industrial locomotives appeared in East Devon. These were used at Exeter gas works. The works had been established adjacent to the Canal Basin in 1836, and when the South Devon Railway's canal branch had opened in 1867, a siding had been laid to the gas works. Internal shunting was undertaken by horse traction until 1903, in which year a second-hand 0-4-0ST was acquired. Between then and the cessation of rail traffic into the gas-works in 1971, a total of five steam and two diesel locomotives saw service at the site at different times. In the 1930s most of the coal arrived by ship and the locomotives shuttled backwards and forwards with wagons between the works and the sidings in the basin. Three of the steam engines were Peckett's 'M5' class 0-4-0STs which were purchased new in 1912, 1942 and 1946 respec-

tively. The last of those to remain in action at Exeter was the 1942 locomotive, Works No 2031, which was sold to the Dart Valley Railway for preservation in September 1969.

Diesel traction first appeared at Exeter gasworks in 1964, when a new Hunslet shunter was purchased, and a Ruston Hornsby diesel was transferred from Torquay gasworks in 1968. The gasworks at Torquay were smaller than those at Exeter, and locomotives were used only from 1956. In that year, Exeter's 1942 Peckett 0-4-0ST was transferred temporarily to Torquay and the Ruston Hornsby diesel was bought new. The closure of Torquay gasworks in 1968 prompted the transfer of the Ruston Hornsby locomotive to Exeter; along with the Hunslet diesel, it hung on at Exeter until the change to road transport in 1971.

Elsewhere in the area, Exeter City Council's sewage works at Countess Wear was equipped with a 2ft gauge tramway, and four-wheeled petrol locomotives were used between 1933 and 1962, in which year road haulage took over. One of the two locomotives to be used at the sewage works had previously seen service with the Forestry Commission at Mamhead, near Dawlish. Another 2ft gauge line was once operated in the city by the Western Counties Brick Co at Pinhoe Brickworks, and the first of its two Lister-built petrol locomotives was delivered in 1935. A third location in Exeter at which privately-owned industrial locomotives were used was the coal concentration depot at Exmouth Junction, which was established on

the site of the Southern Railway's old concrete works in 1967. Motive power was provided by a 0-4-0 diesel purchased secondhand from Messrs William Cory, who had used it at Gallions Jetty in London's dockland. The sidings at the coal depot were all standard gauge, but the popular 2ft gauge made another appearance some 24 miles to the east at Chardstock, where a sand quarry was equipped with its own locomotive-operated tramway. A four-wheeled diesel locomotive was purchased in 1940, but was sold when the quarry closed in 1945.

At Pinhoe Road in Exeter, Devon County Council had its main plant repair depot at which its own locomotives were serviced and administered. In 1929, the Council purchased six secondhand 2ft gauge Kerr Stuart 0-4-0STs, all of which had been bought new in 1922 by a firm of contractors in Essex. Carrying Works Nos 4250/51/56/58/60/65, they had 1ft 8in wheels, outside cylinders of 6in x 9in apiece, and weighed in at just 3½tons apiece. The Council had two quarries of its own at which the locomotives were used. One was Wilminstone Quarry, north of Tavistock, at which the railway tracks were lifted in 1952, and the other was Beacon Down Quarry, near Parracombe in North Devon, where operations ceased in 1958. Although Beacon Down was near the Lynton & Barnstaple Railway, it never had a direct connection to the L&BR, and it is arguable that, had a connection been laid, the benefits to the L&BR might have provided a slightly longer life for the famous little company.

In between quarry duties, three of the 0-4-0STs were used on road widening work in the Barnstaple and Bideford areas. The three, named *Bunty*, *Maid of Skeer* and *Rose of the Torridge*, were sold to a contractor in 1934, and were used during the building of Teignhead Reservoir before being transferred to a construction site in London. Devon County Council purchased a new Ruston & Hornsby diesel shunter in 1946 and named it *Josephine*, but this was sold in 1960 along with the surviving Kerr Stuart 0-4-0ST, *Lorna Doone*. The other two 0-4-0STs, *Pixie* and *Peter Pan*, had been sold in 1957 and 1959 respectively.

Left:
Exeter gasworks' shunter, Peckett 0-4-0ST (Works No 2074), was photographed on site on 4 September 1956. *E. H. Sawford*

Below:
One of Devon County Council's diminutive Kerr Stuart 0-4-0STs, *Lorna Doone*, was photographed at Wilminstone Quarry, near Tavistock, in the early 1950s. *Frank Jones*

8. The Preservationists

Devon has its fair share of railway preservation centres and, furthermore, miniature and pleasure railways are well-represented in the county. Theoretically, the preserved lines of Devon have an advantage over some others elsewhere as they are situated in a very popular holiday area but, as we shall see, it has not always been plain sailing. Nevertheless, the general emphasis in the county has always been on traditionalism, and this should satisfy those who like to see, for example, ex-GWR locomotives at work on ex-GWR lines. As none of Devon's preserved railways operates all year round, it is suggested that details are obtained in advance, particularly if an off-season or long-distance trip is planned and so, being helpful to the last, most entries in this chapter are accompanied by their full postal addresses and telephone numbers. Despite that, this writer had remarkable difficulty in contacting two or three of the organisations listed, and can only assume that those particular ones are terrified of publicity.

The South Devon Railway

The Railway Station, Buckfastleigh, Devon TQ11 0DZ, Tel: (0364) 42338.

The South Devon Railway is the recently-adopted working title of what used to be called the Dart Valley Railway. The DVR was one of the pioneering preservation organisations and, from the outset, its directors could never stand accused of lacking a sense of humour. For the opening ceremony of the preserved line on 21 May 1969, their choice of guest speaker was one Lord (formerly Dr Richard) Beeching whose speech included the observation that, had he not closed the line, he would have been unable to reopen it. Beeching's remark was seen, by some, as a perfect example of how ill-informed he was, as the line in question had been closed to passengers on 3 November 1958, and to freight in September 1962. The infamous 'Beeching Report' was not published until March 1963!

The original intention of the DVR was to reopen the Totnes-Ashburton branch in its entirety, but a major improvement scheme to the busy A38 trunk road adjacent to Buckfastleigh station put a very early damper on the hopes of ever running north of that point. Nevertheless, the seven-mile section between Totnes and Buckfastleigh offered

enough of a challenge to the preservationists. During the late 1960s, numerous preservation organisations sprang up all over the country, but the majority were administered by well-meaning enthusiasts who, to be honest, were not seasoned in the business of doing battle with the authorities. The DVR was different. Although volunteer working groups were formed to support the company, the directorate included a number of experienced businessmen, and a nucleus of full-time employees handled most of the administrative work.

Despite the boardroom expertise, the reopening of the Totnes-Buckfastleigh line was far from a doddle. One of the major problems was at Totnes, where BR refused permission for the DVR to use the main line station. The DVR had little option but to plan its own station, Totnes Riverside, on the other side of the river to the BR station, but this was not viewed as a long-term measure as passengers on the DVR were unable to join or leave trains there. After some years of this unsatisfactory arrangement, BR unexpectedly announced that, from April 1985, DVR trains would be granted access to Totnes station, but this lasted only until 1988. The rethink was prompted not only by the problems of integrating with BR's timetables, but also safety legislation which insisted that, if DVR locomotives and rolling stock were to use BR tracks, they would have to be maintained to main line, and not Light Railway,

Above:
Preserved '45xx' class 2-6-2T No 4555 is seen at Buckfastleigh in charge of the Dart Valley Railway's inaugural special on 21 May 1969. *Rail Archive Stephenson*

Overleaf:
On-loan 0-6-0PT No 7752 was photographed running round its train at Buckfastleigh in July 1992. The South Devon Railway's locomotive and carriage sheds can be seen to the right of, and behind, the water tower. *Author*

standards. The DVR considered the costs prohibitive and, instead, returned to the idea of a new station of its own at Totnes. The purpose-built DVR station was christened Littlehempston after the nearby village, the decision to drop the name 'Totnes' being taken to avoid implying that there was easy access between the DVR and the BR stations in the town; however, at the time of writing, plans are underway to provide a footbridge between the two stations at Totnes.

At Littlehempston, a reversing loop was laid and the station building from Toller Porcorum, on Dorset's Bridport branch, was re-erected. At the other end of the line, Buckfastleigh station was supplemented by a museum, café and gift shop, and it now acts as the focal point for operations. The com-

The timeless charm of Staverton station, on the Totnes-Buckfastleigh line, is very evident in this picture which was taken in July 1992. *Author*

The only preserved locomotive of the original broad gauge South Devon Railway is the diminutive 0-4-0WT *Tiny*. It was photographed on 13 April 1980 whilst being loaded at Newton Abbot station for its journey to its present home at Buckfastleigh. *P. W. B. Semmens*

pany's stock shed and workshop are in the station yard, and all areas are accessible to the public. The only intermediate station on the line is at Staverton which, with its traditional oil lighting and manually-operated level crossing, was restored to such a high standard that it won the 'Best Preserved Station' award in 1980 and, unsurprisingly, has been used by numerous film crews as a perfect 'period country branch station'.

Although the DVR's relations with the local residents fluctuated at first, some of the line's neighbours were very accommodating. After BR had closed the line in 1962, the parish rector at Staverton had acquired the old station signal box for use as a garden shed, but the DVR's offer of a gleaming new shed was enough to persuade the rector that the railway company could reclaim the old one for restoration. At Napper's Crossing, near Staverton, the gates were operated for many years by a local lady who rescinded her voluntary duties only because of ill health. She was in her eighties.

The DVR expanded its sphere of operations in 1972 by taking over the Paignton-Kingswear main line from BR. The prospect of the same organisation having two unconnected lines, only a few miles apart and seemingly in competition with each other, might have raised some eyebrows, but those who were familiar with the routes understood the reasoning. While the new addition was a main line which could accommodate the heaviest locomotives, the Buckfastleigh route was the epitome of a West Country branch line. However, the corporate support and enthusiasm gradually swung towards the Kingswear line and, during the 1980s, it was claimed that the Buckfastleigh operation was losing money.

By 1989, firm action had to be taken to halt the apparent financial decline of what had been one of Britain's most popular preserved railways. Most of the duties were taken over by volunteer workers, but even that economy was not enough. The DVR's directors made it clear that the Buckfastleigh line would have to close but, instead, the support association took over the running of the line and looked towards creating a charitable trust, hopefully in time to open for the

1991 summer season. Fortunately, a suitable trust was already in existence. The 'Dumbleton Hall Locomotive Ltd' trust had been around for some 16 years, primarily to preserve steam locomotives, but its constitution permitted it to operate a railway. It therefore took over the lease of the branch on 1 January 1991, but the small print forbade it from using the words 'Dart' or 'Valley' in the railway's new working title. The obvious alternative name was that of the company which had opened the branch in 1872, the South Devon Railway.

Since 1969, a variety of former-GWR and industrial tank locomotives had become familiar sights on the preserved Buckfastleigh branch but, after the reorganisation of 1990/91, some of the regular steeds were drafted to the Paignton-Kingswear line. During the summer of 1992, '57xx' class 0-6-0PT No 7752 was on loan from the Birmingham Railway Museum and it is anticipated that this locomotive will be in action during 1993. Also expected during 1993 are '55xx' class 2-6-2T No 5526, which spent many of its GWR years in Cornwall, and '1366' class 0-6-0PT No 1369 which was built in 1934, and is a representative of one of only two types of GWR 0-6-0PTs to have outside cylinders. No 1369 spent many years at Weymouth, where its short wheelbase was ideal for hauling boat trains through the streets to the harbour; it finished its working life in November 1964 at Wadebridge, where it had been one of the replacements for the veteran Beattie 2-4-0WTs. Coincidentally, one of the Beattie well tanks, BR No 30587, is a static

exhibit at Buckfastleigh museum, where broad gauge 0-4-0WT *Tiny* also resides after its transfer from Newton Abbot in 1980.

In 1992, the SDR purchased Austerity 0-6-0ST *Errol Lonsdale* from the Mid-Hants Railway, and '4MT' 2-6-4T No 80064 returned to Buckfastleigh, the site of its original ex-Barry restoration, after 10 years' work on the Bluebell Railway. The protracted overhaul of the delightful '14xx' class 0-4-2T No 1420 is scheduled to be completed for the 1994 season and, to the relief of purists, its nameplates of *Bulliver* will have been pointedly discarded by the new operators. The SDR's stud of industrial steam locomotives comprises three other Austerity 0-6-0STs, two from Hunslet and one from Bagnall, and two Peckett 0-4-0STs, one of which was the shunter at Exeter gasworks. In the diesel stakes, there is a Fowler industrial 0-4-0, Class 20 Bo-Bo No D8110 and a Class 127 DMU.

During GWR and BR days, the Buckfastleigh branch was subjected to a 16-ton limit on axle weights, but work to strengthen the weakest bridges on the line is in hand so that 18-ton axle weights can be accommodated. This will enable '28xx' class 2-8-0 No 3803 to be used after its return from Tyseley. Finally, the rolling stock of the SDR should not go unmentioned. It includes the superb GWR Ocean Liner saloon *King George* which was built in 1932 for the express services to Plymouth docks, and a GWR directors' saloon of 1894 which, in 1897, was allocated to the roster for royal train duties.

Fortunately, the SDR seems to be well on its way to a return to financial stability. The Buckfastleigh line is a perfect country branch route, and the new Trust appears intent on maintaining the quality of timelessness which was one of the great strongpoints of the original Dart Valley Railway. Traditionalists will probably be relieved that the Class 20 diesel is unlikely to be used on service trains, and so the order of the day will be, on the whole, ex-GWR locomotives, a plethora of chocolate and cream stock, and a reliance on semaphore signals. An even greater bonus is that, unlike some humdrum preserved lines, there won't be a blasted 'Black 5' in sight!

Below:
Preserved '4MT' 2-6-4T No 80064 was photographed leaving Kingswear on 17 July 1982. The restored ex-'Devon Belle' Pullman observation saloon offers passengers a delightful panorama on the southbound journey and, as can be seen, it enables a close inspection of a locomotive's bunker or tender on the northbound run. Passengers on the Mortehoe banks and between St Davids and Central stations used to be able to get a similar view in the days of steam.
Brian Stephenson

The Paignton & Dartmouth Steam Railway

Queen's Park Station, Paignton, Devon TQ4 6AF. Tel: (0803) 555872.

In 1972, BR announced that, at the end of that year, it planned to withdraw the railway services between Paignton and Kingswear and also the ferries between Kingswear and Dartmouth. Almost immediately, the Dart Valley Railway stepped in and took over the railway operation under the banner of the Torbay Steam Railway. The commercial experience which the DVR had gained with the Buckfastleigh branch proved invaluable in the 'reopening' of the line, but the fact that BR had bequeathed well-maintained permanent way to the preservationists was highly advantageous. The only thing which couldn't be saved was the railway-owned ferry service across the river from Kingswear to Dartmouth. At Paignton, however, it was not possible for the Torbay Steam Railway to use BR's facilities and so a new station, christened Queen's Park, was constructed in the yard alongside the BR premises. A run-round loop was laid and, in the station yard, the TSR provided full servicing facilities for its locomotives.

When the original broad gauge line to

Below:
A Paignton train headed by 2-6-2T No 4588 and a Kingswear train behind No 7827 *Lydham Manor* are seen crossing at Churston on 31 August 1984. *Roger W. Penny*

Kingswear was opened in 1864 it had, from the outset, the status of a main line. Nevertheless, a couple of the gradients were quite ferocious and, in view of the countryside through which the line passed, this was unavoidable. Heading south from Churston, there was a ¾-mile stretch of 1 in 60 while, in the opposite direction, the gradients peaked at 1 in 66. The engineering works on the line necessitated the construction of three substantial viaducts and the 495yd Greenway Tunnel, and these form part of the route's attractions today.

As already mentioned, the Dart Valley Railway PLC's other line, the Buckfastleigh branch, departed from the corporate fold in 1991, and one consequence of the split was that the working title of the Paignton-Kingswear line was changed from the Torbay Steam Railway to the Paignton & Dartmouth Steam Railway. However, the preserved railway did not actually operate into Dartmouth and, unlike BR and before it the GWR, it did not run its own ferry services across the River Dart from Kingswear. Nevertheless, privately-owned ferries were available to transport the preserved railway's passengers across the estuary to the attractive town of Dartmouth, and the line quickly became a commercial success. During the last decade of BR ownership, the Paignton-Kingswear route had been reduced to 'basic railway' status, and even the passing loop at Churston station had been considered superfluous. By contrast, the passenger figures during the first decade of preserved steam operation were so great that it became necessary to reinstate Churston's passing loop and also to provide a new signalbox. For signalling traditionalists, the line's commercial success was, perhaps, too great. In order to cope with the heavy summer traffic, colour light signalling

was installed throughout in 1990, and a new box was constructed at Britannia Crossing, near Kingswear, to control the entire line.

For many years, there was a degree of interchangeability between the locomotives which operated on the Totnes-Buckfastleigh and the Paignton-Kingswear lines, but the heavier steeds were always restricted to the Kingswear route. However, since the split between the two operations, their respective stock lists have become more personalised. On the Paignton & Dartmouth Railway, the flagship of the fleet is 'Manor' class No 7827 *Lydham Manor* which was rescued from Woodham's Yard at Barry in 1970 and restored at Newton Abbot. 'Hall' class No 4920 *Dumbleton Hall* entered traffic in 1992 after a restoration programme that started in 1976. The irony surrounding No 4920's return to steam on the Paignton line is that the Dumbleton Hall Trust, which was created to preserve the locomotive in the first place, is now the body in charge of the South Devon Railway at Buckfastleigh.

In terms of tractive effort, the P&D's most powerful locomotive is '5205' class 2-8-0T No 5239, which was named *Goliath* when its five-year restoration programme was completed in 1978. A pair of '45xx' class 2-6-2Ts, Nos 4555/88, are regular performers, the first of those having been bought straight from BR service by the Dart Valley Railway in December 1963 for service on the Buckfastleigh line; the other was restored to running order at Swindon Works. One 0-6-0PT, '64xx' class No 6435, is now in regular use on the Kingswear line after spending many years on the Buckfastleigh route. Two other locomotives owned by the DVR, but since sold include '16xx' class 0-6-0 PT No 1638 – to which the major honour of hauling the reopening train into Totnes (BR) station in

Left:
On 26 April 1990, '4575' class 2-6-2T No 4588 was photographed crossing Greenway Viaduct on the Torbay Steam Railway. *Paul Chancellor*

been transported to Marsh Mills where they are awaiting re-assembly.

In 1981 the PVR acquired its first locomotive, Bulleid Pacific No 34007 *Wadebridge*. The following year, '4MT' 4-6-0 No 75079 arrived, the funds for its purchase being generated by a lottery run in conjunction with Plymouth City Council. By way of a thank you, the PVR undertook to name the locomotive *City of Plymouth* when it eventually steams again. Work on No 75079 is continuing at Marsh Mills but, in 1992, No 34007 was transferred to a factory site at Bodmin for completion of its restoration. A Hawthorn Leslie 0-4-0ST, which had worked at Falmouth Docks until 1986, was acquired in 1987 and claimed the distinction of being the first locomotive to be steamed on the PVR; it is anticipated that this locomotive will be the first steam engine to perform regularly over PVR metals. On the diesel front, the PVR owns a Class 08 shunter, now No 13002, which was used at a Somerset quarry after withdrawal by BR in 1972, and a Thomas Hill 0-4-0, which formerly worked at the Blue Circle Cement Works at Plymstock.

April 1985 fell. The other locomotive was '14xx' 0-4-2T No 1450.

The more pedantic amongst us may whinge that the Paignton & Dartmouth Steam Railway does not actually go to Dartmouth. If they really wanted to split hairs, they could point out that the steam railway owns a pair of ex-BR diesel shunters, Class 03 No D2192 and Class 08 No D3014, and also keeps Class 25 No D7535 in immaculate condition for standby and special duties. However, a much safer topic for discussion is the rolling stock, which includes a Pullman observation saloon used, at one time, on the 'Devon Belle' and, later, on the magnificent route between Inverness and the Kyle of Lochalsh in Scotland.

The Plym Valley Railway

Marsh Mills Station, Plympton, Plymouth, Devon PL7 4NL. Tel: (05035) 539.

The Plym Valley Railway was formed in 1980, and its initial hope was to reintroduce steam operations on BR's Gunnislake branch on Sundays but, sadly, BR didn't want to play. Therefore, the preservationists had to find an alternative site and they homed in on Marsh Mills, just to the northeast of Plymouth on the long-disused Launceston branch. The long-term target was to relay a line as far as Plym Bridge, and a major milestone was reached in October 1989 when BR finally agreed to sell a rusting but, nevertheless, intact ¼-mile spur at Bickleigh. The plans for the PVR's proposed line and its new station at Marsh Mills were formally approved in April 1991. Since then, work has progressed steadily, and the old station buildings at Billacombe, on the Yealmpton branch, have

Below:
Preserved 2-6-2T No 4555 is seen making use of the new water tower at Paignton (Queen's Park) station on 3 October 1981. *Mark S. Wilkins*

The Bicton Woodland Railway

Bicton Park, East Budleigh, Budleigh Salterton, Devon. Tel: (0395) 68465.

The Bicton Woodlands Railway falls decidedly into the category of a miniature railway but, nevertheless, the origins of its locomotives are of interest. The railway was opened as a tourist attraction in 1963 and now meanders over a route of over 1¼ miles through Bicton Gardens. The gauge of 18in was dictated by the availability of locomotives and rolling stock as, when the railway was in the planning stage, the most suitable engine available was an Avonside 0-4-0T which had been built in 1916 for the internal 18in gauge system at Woolwich Arsenal; that locomotive now carries the name of *Woolwich* in recognition of its heritage. During the 1960s and 1970s, three further locomotives were acquired. One was an articulated 0-4-4-0 Hunslet diesel which had actually replaced *Woolwich* at the Royal Arsenal in 1954, and the other two were Ruston & Hornsby diesels, one of which had also worked at Woolwich.

The Exmoor Steam Centre

Cape of Good Hope Farm, Bratton Fleming, Barnstaple, North Devon EX32 7JN. Tel: (0598) 710711.

The newest addition to the roll call of Devon's steam railways opened to the public in August 1990. However, the Exmoor Steam Centre is not a true preservation organisation, as the track was laid and the locomotives built by the company's joint proprietors, father and son Trevor and Tony Stirland. The Centre's line is about one mile in length, and takes the form of a double spiral which negotiates gradients of up to 1 in 37. Its gauge is 12¼in and, whether by design or coincidence, the external appearances of the three locomotives owe more than a little to the engines which were once used on the Lynton & Barnstaple Railway. The locomotives are 4-4-2T *Bray Valley*, 2-8-0T *Yeo Valley* and 0-6-0T *Lorna Doone*. The railway operates daily during the summer months, but seasonal events such as Santa Specials are also scheduled.

The Seaton & District Electric Tramway

Seaton & Distric Electric Tramway Co, Riverside Depot, Harbour Road, Seaton, Devon EX12 2NQ. Tel: (0297) 21702/20375.

Part of the trackbed of the disused Seaton branch in East Devon was acquired by Modern Electric Tramways in 1969. A 2ft 9in gauge track, complete with three passing loops, was laid for 1½miles between Seaton and Colyford and services commenced in August 1970. The company had previously operated a line at Eastbourne which had been powered by a 120V dc overhead system, and the power equipment, tramcars and track were subsequently transferred to Seaton. However, the overhead power system was not installed at Seaton until 1973 and so, for the first 18 months of its operation in Devon, the company had to rely on battery trailers. The line was later extended at both ends, thereby providing a run from Harbour Road in Seaton to Colyton; the service is worked by a fleet of seven ⅔-scale double-deck tramcars and is aimed principally at the tourist market.

The Lynton & Lynmouth Cliff Railway

It is not strictly correct to include this railway in a chapter which is devoted primarily to preserved lines, as the privately-owned Lynton & Lynmouth Cliff Railway has operated continuously since its opening over 100 years ago. The only reason why this well-managed railway has been left until this late in the book is simply that it is so hard to categorise.

The railway consists of two parallel tracks of 3ft 9in gauge which climb for 862ft on a 1 in 1¾ incline between the towns of Lynton and Lynmouth. One passenger car operates on each track; they are operated by water ballast and are connected by a pair of steel cables. The principle is that, with 700 gallons of water in its tank, the weight of the descending car will lift the ascending car on the counter-balance system. For some purists, it may not be a 'proper' railway, but it offers spectacular views across one of the most beautiful bays in North Devon and, understandably, has been a major tourist attraction ever since it opened. Having said that, to the residents of Lynton and Lynmouth, the railway is an efficient means of everyday transport, and its long life reflects its year-round usage.

The cliff railway was the brainchild of publisher Sir George Newnes, who was also the guiding light behind the Lynton & Barnstaple Railway. It was designed and constructed by Bob Jones, who was a local builder; his grandson is now the Managing Director. It was opened on 9 April 1890 and, at several points in its history, has been used to carry small amounts of goods as well as passengers. After the terrible floods of 1952 in which 34 people lost their lives, the cliff railway provided a means of transporting stranded cars from Lynmouth to Lynton. The railway's proud boast is that, in over a century of operations in which millions of passengers have been carried, there has not been one single accident.

Other sites

Although not a railway preservation centre, the National Trust property of Saltram House in Plymouth warrants inclusion as it has one of the 4ft 6in gauge Lee Moor Tramway locomotives on static display, along with a small collection of artefacts from the tramway. The external renovation of the locomotive, Peckett 0-4-0ST *Lee Moor No 1*, was completed in 1970 by the Lee Moor Tramway Preservation Society, and sister locomotive *Lee Moor No 2* was subsequently dispatched by the Society to a china clay museum in Cornwall. The Society had been formed in 1964 and had had its base at

Left:
The Plym Valley Railway's former Falmouth Docks shunter is seen at Marsh Mills in June 1987. *B. Mills*

Left:
Avonside 0-4-0T *Woolwich* now works on the 18in gauge system at Bicton Park. *D. K. Jones Collection*

Below:
During 1992, BR had a surprise change of heart about allowing main line steam workings on the Waterloo-Exeter route. On Sunday 18 October, preserved 'King Arthur' 4-6-0 No 777 *Sir Lamiel* hauled a special train from Andover to Exeter, and rebuilt Bulleid Pacific No 34027 *Taw Valley* was in charge of the return leg. In this picture, the latter is seen leaving the yard at Exeter Central to link up with its train. *Author*

Torycombe; on disbanding, many members regrouped to join the Plymouth Railway Circle. Another locomotive on static display in Devon is ex-GWR '14xx' class 0-4-2T No 1442, which can be seen in Tiverton.

Arguably the best remembered of all Devon's long-lost lines is the Lynton & Barnstaple Railway. The L&B Railway Association, which has been in existence since 1979, has realistic hopes of relaying a 1ft 11½in gauge line as far as Snapper, despite a couple of false starts so far. The Association's main problem is that, as the line has been out of use for so long, its route is now divided among countless landowners, a number of whom are sadly unsympathetic to the Association's aims. The prolific division of land is illustrated by the fact that, in the first two miles from Barnstaple, the route is owned by EIGHT different landowners. The obvious ultimate goal of the Association is to relay a line to Lynton but its members are realistic enough not to hold their breath waiting for that to happen. In the meantime, the target of a line from Barnstaple to Snapper presents a stiff enough challenge. The Association has an interesting exhibition at the old signal box at Barnstaple Town station, but this is usually open to the public only during the summer period.

At Bere Ferrers, there is a privately-owned collection of railwayana. It is housed on a stretch of the demonstration track which was laid adjacent to the station for the Lydford-Devonport line's centenary in 1990. The collection comprises the Hunslet 0-4-0 diesel

Above:
The exquisitely restored 'King Arthur' No 777 *Sir Lamiel* was photographed after working a steam-hauled special to Exeter Central on Sunday 18 October 1992. *Author*

shunter which once worked at RNAD Ernesettle, and four carriages, one of which was a camping coach; interestingly, the old signal box from Pinhoe, near Exeter, has been reconstructed at the station. It is hoped that the site will be ready for opening to the public in 1993.

A little to the north of Bere Ferrers, there is the Morwellham Centre at Morwellham Quay. Once again, this site is not dedicated specifically to railway history, but the Centre's presentation of the stories of Devon Great Consols and the Tavistock Canal includes a number of tramway artefacts, and some parts of the long-lost routes can be clearly identified. Restoration work at Morwellham Quay started in 1970 and, today, the Centre offers a fascinating day out, not just for the industrial archaeologist but also for

the whole family. There is a small pleasure railway at the site, and some of its track was salvaged from the area's 19th century industrial tramways. Perhaps the most intriguing aspect of the Morwellham Centre is that the present-day layout is hardly any different to that shown in the 25in 1885 Ordnance Survey map, which appears in Chapter Seven of this book.

Two schemes which did not come to fruition, however, were, firstly, the plan to preserve the Barnstaple-Ilfracombe line. This busy holiday route was closed on 5 October 1970 and a campaign was launched to save it. The scheme failed and, after a few years, the bridge across the Taw in Barnstaple was demolished. The second proposal occurred a decade later when the Barnstaple-Torrington line was finally closed. Although preservation

emerged as an option the line was not to survive, although much of the trackbed is now a footpath.

Finally, mention should be made of the Launceston Steam Railway, just over the border in Cornwall. It operates a 1ft 11½in gauge line on the old standard gauge trackbed westwards from Launceston station and has three locomotives, all of which were acquired from slate quarries in North Wales.